O9-BTN-981

Liberty for Latin America

LIBERTY FOR LATIN AMERICA

How to Undo Five Hundred Years of State Oppression

ALVARO VARGAS LLOSA

Farrar, Straus and Giroux

New York

Farrar, Straus and Giroux
19 Union Square West, New York 10003

Distributed in Canada by Douglas & McIntyre Ltd.
Printed in the United States of America
First edition, 2005

Library of Congress Control Number: 2004114704

ISBN-13: 978-0-374-18574-9
ISBN-10: 0-374-18574-3

Designed by Jonathan D. Lippincott

www.fsgbooks.com

10 9 8 7 6 5 4 3 2 1

For Susana, Leandro, and Aitana

The thing is, to outgrow governments; the people, left to themselves, don't act that way.

—Albert J. Nock, from a letter to Ruth Robinson, June 11, 1915

Contents

Liberty for Latin America

Introduction

A few years ago, Latin America was thought to be finally moving toward prosperity and, of course, many Latin Americans fooled themselves too. The sweeping reforms taking place from the Rio Grande to Patagonia under the so-called Washington Consensus and the craze over "emerging markets" practically made it a capital offense to predict that this might be yet another illusion. "Stabilization," "liberalization," and "privatization" became the buzzwords of the day. Development was around the corner.

Thus far, however, the shift to capitalism and democracy has been a modern-day verification of Lampedusa's dictum, as delivered by a character in his famous novel *The Leopard*: "If we want everything to just stay as it is, everything must change."

If the left and the right, socialists and conservatives, social planners and champions of private enterprise, had, through delusory swings of the ideological pendulum, helped to make Latin America home to more than 200 million destitute people and a symbol of oppression even under democracies that periodically reduced the horrors practiced by dictatorships, was there not a danger that these transformations could end up essentially reshuffling elites and power interests? Would a rude awakening not eventually open a fuming chasm between ordinary citizens and their leaders and governments?

The new millennium brought home the naked truth. Argentina, only a century ago one of the twelve wealthiest nations on earth, descended into a state of collective hysteria as its economy collapsed and almost six out of every ten people became unable to meet their basic needs. Brazil, the world's eighth-largest economy, saw its currency drop 40 percent in 2002, and its underclass, comprising at least

60 million people trapped in poverty, turned to President da Silva, whose essential message at the time was to blame globalization. Mexico, recently the stout partner of the United States, started to lose jobs to China and began to voice concern about the benefits of North American free trade as millions risked everything trying to cross the border into America, a land traumatized by foreign hostility and single-mindedly bent on security. Oil-rich Venezuela, the United States' third-largest supplier of petroleum, with a reputation for prosperity and democratic stability during part of the second half of the twentieth century, was engulfed in protracted and bloody civil strife and suffered a double-digit drop in economic output during 2003. Colombia had little time for anything other than waging war against drug-financed terrorist guerrillas. Peru's new democratic government, marred by corruption, and its nascent democratic institutions quickly became the most unpopular in the nation's history. In Bolivia, a Jurassic anti-American coca grower almost made it to the presidency, and the man who did was nearly assassinated not long after taking office by a bullet fired into the palace in the heat of riots against taxes proposed by the International Monetary Fund; a few months later, another revolt led him to resign. In Ecuador, the former leader of a military coup was actually elected, just as had happened in Venezuela.

The year 2003 brought more stability to countries like Argentina and Brazil but little economic growth to Latin America as a whole, not even reaching an average of 2 percent; international bodies started to refer to this period as the "lost half-decade," after the "lost decade" of the 1980s. In 2004, the rise in the price of certain commodities triggered a temporary recovery that had nothing to do with reform.

Why should we be surprised? A look at the region's past should have told reformers and their international supporters that there had been many attempts at reform in two centuries of republican life and that the key to making it work was understanding what had failed before. An understanding of the causes of underdevelopment and of what made the leading nations wealthy should have suggested that the intangible—the way power is organized, the rules people use to relate to one another and to those who call the shots, whether the law is simply what lawmakers decide it is and whether rights are allocated vertically or horizontally—constitutes an infinitely more important factor for prosperity than the tangible: investment, production, and growth are simply the outward manifestations of development. A knowledge of how transformations play out at the grassroots level would have told them that the majority of people, desperate to own and trade goods and services, were being excluded even as opportunity was knocking at the door of new beneficiaries and capital was changing hands, sometimes spectacularly. An awareness of the vibrant, amorphous civil society emerging from the rural migrants (and their children's survival in the cities through a web of voluntary associations and communities that provide the social services the state is incapable of providing) would have told them that the poor need less legal and political discrimination. Observing the moral and spiritual fatigue caused by disillusionment would have warned them of the danger of trampling on the rights of ordinary citizens—the Latin American republics might come to be seen as illegitimate, the type of institutional divorce that has reduced peaceful coexistence to ashes in many parts of the world, including Latin America.

These reforms left Latin America resembling Florida stone crabs that are thrown in the water with all their legs tied except for one pair, which develops into a fine, fleshy delicacy at the expense of every other part of the body.

Nothing is more critical to the task of liberating Latin America than understanding why the last two decades of political and economic transformation have benefited only a small elite. Only by comprehending why democracies behave like dictatorships and private enterprises like government bureaucracies, why laws and constitutions amount to fiction and real people are forced to spend their lives struggling to survive in hostile environments rather than create, own, exchange, and exploit the possibilities of the human condition, can we grasp what has created Latin America's present state and perceive why the most recent experiment at liberation was pregnant with menace from the very beginning.

Is economic development the child of institutions or of culture? In other words, can a country prosper by removing institutional barriers that hinder development, or must the culture first be transformed so that institutional change becomes politically sustainable and can be met by an adequate response from the members of society? The truth is that, whatever factor one chooses to establish as the more decisive in this chicken-and-egg conundrum, institutions and culture desperately need each other. Excluding either one from a discussion about underdevelopment is a mutilation.

If, loosely defined, institutions are the rules by which individuals relate to one another, and culture is the set of values that determine human conduct, reforming the institutions governing underdevelopment is meaningless unless individuals act according to the corresponding values of the reformed institutions. The values that influence behavior will not change unless people view the new values as relevant to their lives through incentives and rewards made possible by institutional change.

Some scholars look at development from a cultural point of view, while others prefer an institutional approach.

The "culturalists" believe that the spread of certain values and beliefs, particularly those introduced by the Protestant Reformation, brought about prosperity in the West. They insist that the political institutions of a market economy will not spark development unless they are preceded by a transformation of people's minds, and that choices—political, economic, and otherwise—are determined by culture. For them, development, if reforms are even feasible without a new system of values, will be wasted or interrupted by the prevailing human conduct.

The "institutionalists," on the other hand, believe that the rise of the West on the wings of sustained productive investment was made possible by social and political arrangements based on property rights and contracts. The institutions limiting freedom need to be removed before the members of an underdeveloped society can realize their potential, and only through the system of incentives in a free society do individuals prosper in the long run.

Institutionalists think, as John Waterbury has written, that "culture modifies but does not determine" and that culture "cannot be dissociated from institutions that themselves may be acultural or extra-cultural." Likewise, culturalists think, in the words of Daniel Etounga-Manguelle, that culture is the mother and institutions are the children (even for Tocqueville, "too much importance is attributed to legislation, too little to customs"). Each side emphasizes either culture or institutions.

There are strong arguments supporting both viewpoints. It seems beyond dispute that the Puritan spirit helped shape many capitalist institutions. But it is equally true that there were manifestations of capitalist enterprise in northern Italy long before the Reformation and that, thanks to the relative freedoms they enjoyed, the people—Muslims and otherwise—of the Saracen civilization were already involved in scientific discovery and vibrant trade when most of western Europe was still living in the Dark Ages. It is true that the Ibero-Catholic tradition weighs heavily against Latin American development, but it is also true that Spain and Portugal, where that culture originated, have since prospered while Latin America has not. Iberian heritage has played a key part in Cuba's underdevelopment (Spain controlled Cuba for the whole of the nineteenth century), but Cuban immigrants in the United States quickly and successfully adapt to American institutions. The very same Confucian values that today account, in the eyes of many, for the social capital on which development has rested in East Asia were present in that part of the world before the 1960s, that is, in the midst of underdevelopment.

Looking at the world from the other side, however, is it not true that an intolerant cultural tradition in Latin America played a part in undermining the liberal reforms of the nineteenth century? What good does it do to change institutions that make the government an instrument of privilege and predation if those changes are reversed by a culture unwilling to trade the security of a given situation, however dire, for the uncertainties and adjustments of free choice? That is exactly what happened to Argentina in the 1930s: after half a century of substantial free-market capitalism, it chose the opposite path. Growth cannot be sustained if, once the productive capacity of a nation is liberated from institutional constraints, citizens, lacking notions of saving and investing with a view to the future, squander their surpluses.

In any case, liberty is never won forever. We can point to the growth of government in the United States throughout the twentieth century as a sign that limited government, hard work, and personal responsibility never quite displaced the instinct of relying on political coercion to obtain wealth from fellow men, a supposed cultural trait of Latin America. This indicates that the individualist culture and institutional reforms not preceded by cultural change are reversible.

This book aims to answer a simple question: Why did the market reforms of the late twentieth century, seen at the time as a universal model for underdeveloped countries, fail in Latin America? In answering the question, I use both the culturalist and institutionalist perspectives. The emphasis varies according to the particular area of discussion. The final proposal for a new, unprecedented type of reform is ultimately institutional because postponing the removal of the direct causes of oppression until the "right" values impregnate Latin America will condemn us to impotence and cede the ground to those who would be tempted to use those very instruments of oppression to bring forth cultural change. Furthermore, a free institutional environment will foster a system of opportunity and reward that encourages those basic human instincts of survival and personal gain through social cooperation that straddle different types of cultures and coexist with less-civilized impulses. But, of course, culture is not absent from a proposal that simply places the responsibility for generating a new system of values on the choices of the free society rather than on the impositions of the old state.

Part I explores the failure of Latin America from ancient to modern times. The first two chapters trace the roots and follow the itinerary of what I call the five principles of oppression that have defined Latin America: corporatism, state mercantilism, privilege, wealth transfer, and political law. Understanding how these five principles survived the transit from pre-Columbian to colonial times, from colony to independence to the present day, is critical to understanding why recent reforms have failed and why real reform must confront them head-on before progress is made. The third chapter, which ends Part I of the book, looks at the tortuous relationship between the developed and the underdeveloped worlds, highlighting the unwitting, and sometimes all too intentional, ways the leading nations, particularly the United States, have promoted values contrary to those that triggered the rise of today's major economies.

Part II looks at how developed nations achieved their success and what elements in Latin America point the right way. The fourth chapter examines the reasons why certain Western countries became prosperous in a relatively short time while other nations went in the opposite direction. The fifth chapter, which closes Part II, tries to rescue a lesser-known tradition of liberty from the midst of past and recent defeat in Latin America, and also from within the straitjackets of contemporary society, using it as a reference from which to draw inspiration for definitive reform.

Part III, which comprises the next four chapters, plunges into every aspect of reform. It deals with the so-called capitalist revolution undertaken in Latin America, including massive privatization as well as monetary, fiscal, tax, trade, financial, investment, and labor reform, started by Chile in the 1970s, followed by Mexico in the 1980s, and taken up with crusading fervor by the rest of the region in the 1990s, up to the new millennium. Since these changes echo old experiments in some regards, an overview of deceitful capitalist reform undertaken in the past serves as an introduction for the criticism of this new, more powerful attempt and as a reminder of the tenacious persistence of those five principles of oppression that turn reform into the perpetuation of that which reformers are supposed to be changing. This paradox is further illustrated by the reforms of the last two decades, which these chapters dissect. Part III ends with an assessment of the moral and cultural abyss into which Latin America has been thrown by the institutions of spoliation and oppression in the absence of individual rights, a reminder of the human toll that the accumulation of illusory reforms has had on citizens.

Part IV is a call to arms. The purpose of this book is to help shake off some of the cynicism regarding the future of the underdeveloped world. It ends, therefore, with a proposal for change, establishing the principles of government that might allow Latin America to change course. The proposal involves an assault on the political system in order to transfer power back to the individual in all spheres of human endeavor, an institutional vindication of the creative ways of the victims of the present system, the transformation of the role played by the judicial courts, and a careful transition for those who depend on the current state of affairs. The proposed change—at heart an exercise in humility on the part of any political decision maker—points the way toward a free and ethical society.

PART I

What Failed

1

The Five Principles of Oppression

If no other evidence were available, the history of Latin America would be enough to lend credence to the theory that sheer force, through conquest and expropriation, was the origin of the state. No matter what periods of peaceful, decentralized, local, or clan-based endeavor one can point to, and there are many in Latin America's long history, a pattern of oppression in which a particular class of people dominates a wider number emerges. It is possible that the prehistoric states arose not as the result of force but out of consent and self-interest on the part of those living under their rules, but if so, we need to explain how and why the state degenerated from a harmless arrangement into the machinery of exploitation incarnated in the chiefdoms, kingdoms, and empires of the last six thousand years.

As in other seats of ancient civilizations, such as Mesopotamia, Egypt, and China, it seems that in the valleys of Mexico and Peru—where natural barriers made it impossible for the losing side in a war to flee to other arable lands—political domination by one party led to an incipient form of state. In more open spaces, what forced the losing side to become subordinate rather than emigrate was probably the fact that resources were concentrated in a particular area, or the existence of dense population around that stood in its way. The subordinated were forced to produce a surplus in order to pay taxes, and the powerful, who no longer needed to work for their own subsistence, made up the ruling class. Some chiefdoms eventually grew and conquered others. They became in effect states capable of imposing taxes and forced labor, drafting soldiers, and enforcing their laws. The sequence of events was by no means linear, nor did these states come about simultaneously in every region. Peaceful subsistence communities continued to exist in some parts as states emerged in other areas.

But the state had been born: its tendency was to grow and to last. Between the third and ninth centuries A.D., the Maya city-states of southern Mexico and Central America, and, much later, the Aztec and the Inca empires of Mexico and Peru, became, in their respective areas, ultimate examples of state power.

The Maya temples of Tikal, the Aztec pyramids, and the Inca fortresses of Machu Picchu and Sacsahuamán are markers of cultural greatness. We admire the Mayas' mastery of agrarian life with their canals and ditches to control the flow of water, the Aztec capacity to build aqueducts and drawbridges, and the terraces with which the Incas overcame the difficulty of retaining water in a mountainous geography lacking flat arable land. We marvel at the corn surpluses of the Mayas and the even greater surpluses of the Incas, who stored large amounts of food with a prudence that is missing from modern Latin America's fiscal policy. And yet we disregard two facts about these very symbols of success: they were the result of collectivism, of systems where political power organized the population into herds, and they constituted a wrenching redistribution of resources (similar to the Soviet empire in recent times with respect to its military-industrial complex), which condemned much of the population to mere subsistence, leaving little space for other, less collective, endeavors.

Indigenous Oppression

One can identify, as far back as those ancient civilizations, five principles of social, economic, and political organization that oppressed the individual: I call them corporatism, state mercantilism, privilege, wealth transfer, and political law. The state had a corporatist view of society—its laws and power did not relate to persons but to groups, determined by function. The machinery of the state was mercantilist because it was not a neutral entity that existed for the people's convenience; it required instead that the commoners, the vast majority, devote their efforts to the maintenance and enhancement of it and its cronies. Privilege governed the relationship among the different "corporations" of society and between them and the state. The economic principle of bottom-up wealth transfer stemmed from this institution. And, finally, the sacred nature of authority, embodied by a supreme ruler who was either a descendant of the gods or a godlike figure, meant that the law was supreme.

These five principles worked against the individual in pre-Columbian times. As we will see later, their endurance has been remarkable.

A person was not a person. He or she was primarily a cog in a larger mechanism. The individual existed only insofar as he or she belonged to a collective entity. The nobleman was different from the priest, the priest from the warrior, the warrior from the artisan, the artisan from the peasant, and the peasant from the slave. Most people were agricultural laborers; under the Incas, some worked in the mines, and others, where possible, fished. Women, who also toiled on the land, weaved cloth. But not only the commoners performed a function; the nobles did too. They organized and manned the bureaucracy, managed the empire or the kingdom, and, in the case of priests, oversaw religious matters. The entire social fabric was fragmented into groups that had specific functions, even if the bottom "corporation" consisted, as in central Mexico, of groups of families working on their separate plots of common land.

Such was the principle of corporatism.

People did not work for themselves but for the maintenance of an entity that exercised power over them. They did not work in order to subsist; they subsisted in order to work for the state and its attached parasites. Through taxes and services, their capacity to produce was expropriated by the government, which was not distinct from the state. Surpluses beyond subsistence, whether in the form of products or labor time, were taken over by those in power. The Maya chief collecting taxes from the people, the Aztec capital of Tenochtitlán drawing tributes from dozens of provinces, and the Inca state forcing peasants to pay their dues by laboring on state property were all varying manifestations of the same principle of state mercantilism. Within the same geographical region, the principle could translate into different shapes. The Tarascan state of central Mexico was more akin to the totalitarian structure of the Inca state in Peru than to that of the Aztecs, who respected local autonomy.

The Inca system was particularly sophisticated. The government split the land into three parts. One part, of poor quality and of a size calculated to sustain life and nothing more, was left to the people, who held it under community-based custom. The other two were reserved for the state and for religious activities. The *kuraka,* or local chief, was charged with enforcing the obligations of the community, such as laboring on state lands. Every year, in order to avoid inequalities derived from differences in productivity, land was redistributed and people found themselves laboring on new parcels. The Inca state decided what public works were needed across the territory, and the state engineers mobilized the population to build terraces and canals, fortresses and temples. With each new conquest, people were forcibly relocated in order to break traditional loyalties and accentuate dependency on the state.

Under the Aztecs, Moctezuma's code regulated clothing with implacable restrictions, just as the Incas regulated water, wood, and animals. Even in areas where the state left some breathing space, as among the merchants who managed the market in Tlatelolco, the tributes taken away by the state and political interference in the conduct of affairs considerably reduced the possibility for growth and improvement.

Such was the principle of state mercantilism.

The third and fourth characteristics of ancient Latin America—the principles of privilege and wealth transfer—are closely linked. Nobility was of course hereditary, and nobles enjoyed many privileges apart from the labor and tribute of the common people. Aztec nobles could wear cotton clothing and jewels, drink cocoa and eat sumptuous foods, and use slaves as pack animals. In Inca society, only the nobles were educated, and they too enjoyed exclusive rights to clothing and jewelry. Everything, from the economic system to outward appearance, was designed to distinguish the noble class from the common people. It was not so much a feudal privilege as a state-sanctioned privilege. The noble class was protected by the state, to which it also belonged because it managed the bureaucratic empire and, through the network of priests, controlled religion.

Such was the principle of privilege.

The nobles constituted a privileged minority. They were paid tributes or enjoyed the services of the commoners, in the form not only of slaves but, more extensively, of laborers who produced goods for them. Among the Aztecs, the nobles received rights to land, labor, and tribute under state privilege. Wealth was thus redistributed, in the form either of goods or of services, to the top rank in society. The system was enforced by a machine we call the state.

Such was the principle of wealth transfer.

The king or emperor descended from the gods and therefore wielded an absolute authority. The law was an extension of the king: not an ideal against which everyday rules could be measured, or an offspring of living, ever-evolving institutions and customs, but the incarnation of divinity itself as dictated by the godlike will of the ruler. The law and the will of the powerful were one and the same. The Inca ruler, for instance, was believed to descend from the sun: the empire, a heliocentric constellation of worldly stars, revolved around the will of the emperor-sun.

The legitimacy thus conferred on the head of state and his courtiers enabled the state to rewrite history and establish an official truth. Both the Aztecs and the Incas practiced this subtle art of rewriting history so that the past became synonymous with the will of the supreme ruler. And, finally, if the ruler had power over the truth, he also had power over life. That is why the Mayas and the Aztecs practiced massive human sacrifices (the Incas, who committed many cruelties with the people they conquered, did not practice ritual human sacrifice).

Such was the principle of political law.

All five principles made the ancient Latin American state an instrument through which one class exploited lower classes to satisfy its desires. Borrowing Franz Oppenheimer's definition, one could say that the principles point to the use of "political" means of predation rather than "economic" means of production and exchange in order to sustain an elite.

Iberian Oppression

In Spain and Portugal, the countries that conquered what is today known as Latin America, the five principles of oppression also contrived to rein in the individual spirit. They were greatly boosted by the emergence, in the fifteenth century, of a central, unified monarchy that began to dominate a good part of Europe under the Hapsburgs.

In that world, rights and liberties were corporate, not individual. Under the title of *fueros*, local kingdoms had given many liberties or rights to various groups, which included municipal corporations, religious and military orders, and guilds representing economic activities. The central, unified monarchy continued and expanded the tradition of negotiating not universal but rather horizontal rights cutting across the different sectors of society, but very specific concessions were made to groups according to the standing or recognition the state wanted to grant them. This system, which looked at the world in terms of functions rather than of persons, facilitated taking rights and liberties away according to necessity at a minimum cost, because one corporate group's loss could be another group's gain, and at no point was everyone angered simultaneously. It also kept the various corporations competing with one another for state concessions.

All consultative or representative bodies, including the local assemblies, or cortes, that existed before the unification of the regional kingdoms, had been made up of group representatives with whom the various kings chose to deal. At the close of the fifteenth century, the unified monarchy simply reproduced at the national level a corporatist tradition that already existed at the local level in those places that the Christians claimed back from the Saracens. When they conquered Central, South, and part of North America in the sixteenth century, Spain and Portugal were at the zenith of a long corporatist tradition that had placed a tight corset on the individual spirit.

Such was the principle of corporatism in Iberia.

The nation-state emerged in Spain at about the same time that the New World was discovered. It immediately faced the question of how to sustain itself and grow. The state began to appropriate the wealth of the country. Fiscal revenue, an obsessive pursuit from the beginning, grew more than twenty times in a matter of three decades, making it clear that the nation's resources were destined to satisfy this new entity, which had acquired a life of its own independent from the needs of the people over whom it ruled. The state acquired mythical overtones, a "national" soul, something that went far beyond the contract relations that, however lopsided, had kept some sort of balance between the small kingdoms and the emerging groups into which the communities were fragmented. Society was geared toward the maintenance of the state and its dependents, who concentrated all the economic resources.

As a consequence of the rapacity of the state—which was engaged in all sorts of military and religious crusades across the region—a direct and fundamental conflict emerged between fiscal necessity and property rights. In this tug-of-war, the individual again succumbed. The state decided that either the individuals and different groups became wealthy and the state perished, or the state and its satellites became wealthy and society had to pay the bill.

It is not true that there were no property rights and that no private economy existed, a frequent misunderstanding of the system that was soon transplanted to Latin America. Both existed, but they were considered an auction mechanism by which only the party or parties most able to provide what the state needed could benefit from an exclusive concession. The state realized that it could not take money from all sectors all the time. In order to obtain funds, it chose to assist particular groups, the ones immediately able to provide fiscal revenue, at the expense of the others. The property rights of one party were the price the state was willing to make another party pay in order to obtain wealth.

Among the various guilds, none was more powerful than the sheepherders, Spain's principal source of fiscal revenue. Raising sheep and producing wool was the major industry. In order to drive their sheep from the cold parts of the north to the warmer south during the fall and winter, the members of the *mesta* guild were required to obtain rights from the government. Those rights limited private property and the possibility of expanding agriculture along the vast lands trampled on by the migrating flock at a time when the population was steadily growing—a perfect case of corporate rights taking precedence over individual rights.

As a consequence of the emergence of the nation-state and its fiscal rapacity, property rights became a mercenary transaction between the central authority and particular groups to a much greater extent than had been the case under the regional kingdoms. The arrangements never completely met the financial needs of the state, and new devices had to be put into place. This meant new taxes, like a sales tax and religious dues. When the time came that selective property rights and general taxation did not suffice, the state expropriated private wealth directly.

Such was the principle of state mercantilism in Iberia.

The other three features of the Iberian conquering powers were closely related to corporatism and state mercantilism. Privilege, wealth transfer, and political law were part and parcel of it. The state became a sanctifier of privilege. The Roman Stoics' tradition of the "gift" became, in medieval Spain, government patronage, a system that the nation-state, endowed with supreme authority, subsequently institutionalized. The encomiendas, large grants of serf labor handed out by the state as a reward for military victories or other reasons, were perhaps the greatest symbol of privilege. The symbol reflected the dominant idea that wealth was not to be produced but appropriated, and its appropriation entailed a form of status. Producing wealth through work and trade was demeaning. Military, religious, and bureaucratic beneficiaries of this system made up the privileged caste. Many of them were, of course, ennobled.

Such was the principle of privilege in Iberia.

It was inevitable that in such a system, bottom-up wealth transfer took place. If the top sector failed to produce wealth, the bottom was left to create it. We have seen how the state obtained wealth through various mechanisms, from exclusive property rights to taxation to direct expropriation. Once wealth flowed from the people to the state, it was redirected toward the different expenses, of which maintaining a privileged class—in exchange for, among other things, military and religious services—was crucial. The state redistributed wealth from the laborers it forced to work for privileged landholders, or from the other peasants, the merchants, or those engaged in various crafts in the cities, whom it crippled with taxes.

There were other, unintended forms of redistribution, such as inflation caused by the money coined out of the incoming bullion from the New World. As a result, price ceilings were set on wheat. The effect on agriculture was crippling and migration to towns torrential. The supposed beneficiaries of the measure, the poor, became the primary victims.

Sustaining the edifice of the nation-state was the divine authority of the king—political law, the fifth principle of oppression. The Crown saw political law as a way to consolidate national unity. Iberia had a mixed tradition of customary law dating back centuries to the Celts and the Iberians and, later, to some extent, to the Visigoths, and of Roman law, especially the more top-to-bottom, codified type. The absolutist monarchy of unified Spain consolidated the latter type and, through the fusion of law and religion, strengthened the "idealism" and "unreality" of the legal system. The spheres of political authority and of the church were so intertwined that they became almost indistinguishable (kings even appointed bishops). The Inquisition, a religious institution, was also an oppressive governmental, that is, political, apparatus. The theological foundation of absolutism was derived from Thomistic thought. St. Thomas Aquinas had revolutionized philosophy with something that came in very handy for absolutist monarchs when the nation-state was born. He had married the idea of natural law, from which civil and political institutions such as property and the patriarchal family were derived, to the idea of Christian morality. In further scholastic thinking, this notion turned the state, the political institution par excellence, into the embodiment of God's revelation and Christian morality. Although many scholars defended the space of the individual, scholasticism became the Christian justification of absolutism, on which rested the godlike will of the Spanish monarch.

It is inaccurate to say that this awesome power was undisputed: a number of rebellions against the Crown took place at the local level, and the philosophical foundation of absolutism and divine right going back to St. Thomas Aquinas presupposed a certain degree of prudence on the part of the king as well as consent on the part of those delegating authority to him. But the divine aura of the Crown was so intimidating that, even in times of rebellion, the subversives chanted, "Long live the king and down with the ministers!" In theory, as in the sixteenth-century scholastic writings of Dominicans like Francisco de Vitoria and Domingo de Soto, and Jesuits like Francisco Suárez and Luis de Molina, absolutism was tempered by natural law (that is, by the very source invoked to justify the divine right of the king), and the "organic" community could not stifle the individual precisely because it was not above that natural law. In practice, since the king was the divine interpreter of those rights and laws, the state had an authority beyond contract or consent.

Such was the principle of political law, the legitimizing factor behind corporatism, state mercantilism, privilege, and wealth transfer in Iberia.

Colonial Oppression

The imposition of the Iberian mold on the pre-Columbian state and society produced a creature that is still alive today despite the many metamorphoses it has experienced. Those five traits seen on both sides of the Atlantic did not vary substantially once the two civilizations were intertwined.

Although individualism had been the stuff of the conquest as much as anything else—the conquistadores were larger-than-life figures with ambitions that often collided with what was expected of them by the Crown—the colony consolidated the corporation over the individual.

There were many different corporations. Indian peasants, the lowest and largest caste, were treated by the authorities as an organic entity, not as individuals. Their function, as laborers on the land or in the mines, was to sustain the economy of the Iberian colonizers through tributes and services. When partial ownership was granted to them, it was under collectivist arrangements. In Mexico, for instance, land ejidos were given to the communities to be held in common in exchange for service to the government. In order to colonize certain areas, such as New Mexico, community grants were given to groups of village families who, after dividing up the land, shared a commons—the village ejido—for grazing, hunting, and collecting firewood. Some Indians and many mestizos, or mixed-blood Latin Americans, formed artisan guilds, another form of group entity, in the various colonial towns.

On the other side of the social spectrum, the encomenderos and the owners of repartimientos—Spaniards whom the Crown allowed to control peasants within certain limits and to appropriate the large chunks of the lands of the Indians—represented corporate interests themselves, in constant struggle with the central authorities. Their power later waned, but other corporate interests filled the vacuum. Municipal councils controlled by Spaniards were set up in all cities, constituting corporate institutions with which the central state and its colonial bureaucrats negotiated colonial affairs.

Of course, the church was the most powerful corporate interest group. Its special status gave it clerical immunity from civil prosecution. In the name of the church, the government, indistinguishable from the state, collected a special tax; the church controlled land, influenced education, and held hegemonic positions in the field of intellectual endeavor. It received income from land rents, mortgages, charitable organizations, investments of various kinds, and contributions by parishioners, making it the largest banker. As the foremost corporation in the corporatist family, the church owned more than half the land of Mexico and a quarter of all the buildings in Mexico City and Lima. All church-held land had originally belonged to the Indians. Because the church was such a large institution, it was divided into many smaller corporate entities like university communities, religious orders, the Holy Office of the Inquisition, and others. Indian cofradias (parishioners' associations) were yet another form of corporation stemming from the corporation that was the colonial church. Their presence was particularly significant in Mexico.

These various groups were heavily related to the government in one way or another, and their existence was due not to immanent rights exercised in the form of voluntary associations but to the part they played in the wider design of the state. This is the reason why the state held the properties of landholders in check and appointed bishops.

Such was the principle of corporatism in colonial Latin America.

The colonial system was not only corporatist but also state mercantilist. It acted through the four viceroyalties spread from Mexico to South America. Local governments existed, but they had no real power and could not levy taxes. The structure was very centralized. Spain's and Portugal's aim was not to develop the colonies but to obtain as much wealth as possible from them.

The Spanish Consejo de Indias (Council of the Indies) held power over all political decisions, and the Casa de la Contratación (House of

Trade) governed all commercial transactions under a monopoly arrangement that forbade the colonies to trade with other countries. It also tightly regulated the movement of people. The primary purpose of the trade entity was to maximize revenue. Until the eighteenth century, only the ports of Seville and, later, Cádiz were allowed to trade with the ports of Portobello and Veracruz, and intercolonial trade was illegal. Special *consulados*, associations of merchants, were given exclusive licenses on both sides of the Atlantic to engage in trade. When the inevitable time came that the revenues no longer satisfied the financial needs of the Crown, the logic of such a system dictated that the state take for itself direct trade in certain products like salt, pepper, quicksilver, and gunpowder.

In Brazil, the mercantilist web grew more gradually than in the Spanish colonies. In the early period, Brazil was not thought to have precious metals, unlike Mexico and Peru, and its population, made up of scattered nomadic Indians, was not suitable for mining and agricultural activities that required organized labor on a large scale. The political and economic organization, therefore, was not centralized: colonization, at least until the reforms of the eighteenth century, was more of a "business venture" and as such not presided over by a grand design on the part of Portugal. Sugar was introduced, trade remained in private hands, and early settlements were left to *donatários* who received concessions to develop specific areas at their own expense. Portuguese interests linked to the metropolitan government subsequently became major intermediaries in the sugar trade. Local government, tied to large estates, was stronger than the central government in Brazil until the eighteenth century, when the discovery of gold led Portugal to increase control very heavily. By then, trading monopolies were set up, the Crown reserved an important proportion of mining revenues for itself, limits were set on local manufacture, and it became illegal to produce goods that could be supplied from the metropolis.

As a result of the dearth of free trade, a century and a half after colonization, contraband represented as much as two-thirds of colonial commerce in Latin America, mainly by the French, the Dutch, and the English (a reason, incidentally, why Buenos Aires prospered). It is not surprising that in such a climate informal street vending prospered despite heavy persecution. The only real market was that of public offices. Local government and colonial bureaucratic posts were constantly bought and sold, an exchange that provided for the only type of social mobility. Colonial society, then, quickly learned that its survival depended on getting around the law of the mercantilist state, because the only productive, rewarding activities were smuggling and buying and selling public office.

In the eighteenth century, when the French Bourbons replaced the Hapsburg dynasty in Spain and the reformist Marquis of Pombal became prime minister of Portugal, some political change occurred in the colonies. But the central command structure remained in place. Intendencias, which replaced local government officials with royal bureaucrats holding wide-ranging powers in Spanish America, were more responsive to metropolitan power since their goal was also to enhance the fiscal health of the Crown. From a spiritual and an ideological point of view, these changes turned out to be the beginning of the end of the colonial era insofar as they split the "soul" of Latin America, in Howard Wiarda's apt phrase, but they did not alter the way of organizing the economy, primordially geared toward extracting rather than producing wealth and channeling it toward the state (in effect, the government) rather than allowing private economic spaces to develop. Although trade barriers were lowered, Spanish monopolies were strengthened at the expense of American Creoles and natives. Only Cubans were permitted to participate in transatlantic trade. The rest of Latin America was confined to intercolonial trade and taxed so heavily that it was impossible to compete with metropolitan interests.

Such was the principle of state mercantilism in colonial Latin America.

Like any system based on fragmented property rights, colonial society was driven by privilege, the third principle of oppression. In exchange for political support back home, the Crown rewarded its chosen ones with riches, honor, and power. The relationship between the Crown and the privileged few was tortuous, because the state did not want the landholders, the clergy, the military, or even its own officials to become too independent. But sustaining a transatlantic empire required concessions to be made. Apart from encomiendas and repartimientos, there were numerous ways of bestowing privilege on individuals. For instance, large land grants were given to some for the establishment of livestock ranches in order to colonize New Mexico; other types of land grants were made as part of a bundle of privileges in exchange for which the beneficiary, usually a prominent person, made the commitment to build a town. The Iberian-born were the most privileged, followed by the locally born Creole Iberians. At the other end of the spectrum, distinctions were made between natives tied to the old power structure, whether it was the ruling caste or the local chiefs, and the rest. In between, the mestizos were discriminated against but slowly found ways of moving up the ladder, something the Indians could not do. Land, money, and access to the legal profession or to the priesthood and local government posts were reserved for top tiers of society, particularly those of Iberian descent. The masses provided labor and services, and a large part of the population was taken to remote locations to work in mines.

Such was the principle of privilege in colonial Latin America.

Privilege begets wealth transfer, the fourth principle of oppression. Although a very few industries developed under exclusive licensing arrangements, and commerce was present through the monopoly rules explained earlier, it was in mining and on the land where upward redistribution was more visible. The colonial elite took land and mines from the Indians, a direct form of redistribution. The state tolerated private encroachments and takeovers, against which the Indians responded—unsuccessfully—through the affirmation of their own types of property titles. In general, the colonial elite were private owners of those assets in limited form: they were allotted a number of Indians to work on a property that was temporarily under their tenure but that ultimately belonged to the Crown. The usufruct of that labor went partially to the Crown and partially to those to whom the Indian labor force was allotted. The Crown thus redistributed wealth produced by Indians by awarding their labor on the land and in the mines to private claimers whom it wanted to please.

In Brazil, a good portion of the land and the laborers was also handed out by the Portuguese state to political associates. Originally, Martim Afonso distributed huge estates of land to a few followers, and these grew into the enormous sugar plantations that came to symbolize the coastal economy. The Indians and, later, the African slaves produced all the goods, and the state rewarded a small elite with property (albeit in limited form), attached to which were wealth and prestige. Unlike in the English colonies of North America, where small agricultural properties made for a more extended distribution of income, Brazil's large estates linked to the sugar export economy concentrated wealth on small groups of people.

This system of rigid wealth transfer stifled the colonial society and created a social divide that lasts to this day and a concentration of property that still constitutes a visible characteristic of the Latin American economy. The Spanish and Portuguese estates in the Latin American territories did not enter the world economy until the eighteenth century. Before that time, agriculture was mainly geared toward the local market; one of its responsibilities was to feed the mining towns. In the case of Brazil, the huge plantations were the basis of an economy dependent on one product alone.

Such was the principle of wealth transfer in colonial Latin America.

Only the countries with a small Indian population and where immigration was less restricted, such as Argentina, Uruguay, and Costa Rica, were spared the gross inequalities that came with bottom-to-top redistribution. They went on to develop larger middle classes than countries like Mexico, Peru, and Brazil, where property was severely concentrated.

Colonial corporatism, state mercantilism, privilege, and bottom-up wealth transfer were underpinned by political law, the fifth principle of oppression. Rules that emanated from the government were holy, unquestionable. The fact that the godlike authority of the government was so separate from the territories and the people over whom it ruled created a gap between law and reality. The authorities in charge of enforcing the rules did not make them (except for minor ordinances), and in many cases fell victim to them. Back in Spain, the Crown produced a labyrinth of norms, including the minute details of every regulation, without regard to the practices, customs, aspirations, and wishes of the people in the Latin American territories. Almost one million laws and norms were passed in three centuries of colonial life. A chasm opened between the letter of the law emanating from the Crown and its interpretation and application by the Crown's representatives and then by the elite in charge of enforcing the endless number of rules. It created a gulf between the law and real life. The colonial officials themselves reserved the right to "obey but not comply with" many of the laws they were meant to enforce. This was true not only of Spanish America but also of Portuguese Brazil.

When independence movements sprang up in the early nineteenth century, there existed a culture in which the law had no real roots. Order was maintained through fear, but also with an elite that, despite the enlightened rhetoric of the leaders, wanted to reproduce or preserve the organic order of the mother country from which the colonies were thought to have perilously deviated. The cause of the problem was taken for the solution.

Such was the principle of political law in colonial Latin America.

Republican Oppression

In the early part of the nineteenth century, the Latin American colonies gained independence. It is often said that things did not change, but they did. The problem was that the change itself, from the maniacal writing of constitutions to extensive commerce with new partners like Great Britain, was nourished by the placenta of corporatism, state mercantilism, privilege, bottom-to-top wealth transfer, and political law. The Latin American republics that fought and defeated the colonial enemy drove a sword through a phantom disguised in human flesh; the sword went through, and the human flesh of the enemy succumbed, but after all that sound and fury, the colonial phantom was still intact. By the time the blood dried, he had become a republican.

The republic—that is, the sphere of public policy—was a very small space. Political representation did not have a substantial meaning. Until the late nineteenth century, only 1 or 2 percent of the Latin American population were allowed to vote, whereas in the United States there was already by the middle of the century eight times that rate of popular electoral participation.

Constitution after constitution reserved "emergency" powers for the government and vested absolute authority in the executive branch. In the absence of grassroots civil society—nothing like New England town hall meetings existed—and of state checks and balances, there was little to tame the beast of political power. And the military, whose roots were in the militias created by the colonial state in the second half of the eighteenth century, was the determining political agent.

Brazil's transition to independence was more peaceful than that of the rest of the region: due to events in Europe, the monarchy simply broke with Portugal and established itself in the former colony. However, authoritarianism remained the dominant trait of the state and continued to be when the republic finally came about in 1889.

Corporatism entailed the concentration of property. Through various means, including the use of violence, discriminatory legislation, elite-dominated municipalities that replaced the local and village colonial governments, and plain encroachment, the land was quickly appropriated by the privileged few. Agriculture emerged in countries that were still primarily rural as a space of highly concentrated property and high marginal product of labor, with little incentive to revolutionize technology. When Brazil offered cheap land in the nineteenth century, coffee plantations surged all the way to São Paulo. An opportunity opened for many new landowners to prosper. But public policy, especially legislation promulgated in the 1850s, prevented small-scale agriculture and favored huge estates under control of a few fazendeiros who employed masses of low-wage laborers and immigrants under *parceria* or sharecropping arrangements. In Peru, local political bosses and wool trade intermediaries helped the formation of powerful haciendas by encroaching on Indian community lands. By the end of the nineteenth century, there were 705 estates, and the number tripled by the early twentieth century, covering most of the Peruvian fertile land. By then, 95 percent of the rural population in Mexico owned no land at all, and one-fourth of all the land of that large country was in the hands of two hundred families. Mexican liberals who had managed to free land from conservative interest groups like the church in the late 1850s had ended up favoring new interest groups that also concentrated most of the property and pushed the wider indigenous population off the fertile lands.

Such was corporatism in republican Latin America.

The republic also perpetuated state mercantilism. A good illustration is provided by the Portuguese monarchy in Rio de Janeiro in the early nineteenth century, which led to the growth of government employment and public expenditure in construction projects, although it also saw the end of some trade controls. Globalization tended to reinforce, not mitigate, that system by which proximity to the state and the capacity to fund it were the conditions private interests had to meet in order to succeed. It is a paradox that would keep recurring in Latin America all the way to the twenty-first century: globalization opened markets for Latin American products in Europe and provided capital for those countries, but because the governing institutions were a bottleneck that slowed or simply prevented the flow of property rights to the wider public, the effects were felt solely among the elite and, in smaller proportion, by the tiny middle class. Only countries like Argentina, where the absence of an indigenous population (to a large extent annihilated in the conquest of the pampas) and massive European immigration coincided with a more horizontal spread of rights, really benefited from globalization.

The expansion of European markets stimulated production in the Mexican haciendas, but modernization and capital formation remained concentrated in those who had exclusive access to ownership. Brazil's ability to sell large amounts of coffee boosted the plantation economy, but because property rights were restricted, the huge wealth divide was consolidated.

Such was state mercantilism in republican Latin America.

Corporatism and state mercantilism enthroned privilege. The Brazilian government, for instance, promoted numerous activities, such as railroad construction, with subsidies and guaranteed rates of return. Immigration was subsidized, and the export economy, which by the mid-nineteenth century was largely dominated by coffee plantations dependent on slave labor, was granted privileges, as were certain industries, with government-guaranteed earnings and exemptions from tariffs for the import of equipment. Coffee producers were closer to the capital than sugar producers had been in the first centuries of the colony, so they were acutely aware of how government affected their interests, which led to a close link between them—and set the stage for strong government intervention in favor of coffee in the next century, including the use, by the state of São Paulo, of proceeds from export taxes and foreign loans to buy large amounts of it in order to withhold it from the market and thereby counterbalance a decline in prices.

Such was privilege in republican Latin America.

Privilege was both a result and a cause of wealth transfer from the productive members of society to the parasites upstairs. And wealth transfer hurt savings and investment, thus keeping domestic markets from developing because of insufficient demand, and widened the social divide by preventing the emergence of a solid middle class.

Such was wealth transfer in republican Latin America.

Because political law was the instrument of the corporatist, state-mercantilist, privilege-driven, wealth-transferring system, the gradual illegitimacy of the republican state was really the gradual illegitimacy of the law. The Latin American countries liberated from Iberia imported, word for word, the legal codes enacted by Napoleon and replicated across the European continent, including Spain. They mirrored the constructivist, top-down approach that derived from certain transcendental principles every possible rule in order to govern the behavior of the individuals without regard to their customs and norms, their comings and goings. The nature of the law demanded that the authorities, either the executive branch or parliament, become its supreme interpreters. In the hands of politicians, who expropriated from the judges the essence of the judicial process, the law became a permanent and devastating intruder. The day-to-day practice of interpreting and writing the law, and leaving judges simply to follow the ever-changing rules imposed by the politicians, increased the divide between theory and reality.

Every new government appointed or removed judges at will, rewrote the constitution, and reinterpreted or extended the codes. This meddling in yet more aspects of people's lives produced fantastic amounts of norms in the presidential palaces and the ministerial offices. The stage was set for a republican tradition of executive norm bombardment: the presidency and the ministries of Peru produce slightly fewer than thirty thousand norms, regulations, decrees, and laws every year, and since the 1980s Venezuela has produced three thousand annual executive orders governing economic activity.

The Latin American legal system that has been in place since the advent of the republics has been described as suffering from idealism, paternalism, legalism, formalism, and lack of penetration. Idealism entails a disconnection between the law and real life. Paternalism stresses authority over freedom. Legalism binds all social relations under comprehensive legislation. Formalism breeds a proliferation of requirements for legal permissions. Finally, lack of penetration signifies that the law and the legal system in general do not reach the common people, who are unable to understand or "discover" them and do not participate in them.

In such a climate, advancement in society was possible only by influencing the political process that dominated the law. It was there, in the theater of political law, and not in the marketplace, that all real competition took place. The energy was geared not toward producing wealth but toward bending the law to one's advantage (or preventing others from doing so).

The colonial system had married political power and the law (viceroys and governors headed the main judicial bodies, and corregidores were local magistrates with political powers), emptying the latter of any universal, general, and abstract character. The dazzling changes brought about by the independent republics—perfect codes, parliaments interpreting the law in the name of the sovereign people, judges overseeing the separation of powers—meant another turn of the screw in the tradition of inequality before the law. Anything governments and parliaments decreed, and they decreed profusely, was the law. But the inflation of laws translated into their debasement, just as the inflation of money debases a currency.

Such was political law in republican Latin America.

A paradox resulted from it all. The stronger the five principles of oppression, the weaker the legitimacy on which they stood and the weaker the state apparatus engineering them.

That nineteenth-century archetype, the caudillo, was larger than the law because he *was* the law. But the stronger he was, the weaker—the less representative and rooted—the law actually was. Whether that caudillo was José Gaspar Rodríguez Francia in Paraguay, General Santa Anna in Mexico (who buried the leg he lost fighting against French troops in a Mexico City cemetery with fanfare), Manuel Rosas in Argentina, or Ramón Castilla in Peru, despotic or democratic, federalist or centralist, liberal or conservative, pro- or antislavery, bigot or anticlerical, from peasant or oligarchic background, he was a variation of the same republic, a republic in which order was not "a balance arising from inside" the society but "a pressure exerted from outside" it. The republic, which had come about as the result of the struggle against the institutions of colonial rule, in fact consolidated the five principles of oppression that constituted the legacy of both the pre-Columbian and the colonial worlds. Just as had been the case in the remote origins of the state, political power was now, if in more sophisticated ways, the instrument by which a powerful ruling class satisfied its desires and ambitions at the expense of the rest.

A few decades after independence, then, the republic began to lose legitimacy without realizing it. So did its image, the law. Once again, the illegitimacy of the state brewed ideas of change.

2

The Twentieth Century: The Hour of the Snail

The twentieth century in Latin America began with what purported to be a capitalist revolution under Porfirio Díaz, who had come to power in Mexico in the last decades of the nineteenth century, and ended with what many took to be a capitalist revolution from the Rio Grande to Patagonia in the 1990s. In between, there were two major developments that shaped most others: revolution and economic nationalism. Revolution, or the rise of the people, led to the new state, which replaced the oligarchic, illegitimate nineteenth-century republics. Economic nationalism, the ideology that seeks to protect a country's economy from the outside world through political means in order to "correct" the adverse terms of trade, became the philosophy of the new state in its effort to reform the old one. There was revolution of the seismic kind in Mexico, Bolivia, Cuba, and Nicaragua, of the radical sort in Chile, of the socialist but somewhat less radical type in Peru and Panama. Economic nationalism swept the region, but perhaps it reached its zenith in Argentina with the populism of Juan Domingo Perón, a man with many imitators, conscious or unconscious. Everything, left and right, democratic or dictatorial, came under total or partial influence from the double phenomenon of the rise of the people's state and economic nationalism.

And the paradoxical result of the insurgence against tradition was the perseverance of tradition, in the form of the five principles of oppression. The spectacular acts of the twentieth century were played out on a stage whose hidden machinery was made of the parts and pieces of pre-Columbian, colonial and republican corporatism, state mercantilism, privilege, wealth transfer, and political law. The way property rights were allocated, the nature of the relationship between power and the individual, the role played by the law—all were traditions that proved resilient to change. The genius of these traditions consisted in allowing the relative strengths of the competing factions of power to vary, and the hierarchies between winners and losers to be upset, according to who was giving the orders. But the fundamental set of rules by which those changes took place was not modified. What varied was who enforced them and under which model.

The Rise of the People

A century of independent republican life had produced an illegitimate state amid a sea of excluded masses. It was only a matter of time before political actors would give expression to that sentiment of the majority. It came, in 1911, by way of the Mexican revolution. A new character came onto the Latin American scene: the people. Most of what followed in the century to come, both in Mexico and in the rest of Latin America, would be done in the name of the people, if not always with the people's participation. And most of what would happen for decades to come, in politics and economics, was influenced by that revolution.

What did that revolution, after the furor, the ashes, and the poetry, accomplish? A new state came to replace the illegitimate nineteenth-century entity. It was the offspring of a compromise between warring interests. Through the formation of an official state party, regional armies and power groups became the columns of a new corporate edifice. Whereas the exclusion of the masses had deprived the former state of legitimacy, the people now had to become the bedrock of the new creation. But how does a state incorporate millions of people? In the absence of universal, individual rights, it can do so only through the use of a juridical abstraction, that remote Roman legacy, operating as a form of representation. Once the state, through its manifold components, represents the interests of the people, it is not necessary for all members of society to represent themselves directly and take responsibility for their own lives. By absorbing individual identities into collective abstraction, the Mexican state became a kind of corporation; that is, a juridical fiction acting in the name of the people, whose legitimacy lay exactly where the previous state's illegitimacy had rested. The rise of the people at the beginning of the twentieth century was not so much the physical rise of the masses as the subsuming of all individual identities into a body politic that now acquired the legitimacy of universal representation.

Prior to the revolution, property rights had been selective and fragmentary. The revolution failed to make them individual and tangible; they became collective and abstract. In the name of the people, the 1917 constitution (a much amended document) reserved under article 27 all rights, whether related to land, the subsoil, or intellectual property, to the state. In the 1920s, President Plutarco Elías established an official party, which, in the name of the people, would monopolize political representation and operate as the link between society and its new representative. In the 1930s, President Lázaro Cárdenas nationalized oil, roads, and other assets. In the 1970s, the enduring Mexican revolutionary state inscribed in the constitution the decision to reserve for the state the planning and conduct of economic activity. Through the decades, the revolution legitimized the state by expropriating rights as well as assets. And when property rights were not confiscated, they were limited by the fact that the government was the repository of all rights, which it might temporarily allow to be exercised by, or might allocate to, private parties.

The revolution chose to redress the exclusion and discrimination of the old order through a juridical gimmick. But representation still needed to be personified by real people acting with the authority of the government. The president and the members of the executive power were, of course, the chosen ones. The constitution concentrated colossal political power in their hands. Congress, the judiciary, and state governorships were subservient powers. They had to be, if the state was going to legitimize itself through the exclusive representation of the people's collective identity. Any effective system of checks and balances would inevitably weaken the state's ability to exercise the exclusive representation of the people. The state, therefore, was really a hierarchy in which some powers were predominant and others obedient, and, since the government was at the very top, there was not much difference between it and the state. If the state was the owner of rights and the state was personified by the president and the executive power, then the political authorities were the effective owners of the people.

This was not a totalitarian state. It was authoritarian, even dictatorial, and sometimes brutal, but not, strictly speaking, totalitarian. Its essence was corporatist in an even stronger sense than in the past. Members of society were divided by function into "peasants," "workers," "functionaries," "intellectuals," "the military," and others. Each group was organized from the top down on a federal, state, and local level. The party, born in 1929 and after a number of name changes known as the Institutional Revolutionary Party, commonly referred to by its Spanish acronym, PRI, was the unifying factor, giving organic coherence to society and integrating it into the state. As always, in the corporatist structure rights were collective. Only by sharing in the corporate identity of the group to which one belonged could the individual go about his or her business.

Of course, the new corporatism affected already powerful corporations and benefited new ones. The new state targeted the church and particular business groups linked to foreign capital, redistributing that wealth to the new beneficiaries. The constitution explicitly directed its hostility toward the church through article 130 and granted explicit rights to organized labor and to peasants. Workers obtained the eight-hour workday, the six-day week, a specified minimum wage, participation in profit sharing, and restrictions on the right of employers to fire them. State and local boards were set up to vouch for workers in their disputes with managers. Peasants made gains too. Under the ejido system, land was taken away from its owners and divided into small parcels. In the 1930s Lázaro Cárdenas redistributed 45 million acres, and in the 1970s Luis Echeverría undertook another massive redistribution of almost 33 million acres, with plots becoming so small that in many cases they could not accommodate even subsistence crops.

Corporatism beckons state mercantilism because, if rights are fragmented, the government must interfere in order to define the new winners and losers and live off those new arrangements. State mercantilism in turn generates privilege, which requires wealth transfer, and political law is what makes all four principles possible. The revolution eventually understood that some "revolutionary" business groups had to be encouraged if somebody was to sustain the statist structure. Through what has aptly been called "backward integration," the state incorporated certain business groups into the system by allowing them to write their own rules, that is, by granting them exclusive privileges. Since the banks had been de facto nationalized, and money and access to foreign credit became a priority, the bankers were allowed to exercise property rights again and write their own rules so that barriers to entry would preserve business in the tight hands of the chosen parties. Industrialists benefited too; they wrote their own rules, and tariffs went up to protect them. The government, which influenced banks and set up a bank of its own, made sure the money flowed toward the business groups it hoped to strengthen. In order to make its commitment more credible, politicians and bureaucrats became businessmen too. Thus, corporatism, state mercantilism, and privilege hinged on wealth transfer, through the tool of political law, in this case embodied in the new state that based its legitimacy on "the people."

In order to avoid the loss of legitimacy that had sparked revolution, this time the corporatist, state-mercantilist system would be wider, more inclusive, and built on the identity of the people. But, after all the death and destruction, and the ensuing years of civil war, Mexico was left with a state under which the rights structure was still defined by the transaction between the political authorities and particular interests, however much those interests had expanded according to the numbers represented.

Like all revolutions, the Mexican revolution sought stability and perpetuity. Once those corporate pillars of stability were in place and the system could be perpetuated, it did not matter what policies were pursued, whether liberal or protectionist, fiscally responsible or profligate, as long as they were all done within a framework of institutionalized interests binding together the new state. Indeed, nothing attests more aptly to the many contradictory ideologies and policy inclinations of the revolution than the fact that by the end of the 1980s there were 318 amendments to the constitution.

In a fundamental sense, the revolution went back to where Mexico was when the first shots were fired, however much the country as a whole had been transformed beyond recognition, however much resources and wealth had changed hands and vast sectors of society had begun to participate in the "official" republic. The capitalist Mexico of Porfirio Díaz and the revolutionary Mexico of Plutarco Elías, Lázaro Cárdenas, and Luis Echeverría had more in common than either party would care to acknowledge.

Other revolutions followed the Mexican revolution in Latin America. The Bolivian revolution in 1952, the Cuban revolution in 1959, and the Nicaraguan revolution in 1979 were revolutionary in the classical sense, although in Bolivia revolution meant nationalism, and in Cuba and Nicaragua, communism. The Chilean revolution triumphed in 1970 through the bourgeois electoral system, whereas the 1970s Peruvian and Panamanian revolutions were military dictatorships that purported to be revolutionary. It is not necessary here to describe the details of the revolutions. What matters is that despite not being able to perpetuate themselves like the Mexican revolution, they all extended across Latin America some of its themes and shared with it characteristics that shaped the region's century.

The many similarities among the revolutions can be reduced to two ideas that came to mark much of the twentieth century. The first is the emergence of the state as the expression of the people's identity. If the state was the people, then redemption of the people from the old, illegitimate republic could take place only through a new, legitimate state that embodied the collective identity. The second idea is an extension of the first. Since the state as the repository of the collective identity and redeemer of the people from the oligarchic republic of the past was a concept that had no meaning until translated into a political and economic structure within a new set of rights and institutions, the revolutions ended up reinforcing rather than correcting what they had rebelled against.

In the early, illegitimate republic, the winners were not those who were better at playing the game but those for whom the rules of the game were made by the state. Now the state, which still made the rules, favored new interests, if sometimes more representative of society in number. Among the interests favored by the rules of the game was the state itself, which became a major winner in the game of economic power. After taking over mining, oil, fishing, banking, insurance, commerce, agriculture, and other business interests, the Peruvian revolutionary government of the 1970s controlled more than a third of the productive economy. The 1952 Bolivian revolution under Víctor Paz Estenssoro expropriated, from both foreign and local owners, many sectors of the economy, including the powerful tin mines whose revenue for the three proprietary families exceeded the entire fiscal revenue of the government. As a result, by the 1970s the Bolivian state was generating 85 percent of fiscal revenue and one-third of all the jobs in the country. Chile's revolution under Salvador Allende was truncated overnight by Augusto Pinochet's 1973 coup, but in the three years of Allende's rule, the state also took over vast parts of the economy. In the more extreme case of totalitarian Cuba, which was followed by Nicaragua (but not to the same degree), no corner of society was free from government control.

Aside from the minute size of the electoral franchise, no other sign was as powerful an emblem of the old, illegitimate republic as the concentration of land property. Now, inspired by revolution, land reform became the battle cry across the region. As we have seen, the Mexican Revolution undertook reform early and continued to expropriate land until the 1970s and distribute it through the ejido system at various stages. Vast tracts of land were handed out to peasants, but they were not given full ownership rights and they were organized into movements that came to fit perfectly the corporatist structure masterminded by the state (the Confederación Nacional Campesina created by Lázaro Cárdenas is a perfect case in point). After 1950, other countries implemented their own land reforms, from Guatemala in 1952 and Bolivia in 1953 to Peru in the early 1970s. The methods varied—Bolivia legalized invasions, Peru expropriated land from the hacendados and turned it into six hundred government-run cooperatives—but the result was generally the same, except that in Bolivia peasants were more successful at withstanding their government and taking private initiative.

The transition that took place was not from exclusive property by few private owners to full property by millions of private owners, but to a symbolic form of property by the peasants, while the state, the entity that embodied the collective rights of the masses, became the real owner. This new form of concentration, and the fact that much of the land untouched by this transfer was so small that almost no economy of scale could take place, explains in part why in the three decades after the Second World War agriculture grew at only half the rate of industry, the new star of the Latin American economy. It was only when, as happened in Peru after 1976, the government-run cooperatives began to sell the land on an illegal basis to peasant associations that some peasants became landowners. But since the parceling of land was illegal, transaction costs were high and access to credit, investment, and transfers of rights was severely limited on these small, undercapitalized, low-production plots. That is why, despite informal privatization, Peru's land reform accounts for a drop of 2.3 percent per capita in agricultural output between 1971 and 1983.

The concentration of property did not start with the revolutions and land reforms. It had been one of the evils of the old republic, a trigger of reform movements and wide protest in countries that eventually underwent revolution and in those that did not. By the 1950s, 60 percent of Argentina's land was owned by 2 percent of the country's estates or estancias; in Brazil, 1.6 percent of fazendas owned 50 percent of the land, and in El Salvador, 1 percent of the haciendas owned 50 percent of the land. In Peru, before revolution and land reform, coastal sugarcane estates took almost all the agricultural credit. As Ernest Feder wrote, latifundismo, a sort of land monopoly in the hands of the state-backed elite dating back many centuries, had been responsible for exploiting peasants through one-sided sharecropping, labor dues, evictions, and violence. The result was much less efficiency and productivity on the great estates than would otherwise have been the case and, more important, a landless mass of peasants shut off from the market. Given the situation, defenders of the status quo thought that any type of reform would violate the property of the big landowners, whereas land reformers, in many cases backed by programs such as the Alliance for Progress, failed to realize that substituting state bureaucracy for elite landowners would only aggravate the problem. Millions of Latin American peasants became the victims of this false dichotomy.

The old legacy of elitism continues to haunt countries like Brazil, where nearly half of the arable land is held by just 3 percent of all landowners. The Landless Movement founded in the mid-1980s has forced the government to give the poor some of the land it deemed unproductive, but the problem remains and is the cause of violence by landless peasants who invade property and powerful ranchers who seek to preserve the status quo.

"At times," wrote the Colombian writer Germán Arciniegas in 1958, "something worse than instability occurs: stability." No one would dare call all those twentieth-century decades marked by revolution "stable." And yet, in a deep sense, stability of the wrong kind was the ironic by-product of those tumultuous years. The seeds of illegitimacy, which had grown to make the early independent republic untenable, were still deeply ingrained in the Latin American soil, except that whole new masses of people had gained an entry into the new state of affairs. The oligarchic state had become the bureaucratic state.

Only one revolution produced a different kind of stability, or rather, a less deceptive kind of instability: the 1948 Costa Rican revolution. There, civilized coexistence, relatively secure institutions protecting certain rights from government intrusion, and a rejection of authoritarianism were the legacy of the 1948 insurgence of José Figueres. A few decades later, Costa Rica's superiority over the rest of Central America would come to be seen as a by-product of that revolution (and of a legacy of small and medium proprietors on much of the land). But even Costa Rica was later impregnated with the tradition of economic nationalism rising out of, and nurturing, revolutionary Latin America; underdevelopment would continue to be the Costa Rican condition as it sought to redress social ills with taxes and subsidies, with the nuances just mentioned.

Economic Nationalism: The Hour of the Snail

There was a moment in the early twentieth century when, after four centuries of intense relations with the rest of the world, three of them as a colony and one as a group of republics, Latin America decided to change course. It was not a tentative gesture of coyness or flirtation; rather, it was a conscious, thought-out drive for inwardness. The future, it was certain, lay not in the free dance of the gazelle across the global forest but in the hardened shell of the snail. It would from now on look inside its own sheltered space and extract from it the energy to move and to grow.

It is not easy to pinpoint at what precise moment that act of introversion—which was spiritual as well as political, as its depth, scope, and perseverance would show—took place. It may even have taken place in the waning years of the nineteenth century, when Argentina, Brazil, and Mexico sought to protect new industries with tariffs and encourage the import of machines to help develop the "national" economy, while Chile wanted to wrestle control of nitrates from England. Or perhaps it was later, after World War I, when the germs of European fascism traveled across the ocean and found a friendly body in the already corporatist organism of Latin America, paving the way for the nationalist epoch-making regimes of the next decades. Or was it after 1930, when all the aforementioned precedents found their hour in the hostile world of the Depression, when Latin American primary products were no longer in demand and the meddling of rich countries in the capital markets foreshadowed the drying up of the investment and financial well?

The reality is that by the 1930s, the Latin American outlook had dramatically changed. At the time it might not have been obvious that there was a connection between the right-wing corporatist regimes that were about to embark successively on a half century of economic nationalism and the left-wing movements, some of them violent and triumphant (as we saw earlier), that were either shaking or about to shake the various corners of the continent. But they were akin, just as the liberal and conservative enemies who soaked the soil of the nineteenth century with their bitter blood were akin underneath their very different outward expressions and manifest causes. These twentieth-century right- and left-wing currents were tied not only by a long tradition weighing against the individual. Whether in the name of the people and their symbol, the state, or in the name of the motherland, whether in pursuit of social justice or in pursuit of order, whether in the light of proletarian universality or Hispanic nostalgia, economic nationalism was born. Its breath enveloped every party, every church, every class, and every mind. Its philosophy acquired the proportions of an accepted truth; any sign of dissidence was a heretical affront.

The protectionist policies that crept into Latin America in the post–World War I period and gained momentum in the 1930s became a regionwide creed by midcentury. Raúl Prebisch, the Argentinean who in 1948 headed the Economic Commission for

Latin America and the Caribbean (ECLAC) and later became the first secretary-general of the United Nations Conference on Trade and Development (UNCTAD), was the ideological engine behind the new philosophy of structuralism, which impregnated governments, social institutions, intellectual circles, and public schools. No other body of ideas in the field of political economy had a greater, more pervasive, and longer-lasting influence on the century.

It is not the focus of this book; suffice it here to briefly describe its main tenets. Structuralism sought to explain underdevelopment as a condition derived from, and preserved by, unjust terms of trade between cheap primary exports coming from the "periphery" world and expensive manufactured goods going out to poor countries from the "center." Since rich countries "monopolize" capital and technology, poor countries are at a "structural" disadvantage—with their low-priced primary exports they do not earn enough foreign exchange to pay for the capital and technology they need in order to maintain appropriate levels of investment and to buy the manufactured goods that rich countries also "monopolize" (apart from the fact that domestic markets in underdeveloped countries are too small to sustain industrial growth and that multinational corporations take away much of the wealth derived from primary products). And why are these terms of trade ever widening against underdeveloped countries? Because the rise in population and the technological advances that enhance production in poor countries increase the quantity of primary products in the international market, while the rise of income in rich countries does not increase demand for those products; and because technology in the developed world encourages the substitution of primary products anyway. Trade barriers of various sorts and boom-bust cycles in rich countries are added to the "structural" impasse, causing poor countries to suffer continuous fluctuations in their export earnings. According to the ECLAC model, the shift in trade patterns was the main mechanism transmitting the Depression from the "center" to the "periphery" in the 1930s: the inflexible wages in rich countries and the very flexible wages in poor ones meant that unemployment was worse in the developed world, affecting the profitability of primary exports from the underdeveloped world.

Structuralism would "correct" the terms of trade through the use of tariffs, quotas, and exchange rates, all of which would create an environment in which domestic industrial production could thrive unhampered by foreign manufactures. Imports would still be necessary but would be limited to capital goods essential to sustain investment. Since this realignment of the economy could be achieved only through government actions, the state became the guarantor of national economic growth. It could not direct one area and leave others untouched because the model required an organic, systematic way of fitting all the elements into the puzzle. If industry, the muse of the era, was going to be adored, sacrificial lambs had to be offered. Government had to subsidize urban consumers at the cost of agricultural production. It needed to make sure that resources were allocated in the "right" place; therefore, it had to, either through direct ownership or indirect stimulus, favor certain investments—what the Swedish economic nationalist Gunnar Myrdal called "careful segmental planning." In short, economic nationalism pointed to the same phenomenon as the Mexican revolution: the enthronement of the state (really the government) as the body concentrating the collective identity of the people and the nation as a whole.

This nationalist view of political economy quickly became tinged with Marxist elements that echoed J. A. Hobson's and especially Lenin's view of imperialism as an international version of domestic class struggle. Terms of trade were not disadvantageous to Latin America by chance. Behind the economic realities there were active, imperialist forces. A later development of structuralism, of which Fernando Henrique Cardoso, who later became the president of Brazil, and others were primary intellectual powerhouses, came to be called the dependency theory. Since Latin America and other underdeveloped zones were the victims of a structural dependency that not even the import-substituting measures could entirely remedy, the solution was foreign aid. Raúl Prebisch himself had proposed, through UNCTAD, that rich countries contribute to the development of poor countries by devoting 1 percent of their national income to foreign aid. The dependency theory gave a philosophical justification to the need for an international reallocation of resources parallel to the one the governments of the underdeveloped world needed to conduct at home via economic nationalism.

The moral power of structuralism and the dependency theory was such that institutions of various kinds, including the church (liberation theology), political parties (from Marxist to Christian Democratic), and international bodies (the United Nations itself), espoused it and contributed to giving it credence across the region. All manner of organizations and leaders, of very contradictory natures and ideological dispositions, embraced import substitution, government-planned industrialization, and foreign aid directed toward myriad government programs as a way to break the structure of primary export dependency. The old export-led model was gone. The corporate beneficiaries of the old model were soon to be replaced, as we saw in the case of the Mexican revolution, with new corporate satellites of political authority—local industrialists, government functionaries controlling the import of capital goods and state enterprises, worker movements in certain areas of industry, and middle-class sectors tied to particular services linked to the nascent industries.

Economic nationalism had two decisive phases. The first one took place in the 1930s, and the second, really an expansion of the first but on much more systematic and ideological ground, came after World War II. Latin America's export economy was devastated in the 1930s by the world crisis. By 1932, the region was exporting 65 percent less than in the late 1920s. The disruption of exports, the contraction of foreign capital, and the rise in domestic public spending created such balance-of-payment problems that most countries in the region began to move in the direction of economic nationalism almost at once. The gold standard (which by then existed in limited form) was dropped in most countries. Devaluation ensued, multiple exchange rates were adopted, capital controls set in, tariffs were erected against foreign products, and other types of import control emerged. Up to the 1930s, high unemployment could easily be attributed to "external factors" since monetary policy was not discretionary and tariffs served a purely fiscal purpose. After the 1930s, politicians gained control of monetary policy, finding it useful in times of recession and unemployment, and saw the use of tariffs in a strategic new light. The export model under British influence had made Latin America the overwhelming supplier of primary products until World War I (accounting for 84 percent of coffee in the world markets, 64 percent of meat, 97 percent of nitrates,

50 percent of bananas, 30 percent of sugar, 43 percent of corn, and large volumes of metals). In the 1920s, the model survived, with somewhat less fluency and more hitches but no essential revision. By the 1930s, the model had collapsed.

Brazil experienced the Estado Novo (New State) under Getúlio Vargas, who rose to power in 1930; Mexico came under the grip of Lázaro Cárdenas in 1934; more than seven decades of free trade and liberalism in Argentina came to an end with military rule in 1930, and the era of the social-democratic Radical Party dawned in Chile. All of them engaged in, and symbolized, import substitution, an attempt to break away from the export-oriented heritage. Not all countries in Latin America pursued the same policies with equal vigor. The Southern Cone countries of Brazil, Argentina, and Chile were much more radical than smaller countries in Central America. Mexico, geographically much closer to the latter ones, belongs in political economy terms with the first group.

Although measures were adopted besides tariffs and exchange controls (including nationalizations in Mexico, state councils and the incorporation of corporatist functional representation in Brazil, and the creation of a central bank in Argentina), this first phase of economic nationalism was still "moderate" and lacked the pervasive, organic nature of the second phase, inaugurated after World War II under the ethos of structuralism and *desarrollismo* ("isms" are a rich contribution of twentieth-century Latin America).

Fiscal profligacy, although not as wild as after World War II, came into the nationalist economic scene, with the combined help of currency devaluation and deficit spending. Revolution was feared in many countries, a fear stemming from the ripples of the Mexican conflagration, the emergence of mass worker movements such as the APRA (Alianza Popular Revolucionaria Americana) in Peru, and the ideological penetration of communism in the hemisphere. The introduction of social welfare programs, a major reason for the expansion of public expenditure, was in many ways the child of that fear. It is not Latin America's first or last historic irony that economic nationalism was in fact deeply connected to the revolutionary spirit in its revolt against old corporate interests tied to the government and its replacement by new ones, and in the common vision of the state as the redeemer of the collective identity. The methods, the intensity, or the rhetoric might vary, but the essence of what was happening in the region was the same everywhere, whether it was revolutionary or reformist economic nationalism.

After World War II, import substitution gained new momentum and followed a logic of its own, an inertia dragging the Latin American governments toward ever-increasing intervention in the economy. If the government was going to play a key role in directing investment toward particular industries, then it might as well take direct ownership of those areas or exercise indirect control through cooperatives. If the government was going to determine what products were to be freely imported and what foreign products domestic consumers should avoid, then it might as well establish state trading monopolies. If particular activities were to be encouraged outside the sphere of state enterprises, then strict industrial and commercial licensing needed to be imposed. If unfavorable terms of trade and the developed world's monopoly of capital had been at the root of underdevelopment and import substitution was the answer to the third world condition, then capital and exchange controls (including differential rates) were imperative. If public spending was to be boosted, price controls were necessary to stem the effect of inflation. If credit was essential for greasing the industrial machinery, then credit needed to be subsidized. If expanding demand was an objective, with a view to goading production, then extensive collective bargaining, in many cases by trade, would help ensure that workers had enough money to buy things.

Brazil, Argentina, and Mexico were the engines of economic nationalism across the region. Juan Domingo Perón in Argentina became an emblem of these policies, which, as had previously been the case with Vargas in Brazil, were accompanied by intense corporatism reminiscent of Italian fascism—including labor codes, functional representation, and the incorporation of mass social movements into the orbit of the state. In Mexico, other PRI governments consolidated the legacy of Lázaro Cárdenas. In Brazil, Juscelino de Oliveira Kubitschek, the "modernizer," gave new impetus to industrialization. By the end of the 1960s, these three nations accounted for 80 percent of industrial production, while five others—Chile, Colombia, Peru,

Uruguay, and Venezuela—produced 17 percent of Latin America's industrial goods.

This second phase of import substitution was supported by considerable foreign investment. Tariffs guaranteed an absence of incoming competition to affiliates of the great industrial holdings and conglomerates of the developed countries. The majority of foreign investors in Mexico were American companies, while Brazil diversified its links, taking European and Japanese investments. Even Argentina after Perón welcomed massive foreign capital: by the late 1960s, eight of the ten most important industrial firms operating in the country were foreign.

As happens when investment is concentrated in a particular area and the government realigns the economy through a selective allocation of resources, many Latin American countries experienced industrial growth between the 1940s and the 1970s. The protection of the domestic market created conditions in which producers of industrial goods could export part of their output (primary exports, in many cases also controlled by foreign investors, continued). Mexico's economy could boast a 6 percent annual growth in those three decades, and Brazil, the only country that can be said to have developed a significant manufacturing export economy, reduced coffee, its former gem, to a mere 10 percent in foreign markets toward the end of the century.

But the basic economics of this model, whose statistical results did not reflect comparable improvements in standards of living and in consumption levels, were flawed. They incubated a crisis that was subdued by massive foreign lending in the 1970s but that eventually exploded in the 1980s. What incentive could there be for efficiency and the use of new technology in companies that operated in highly protected markets? How could high prices and costs resulting from trade barriers and other government guarantees given to domestic industries be sustained indefinitely? How could an economy that was living in a cloud, a fictitious environment, keep importing the ever-increasing quantity of capital goods and even raw materials needed to feed industrialization? How could the foreign exchange pressures caused by these imports allow for the acquisition of first-rate technologies in order to be competitive beyond reduced domestic markets? How could agriculture survive in nations where everything was geared toward industry, including subsidies and price controls favoring urban workers against the Argentinean pampas, the Brazilian land, or the Mexican ejidos? And how could industrialization be sustained in the absence of a solid agricultural base without massive food imports? And if rural areas were going to be depopulated as a result of the urban drive, how could these highly regulated economies absorb millions of new workers?

Economic nationalism—the era of the snail—entrenched new vested interests, powerful groups gyrating in the orbit of the political authorities. Some of these elite groups, mainly the beneficiaries of industrialization, belonged to the private sector; others, mammoth bureaucracies related to the economic state entities, belonged to the government. The latter elites included federal, regional, and local groups, which controlled money and regulatory powers, or directed social movements connected to the state. "Intermediary bodies" (the term used by many institutions, including the Catholic church), supposedly situated halfway between the basic social units of the family and the state but really signifying a new constellation of government satellites, became the new expression of limited individual rights.

Latin America still existed under the grip of corporatism, because rights were fragmentary and based on corporate identities, themselves dependent on the all-encompassing collective identity of the state; of state mercantilism, because the government deliberately determined success and failure among the citizens; of privilege, because the chosen corporations, including labor and business elites, were attached to the political authorities and derived their power from them; of bottom-up wealth transfer, because peasants subsidized the urban world, consumers subsidized the industries, taxpayers subsidized businesses favored by government intervention, and the elites maintained social representation and peace through the state; and, finally, of a legal wilderness, in which political law, ever changing and discretionary, was the tributary of the authorities' will. Within those parameters, part of the hemisphere experimented temporarily with democracy in the decades after World War II: Chile, Uruguay, and Venezuela after 1958; Brazil before 1964; briefly Argentina; intermittently Peru and Colombia despite violent civil strife. Others, especially but not exclusively Central America and the Caribbean, were swept by infamous dictatorships.

The Statistical Mirage

If one sticks to the statistics, it would seem that economic nationalism worked well for Latin America in the post–World War II era (the gross domestic product annual growth rate between 1950 and 1980 was 7 percent for Brazil, 6.5 percent for Mexico, 4.9 percent for Peru, and 3.8 percent for Argentina, whereas Chile's grew at a rate of 3.4 percent until 1970; these statistics compare well to those of the developed world, whose GDP grew at an annual rate of 4.8 percent between 1950 and 1973). But if one looks at the statistics before intense post-war industrialization, when there were very few state enterprises and moderate public spending kept inflation under control, the numbers were equally good (between 1935 and 1953, Latin America's GDP grew at an annual rate of 4.2 percent, and output per capita grew at a rate of 2 percent a year). Some countries, such as Brazil, not only had good growth rates before and after economic nationalism began, but actually boast a statistical average across the century superior to that of the United States (between 1900 and 1987, Brazil's GDP experienced the second-highest rate of growth in the world; in per capita terms the annual growth of its economy was the fourth fastest). The differences in economic growth between relatively free trade policies in the early twentieth century and import substitution later on are not huge, nor can overwhelming variations be observed during the period from 1950 to 1980, between those countries, like Mexico, in which massive industrialization took place, and those, like Costa Rica, in which public policies associated with that label did not reach a comparable apogee (in per capita terms, Mexico's economy grew by an annual rate of 3.5 percent in those three decades, and Costa Rica's grew by an annual rate of 3.1 percent).

It would seem, from analyzing the cold, enigmatic data, that nothing much accompanied Latin America's revolution and reform, that no real evolution occurred behind the ideological pendulum that straddles the spectrum of political economy from the early days of the twentieth century to the critical years of the 1980s. Many transformations did take place, and of course the fact that most Latin American countries went from being primarily rural to decisively urban indicates that there was at least as much shift in sociological terms as there was in the economic model and in patterns of economic production. But one paramount shift did not take place: Latin America was not able to break the chains of underdevelopment. By the 1980s, poor countries were no longer able to repay the petrodollars that had been recycled in the form of bank loans in the previous decade. Due to the oil boom, banks had lent out their excess money to developing nations without paying much attention to their financial health. Between 1979 and 1982, when international interest rates shot up from 11.5 percent to 20 percent, Latin America experienced a major debt crisis. Then the truth became evident: import substitution had failed miserably to achieve development, its single most important goal from the very beginning. Even statistics were no longer able to veil the truth. By the 1980s, Latin America's GDP per capita had fallen to less than one-third of the level in the core countries of the Organization for Economic Cooperation and Development (OECD) from a level of 45 percent in 1950. The planned, deliberate reallocation of resources was no longer able to sustain the growth of targeted sectors and, through them, of the overall statistics of the economy, themselves fractured, elitist, unreal reflections of society, not representative of the individuals' and the families' plight across each nation.

If all manner of public policies seemed unable to do the trick, there must be an underlying factor of underdevelopment that had not been addressed. Or, to turn it the other way around, there must be an immanent stumbling block, something common to the vastly different public policies spanning the century, a set of touchstone principles governing the relationship among Latin American individuals and between them and the institutions of power, that made sweeping transformations of the economy and of society insufficient to break the region loose from underdevelopment. The fact that once industrialization failed, these determining principles were overlooked by almost everyone meant that in the not so distant future, when inevitably the pendulum moved away from economic nationalism and back to free trade and smaller government, reform, however ambitious, might meet with similar frustration. And would it not also mean the second coming of illegitimacy, that devil which struck the nineteenth-century republic and impelled the early twentieth century into massive revolt?

The Absurd 1980s and the Collapse of the State

In the 1980s, for the second time since the beginning of independent republican life, Latin America's political institutions reached the point of collapse. Just as in the early years of the twentieth century the failure of nineteenth-century republics unleashed the destruction of the old regime either through revolution or through the emergence of the new state, in the 1980s, the spirit of revolt against the elitist system could be felt in the streets. The causes of both revolts were seemingly different—the nineteenth-century republic had deliberately excluded the masses; the state of the twentieth century purported to include everything and everyone—but the magnitude of the reaction indicated common frustrations. The state that encouraged participatory government became unable to give real meaning—economic substance—to the promise it signified in its collective embrace of the people. The crisis of the 1980s was what broke the spell of economic nationalism, but the failure had been a long time in the making.

There was no revolution this time, but every institution was subjected to such rejection that there was little doubt something revolutionary was taking place across the region. The manifestations were manifold, from the underground economy overflowing the legal framework of government to the proliferation of evangelical cults gnawing at the roots of the once unshakable Catholic church, from the emergence of mass movements and political outsiders that rose out of nowhere and pulverized traditional parties to word-of-mouth phenomena in the surrounding poverty-stricken shantytowns of major cities displacing advanced technological means of communication. All these symptoms pointed to one basic truth: the people were once again in revolt. It was revolt against the very same entity that had come to rescue them from the illegitimacy of the old republic, pretending to give a sense of belonging to the destitute and the underrepresented, a promise of vindication to those who had been left out of the republican feast.

What would the response of the new political authorities be in the 1990s, once the 1980s brought to the surface the desperate realities the 1970s had only masked, and accelerated the collapse of legitimacy, leaving profound traumas on the political psyche of the region? New attempts at reform, this time in the opposite direction: the so-called capitalist revolution in Latin America. Would those intending to restore the legitimacy of government and of the state understand the real causes of its demise, the subtle, disguised connections between this and the previous crisis of republican institutions, and therefore build capitalism this time upon foundations other than the ones formerly supporting it?

I will return to this later; for the moment, let us examine how the 1980s accelerated and unveiled the crisis of legitimacy. The great achievement of the decade was to expose the Latin American state as a carcass. Everything it seemed to be, it was not. It had grown in size to elephantine proportions. Virtually no area of the economy was free from its captivity. Public payrolls in each nation comprised hundreds of thousands, sometimes millions of people, and most of society depended in some way on commitments made by the government. Entitlements encompassed almost every aspect of people's lives: their job, their retirement, their health, their education, their business, their transport, their consumer needs, their leisure time. Of course, this was fiction. The wealth was simply not there to be distributed. The system through which the government attempted to distribute what was not real wealth was itself a major impediment to wealth creation.

Despite vast amounts of money given to Latin America in the 1970s by governments and banks in the developed world, investment rates did not exceed 16 percent of GDP, whereas other underdeveloped zones, such as Asia, were already approaching 25 percent. The problem was not lack of money, because there was plenty of it. The problem was a system that made it impossible to accumulate capital in a sustained way (capital flight itself being a consequence of bad policies and a cause, among others, of insufficient accumulation). It is no surprise that the asphyxiating distortions hindering capital accumulation held investment rates at low levels and accounted for a mere

0.5 percent rate of growth in per capita income during the 1970s and 1980s, against more than six times as much in Asia.

The fallacy on which economic nationalism was based—the idea that "dependency" was the root of underdevelopment—emerged only when it was no longer possible to sustain it in material terms during the 1980s. The fallacy should have been evident long before its consequences accelerated the loss of state legitimacy, if only because many countries had emerged from backwardness with very different recipes. As Peter Bauer has shown, in the half century between the Meiji restoration and World War I, the Japanese government sought to "import" Western modes and techniques, was able to finance the effort out of real resources, and made meaningful progress. Despite "terms of trade" no more favorable than those in Latin America, and perhaps worse, other countries were able to develop exporting capacities with some success (in fact Latin America itself had not done badly with many of its exports). The rubber industry of Southeast Asia began only around 1900, and by the 1960s it was exporting hundreds of millions of dollars. Hong Kong was but a shell in the first half of the nineteenth century, but by the end of the century it was a major port and an entrepôt, and by the 1970s it had become a potent manufacturing capital.

But Latin America had convinced itself that the problem of underdevelopment lay in "dependency," so it had embarked on the illusion of economic nationalism, as many other underdeveloped nations had done, such as General Gamal Abdel Nasser's Egypt and the Congress Party's India.

The 1980s belied the core tenets of Latin American nationalism through economic irony. At the heart of economic nationalism was the idea, on the one hand, that underdeveloped countries would reduce their dependence on certain imports and, on the other, that they would reduce and even eliminate their dependence on natural resources as key sources of export earnings. Latin American countries, however, did not significantly reduce imports and remained dependent on foreign exchange. In Brazil, for instance, the level of imports as a proportion of GNP decreased only moderately from that existing before import substitution (even if the composition of those imports changed). By the 1980s, some of the biggest Latin American countries were more dependent than ever on natural resources, particularly oil, and on the developed world's funding, except that this time it was not insufficient money resulting from the sale of products in the markets of the rich world so much as generous money lent or donated by those rich countries in order to finance the very same economic nationalism that was supposed to break the chains of dependency.

The real state of some of the weightier economies in the region was so calamitous that only natural resources sustained them, and foreign aid was practically the only compensation for the capital flying out. Oil revenues were four times higher in Venezuela between 1974 and 1983 than they had been in the previous ten years, but virtually all other areas of the economy saw their rate of growth diminish considerably, affecting the overall performance; by 1983, more employment was being lost than created. In Mexico, the growth of the economy was cut in half, and unemployment reached double digits in 1982, despite record revenues from oil in the previous decade. Capital flight in that same country amounted to an estimated $68 billion during the 1980s, more than the combined loans by the International Monetary Fund to the entire developing world between 1982 and 1989 (totaling some $54 billion). The situation, devastating for any notion of dependency reduction, would have been much worse had oil and foreign aid not existed.

The fact that both continued reliance on natural resources and dependency on foreign aid strengthened rather than reduced economic nationalism does not detract from the irony. By 1980, one of every two dollars lent to Latin America was directed toward servicing that very debt, which had grown to suffocating proportions; the panic created by both mounting debt and capital flight spurred governments, such as Mexico's in 1982 and Peru's in 1987, to nationalize the banks, previously heavily regulated but still in private hands. The more money that came in from multilateral institutions and private banks, and the more money that came in from natural resources such as oil, the more the governments spent and were forced to borrow—and the more dependent they became. By the mid-1980s, public spending in Mexico and Venezuela, both rich in oil, reached 61 and 57 percent of GDP respectively; the Venezuelan government employed almost one and a half million people; Mexico's government, four million. Counting all levels of government, Brazil more than doubled this figure.

Latin America was discovering that it was not possible to go down the path of economic nationalism only halfway. The logic of the model drove governments to expand into every sector of the economy in a desperate quest for new resources. Across Latin America, with some exceptions, oil, electricity, railways, banks, mines, water, telephones, steel, airlines, hotels, fishing, sugar, coffee, rice, beans, corn, trading, foreign exchange, and much more were under government control. By 1982, more than one thousand enterprises were owned by the Mexican government; more than 350 in Argentina were state owned. Helping reinforce this logic, in order to meet increasing social demands, were monetary expansion regardless of economic growth and, of course, foreign aid and borrowing. No matter how much money was spent, the quicksand of economic nationalism kept devouring the resources (the Chiapas rebellion in the south of Mexico revealed the uselessness of dozens of billions of dollars' worth of rural subsidies distributed in the 1970s and the 1980s by the Banco Nacional de Crédito Rural).

As Manuel Ayau has reasoned, foreign aid encouraged income and labor tax policies that sought to milk more money from small groups of people who were already paying too much (though income tax did not produce more than 1 percent of GDP in most countries), with millions in the informal and subsistence sectors not contributing fiscal revenue. Such policies propped up multiple exchange rates by which central banks paid those who earned foreign exchange less than it was worth and sold it at higher prices to the various parties depending on it, giving further impetus to rigid labor norms that conferred privilege on those already employed while making it ever more costly for jobs to be created. Corporatism, state mercantilism, privilege, bottom-up wealth transfer, and political law made sure, as always, that particular beneficiaries of the system—this time of everything from subsidies to license monopolies to price controls to specific exchange rates to tax exemptions to labor laws—had a vested interest in perpetuating it. Rent-distributing economies do not exist without rent seekers.

After half a century of acting the snail, the ingrown flaws of the Latin American economy produced the financial debacle for which that region is remembered in relation to the 1980s. This decade could have been remembered as a time when dictatorships were replaced with democracies, a transition that reduced political repression and increased the accountability of public office as well as free expression without bringing about profound institutional reform. But financial chaos and the social indignation derived from a 10 percent fall in per capita income displaced the positive developments from the region's memory. It took many years to understand that fiscal disaster, default, astronomical inflation, and currency debasement were all symptoms rather than causes.

In any case, the financial episodes bear historic relevance insofar as they paved the way for reform in the 1990s. Had Mexico's 1982 default on its $86 billion debt not occurred, had Argentina's, Peru's, Bolivia's, and Nicaragua's four- and five-digit annual hyperinflation not taken place, had external mistrust of the region not reduced capital inflows to little over 1 percent of the combined GDP (or, to put it another way, had net external outflows not totaled $220 billion during the decade), the stage would not have been set in the 1990s for one of the most radical attempts at reform in two centuries. The popular reaction against the illegitimacy of the state and the political class was certainly detonated by the havoc incurred by the crisis in the 1980s. The causes were decades in the making, but the trigger had everything to do with the immediate crisis.

A number of circumstances brought into the open the hidden weaknesses of governments that had grown formidably in size and weight while standing on feet of clay. A slowdown in the world's economy reduced Latin America's exports earnings in the early 1980s, further exposing currencies that had been overvalued since the late 1970s—in part due to oil prices and excessive borrowing from abroad—despite an incessant hemorrhage of capital and fiscal disarray. The 1981 contraction pushed the situation to the brink. It is no surprise that Mexico's 1982 default on its debt shocked the international financial community. The rest of the region, with a few exceptions, followed suit in the following months and years. Three-quarters of the debt (more than $1,000, the equivalent of some countries' per capita income, for every man, woman, and child) was held by commercial banks, many of them in the United States. So Latin America made international headlines.

Default was not the end but the beginning of the crisis. Massive currency devaluation ensued, accompanied by skyrocketing inflation. Multilateral bodies, like the International Monetary Fund, became the last resort for desperate governments, which in turn were accused by hungry hordes in the streets of selling out to those foreign powers perceived as having caused Latin America's instability. It would be a few more years before economic nationalism became known as the culprit. In the meantime, the political and the business elites demanded, and the streets cried for, more economic nationalism.

Absurdly, the multilateral bodies themselves pushed through measures that worsened matters and took governments farther down the devastating path of economic nationalism. In exchange for aid, the IMF demanded that countries devalue their currencies in order to artificially generate export earnings while correcting the imbalance between inflation and exchange rate levels, but in anticipation of devaluation, inflation shot up. Phenomenal pressure was exerted on governments to raise taxes, thus suffocating the slim taxpaying elites and increasing evasion, and further alienating the underground economy from the legal taxpaying economy. High tariffs were tolerated, even applauded, by the IMF as a way to limit the trade gap with a view to achieving an export surplus that would allow for debt servicing. Clearly, no attention was being paid to Chile, which, despite its own financial crisis, was heading the opposite way and, after having slashed tariffs to 15 percent, was showing that export surpluses are not necessary in order to service the debt as long as you have a trusted and stable currency, and enough tax revenues.

In practice, the international financial community ended up backing expansionist monetary and fiscal policies, protectionism, and the growth of government. Because there were no bond markets due to lack of investor confidence, stock markets had tiny capitalization (Brazil's was one-third that of Malaysia), and private banks did not want to lend any more money to countries that had already defaulted or were on the verge of doing so. Whimsical monetary expansion at home and multilateral largesse from abroad were the only sources of capital, barring a radical transformation of the economic model. The latter duly obliged, trying to save the model with the aforementioned conditions that only served to compound it. The snail's shell was reinforced by the outside world from which it was supposed to be protecting the little creature inside—one more irony of economic nationalism.

No statistics can capture the atmosphere of utter failure among the people of Latin America's recently recovered democracies. What had started as social malaise had turned to violence, hatred of the political class, distrust of government, distrust for the law, calls for dissolving the republics that were supposed to have replaced the oligarchies of the past—precisely the social rebellion that the state of the people and economic nationalism had set out to avoid in many countries decades before. Mentioning that the "lost decade," as it came to be known, produced negative GDP growth of –1.1 percent in Argentina and –1.2 percent in Peru, or tiny positive growth of 1.3 percent in Brazil and 1 percent in Mexico (in this case not counting the early reform years from 1986 onward) does not convey the full collapse of the social and economic model. Referring to per capita incomes one-sixth of those in the United States in the 1980s does not begin to express how decrepit the republican state had grown across the region, what a chasm had opened between the authority of government and the respect of the people for anything associated with representative or official institutions.

Government had never been bigger in 160 years of independent republican life, yet it had never been more devoid of meaning and consistency—of legitimacy. There were varying grades and even exceptions. Chile had begun its free-market reforms in the 1970s, so its 1980s slowdown, including the 1982 financial crisis, in the midst of military dictatorship was of a different nature and found citizens in a different situation, marked by economic change. Colombia was the only country that maintained steady growth, not because economic nationalism was absent but because it was somewhat less intense and pervasive, adding to the fact that democracy had been pretty stable since 1957 and a particularly steadfast business elite had kept up investment. Costa Rica, the most stable country with uninterrupted democracy since 1948, did suffer notable economic slowdown during the decade, but its political sanity and the less powerful grip of economic nationalism on its society preserved it from the collapse of institutional legitimacy that took place elsewhere.

The century was to end the way it started, with a massive assault against the status quo. That assault, a combination of daily survival and conscious dissidence, was already happening among the lower ranks of society in the 1980s, but the 1990s would bring about reaction from the elites too. It would be called many things—"capitalist revolution," "liberalism," "neoliberalism," "free-market reform"—and it would constitute, first and foremost, a new attempt to marry the citizens of the republic with the institutions gone adrift. The twentieth century had brought new representations to a stage in which the individual was still the eager actor being pushed out of the scene. But the pieces of the machine making that stage gyrate had remained the same. Would they be different this time?

3

Friendly Fire from the United States

Logic—if logic has anything to do with this matter—suggests that Latin America should have benefited from being in close proximity to the United States and learning the lessons of capitalist development by proxy. Although the United States moved away from small government after World War I, its socioeconomic system has always tended toward individual rights. The success of America is no mystery. Latin Americans admired their northern neighbor during the nineteenth century and at the same time hated all things Spanish. In the twentieth century, their hatred turned to the United States and, perhaps as a result of the Spanish-American War of 1898, in which Spain was humiliated, they began to reexamine their feelings. But whatever their feelings toward the United States, they never sought to emulate or to beat it at its own game.

Equally perplexing is the fact that at no point in the last two centuries has the United States promoted the kinds of policies that could have helped Latin American nations develop into healthy trading partners, solid political interlocutors, and trustworthy neighbors (which does not imply that Latin America's development depends on whether the United States promises the right kinds of policies; promoting the wrong kinds of policies, however, reinforces underdevelopment). When Latin America suddenly became crazy for "capitalist" reform in the early 1990s, after experiencing economic disaster and the collapse of institutional legitimacy, the United States did not have a clue as to the real causes of the crisis. It is no surprise that, when sweeping "capitalist" reform began, the U.S. government, along with Wall Street investors and the media, wholeheartedly embraced it as a sign of the long-awaited transformation of the region. Had they understood the

fundamental flaws of Latin America's political and economic institutions, they might have wondered whether "capitalist" reform mounted on the existing anticapitalist scaffolding would really do the trick.

This lack of awareness grew out of nearly two centuries of ignorance about what was really happening to the south, even if the exterior signs of threatening instability seemed easily identifiable. In order to fully comprehend underdevelopment up to the 1990s in Latin America and the matrix into which reforms were subsequently shaped, it is necessary briefly to assess how the United States related to its southern neighbor as it impoverished itself. In many ways, U.S. policy strengthened the five principles of oppression south of the Rio Grande.

Guns and Loans

In the nineteenth century, the United States had no real policy toward Latin America. Traditional opinion maintains that imperialism began in the early 1800s with the Monroe Doctrine and crystallized with the annexation of Texas, California, Nevada, Utah, and parts of Arizona, New Mexico, Colorado, and Wyoming. Although both episodes testify to the hegemonic impulses of an emerging power (and numerous injustices, including loss of land, befell the Spanish-American settlers once the Anglo-Americans colonized the West and Southwest), the Monroe Doctrine really acted as a warning to Europeans to stop meddling in the hemisphere. The wars with Mexico were not so much the result of a plan designed to deprive that country of its northern half as they were the forceful seizure of an opportunity in territories that were very scarcely populated, which Spain had not entirely controlled in colonial times and which, especially in the case of Texas, included U.S. immigrants with greater loyalties to the United States than to the recently declared Mexican Republic. Unquestionably this was part of a broad pattern of territorial expansion west and south, but it was not necessarily a policy geared toward imperial dominance of Latin America.

In the wake of the Spanish-American War, which inaugurated a more "imperialistic" type of U.S. involvement abroad, the twenti-

eth century brought about specific policies toward Latin America. Throughout the century, the United States moved between interventionism and condescension. Interventionism spans everything from the occupations of Cuba, Nicaragua, Panama, the Dominican Republic, and Haiti to cold war conflict by proxy in the 1980s to the war against drugs in the Andes. Condescension has its roots in Roosevelt's Good Neighbor Policy and Kennedy's Alliance for Progress. Running parallel to these policies is a faint pattern of trade and investment promotion that has never been as consistent and grand as "anti-imperialists" would have it. It started in Washington with the 1889 Pan-American Conference that failed to create a customs union and continues to this day with current efforts to establish a (limited) Free Trade Area of the Americas despite persistent trade barriers on the part of the United States and mistrust on the part of Latin America.

What is the standard by which one should judge American foreign policy toward Latin America during the twentieth century? Presumably, the standard is the extent to which Latin America did or did not become a worthy trading partner, a secure and consistent destination for American capital, and a politically stable democratic region—all of these being manifest objectives of U.S. policy.

Was Latin America by the end of the twentieth century a more worthy trading partner for the United States than it was at the beginning? The United States began to take an interest in the region, in open competition with European countries such as the United Kingdom, Germany, and the Netherlands, at the end of the nineteenth century. That interest increased during the first three decades of the twentieth century, when its southern neighbors were still actively engaged in globalization. By 1929, 19 percent of U.S. exports went to Latin America, while 39 percent of Latin American imports came from the United States and 34 percent of its exports went to the U.S. market. These figures were similar to 1914 figures—World War I had temporarily disrupted trade patterns and by the end of the 1920s they had recovered. What was happening six decades later, by the end of the 1970s? By then, 16 percent of U.S. exports went to Latin America, 31 percent of Latin American imports came from the United States, and 35 percent of Latin American exports went to the U.S. market. Therefore, by the last quarter of the twentieth century, trade relations between the United States and Latin America had not improved.

Did Latin America offer more attractive opportunities for U.S. capital by the end of the 1970s than it did in the early days of the 1900s? By 1929, one-third of U.S. investment abroad was in Latin America. By the end of the 1970s, Latin America represented only 18 percent of U.S. investments abroad, a considerable drop in proportional terms. As in the case of trade patterns, figures from the late 1970s are used so as to avoid the critical 1980s that paved the way for reform, since that decade made matters worse for both trade and investment.

And, finally, can it be said that by the end of the century Latin America had ceased to be a source of political instability for the hemisphere? The very term "Latin America" evokes anything but stability, rendering justice to the title of Andres Oppenheimer's book *Bordering on Chaos*. Although many Latin American governments held elections, they were often not bound by the rule of law and simply meant that communism and military juntas were not in control. Everything else—human rights abuses, political persecution, subservient judiciaries, lack of accountability, widespread corruption, virulent demagoguery, social upheaval, and the absence of individual economic rights—continued, with notable exceptions, to be the salient traits of those nations.

U.S. foreign policy toward its southern neighbors failed to strengthen civil society vis-à-vis government, the extension of economic rights to the less fortunate under politically neutral institutions, and the placement of the authorities under the rule of law (even if in many cases these were the stated aims of U.S. foreign policy). It is often said that American foreign policy is reactive, focusing on short-term measures rather than strategic solutions. Although the primary responsibility for the failure of the economy rests with Latin Americans themselves, a strategy that took into account the corporatist, state-mercantilist, privilege-ridden, wealth-transferring, political law–inspired nature of Latin America's underdevelopment could have at least avoided reinforcing those conditions. Interventionism in the Caribbean and Central America propped up governments that were as corrupt as the enemies they struggled against. And they represented, as in the case of Anastasio Somoza in Nicaragua, Fulgencio Batista in Cuba, and many others, prototypes of state mercantilism favoring particular investors, local and foreign. Interventionism against left-wing South American governments typically served the purposes of right-wing dictatorships, as in Brazil in the 1960s and Chile in the 1970s, not of the democratic alternatives. On many occasions, it must be said, domestic interests openly called for U.S. intervention. It was seldom the case that military action on the part of the northern neighbor lacked local allies. Furthermore, the polarization stemming from the cold war and the dearth of democratic options narrowed the "choices" available to U.S. foreign policy.

But the methods were not always bloody or aimed at overthrowing Latin American governments. On occasion, gunboat diplomacy was used to establish customs receiverships whereby the United States seized control of a debtor country's customs.

Interventionism might have contained communism's spread and prevented the Nazi Party from establishing a foothold in Latin America (many Nazi fugitives took refuge in Argentina after World War II), but it certainly did not favor the interests of the rule of law and capitalism. The effect of interventionism has been twofold. On the one hand, authoritarian, corrupt, and mercantilist institutions were reinforced. On the other, American actions in the region caused many Latin Americans to direct their resentment toward the other values that America purported to stand for.

Direct intervention was by no means the only reactive policy that fed Latin America's traditional institutions and political culture. There were instances of friendly diplomacy too. Those two emblems of U.S. condescension, the Good Neighbor Policy and the Alliance for Progress, were reactive policies but also well-meaning. The Good Neighbor Policy sought to prevent Nazism and fascism from making inroads in Latin America; the Alliance for Progress aimed to suppress communism in the region (Harry S. Truman's 1949 Point Four program, which created foreign aid to underdeveloped countries, also sought to undermine communism). Both programs were funded by the U.S. government and supported by government programs or by organizations that were intertwined with the domestic corporations of economic nationalism in Latin America. The Good Neighbor Policy, which ostensibly sought to promote free trade, provided funds for industrial development, which in practice meant import substitution. The Alliance for Progress stated in its very charter that most of its

$20 billion would come from public funds; therefore it is no surprise that between 1961 and 1965 the amount of U.S. taxpayers' money for the Alliance for Progress doubled. The origin of the money was as much a problem as the destination, because funds provided by a foreign government tend to go to programs blessed—if not run—by the receiver country's authorities. Even when they do not, the result is favoritism and discrimination in the marketplace, not competitive capitalism.

While the Alliance for Progress promoted trade among Latin American nations, the practical effect was that some policies of economic nationalism became regional rather than national. In fact, some of the ideologues of import substitution and the dependency theory responded to the failures of their philosophy by defending the concept of Latin America as a Latin fortress that would reproduce the tenets of economic nationalism on the continental level. The flaws of U.S. policy toward Latin America were compounded by American protectionism at home. Franklin D. Roosevelt protected agriculture, Dwight D. Eisenhower protected oil, and the successive presidents by and large maintained tariffs and nontariff barriers that did not help make the case for Latin American free trade.

Public policy was not the only source of U.S. involvement in Latin America's economic nationalism. In the 1970s, private banks played a crucial role with massive lending of petrodollars to the region. The abundance of money in the banks because of high oil prices and the fact that corporations were relying on commercial paper rather than bank credit to raise capital meant that, in the absence of local companies seeking loans, underdeveloped countries were an ideal outlet for idle dollars. Latin America went wild over easy money and negative real interest rates until in 1979 the second oil shock triggered recession in the developed world. The rise in interest rates and recession in the United States suddenly exposed the fragility of Latin America's economic nationalism. Reform was not yet in the air: Latin Americans, encouraged by multilateral bodies, chose to incur new debt in order to pay the old debt. With regional debt skyrocketing, Latin America was headed for disaster.

Bad Conscience, Bad Economics

Almost every possible type of resource has been transferred from rich countries to poor countries in one way or another, except the intangible one: the secret of development. In fact, the transfers—whether in the form of capital goods, foreign aid, investment money, or loans—had the inadvertent effect of sustaining underdevelopment. Rich countries accepted the idea that Latin America needed capital goods to create its own industrial base, so as not to have to import manufactured goods costing more than the foreign exchange earned from primary products. Even when these "dependency" fallacies became outdated, foreign aid continued to be heaped on underdeveloped nations as a way of providing funds for investment. It was thought that once Latin American countries had the financial resources from abroad it would be only a matter of time before investment spurred development. It should have been easy to determine that simply mounting capital on the scaffolding of underdevelopment would not trigger prosperity. If foreign investment, which has for the most part been far more substantial than aid, failed in the twentieth century, how could international largesse achieve the objective?

Rich countries did not develop because of industrialization. On the contrary: industrialization followed development, which in many Western nations was already under way in the old agrarian economy. Manufacturing, as Peter Bauer has said, is not a "cause" but a "symptom" of development. Importing capital goods in order to augment investment, or using foreign aid to invest in local industry, does not produce development unless the causes of development—the institutions of liberal capitalism—are in place. Throwing money into Latin America in the hope of raising investment levels will develop only those sectors that enjoy secure property rights. Barring the right kind of climate, investment will enhance only certain enclaves, diverting resources from consumption goods, agriculture, or the many services that Latin American nations can provide, including tourism. By the early 1990s, most of Brazil's exports were manufactures, as opposed to less than 10 percent just three decades before, but despite the impressive level of industrialization achieved by that country, it is far from developed. On the other hand, industrialization did become a manifestation of development in environments where institutional frameworks were more conducive to real capitalism, such as East Asia, Spain, Ireland, and Quebec. In any case, the supply and productivity of capital, and the levels of capital formation, depend on the institutions and the capacity of individual enterprise within those institutions, not on investment of funds received from abroad via the World Bank, the IMF, USAID, or any other form of wealth transfer from rich countries. With such funds, a country can temporarily raise levels of consumption and investment, but development does not automatically flow from that effect.

Multilateral bodies such as the International Monetary Fund, the World Bank, and the Inter-American Development Bank have contributed to the region's underdevelopment (something they seem increasingly aware of). The resources they have channeled have had three consequences: strengthening statism, postponing adequate solutions, and displacing political responsibility.

The first consequence comes from funding government programs or government-backed private programs that generate parasitism by encouraging reliance on other people's means rather than one's own efforts in order to sustain an activity. Although both the World Bank and the Inter-American Bank have branches devoted to private projects, they allocate only a fraction of their funds to such purposes. The result of their lending policies is irrefutably expressed in their internal reports, which point to inefficiency, and sometimes corruption, on the part of the recipients of their money.

The second consequence of the loans, the postponement of adequate solutions, stems from the fact that governments, and in no small measure the nongovernmental organizations (NGOs), to which the funds have been channeled have devoted much energy to pushing for big government (and demanding new loans) rather than reforming their own countries.

The third consequence, the displacement of responsibility, is linked to the second: Latin American countries have resorted to blaming international bodies for evils whose major causes lie at home.

Nothing attests so clearly to the failure of development loans than the fact that in the 1990s multilateral bodies helped fund the privatization of state projects that had been originally funded by them.

The case of the International Monetary Fund is telling. That entity was not created to perform the functions of a bank, although it has acted like one in recent decades. In the 1970s, the IMF gave loans to Latin American countries to help them solve their balance-of-payment difficulties. By 1979, it became obvious that governments were not generating the resources needed to pay back their debts. Payments were then "reprogrammed": the IMF lent more money so that countries could continue to service their debt. In the 1980s, "structural adjustment programs" came onto the scene, through which, in exchange for a fiscal tightening on the part of the debtor country, the IMF made yet more loans. Tens of billions of dollars of foreign funding proved useless: it was indeed a "lost decade."

The War on Drugs

In the last two decades of the twentieth century, but especially during the 1990s, U.S. policy toward Latin America came to be dominated by the war on drugs. It was the culmination of a long process that started in 1914 when the Harrison Act forbade the sale of heroin, cocaine, and other substances in the United States, continued in 1937 with the addition of marijuana to the blacklist, and escalated to an outright war under Richard Nixon in the 1970s. At the end of the century, narcotics became the focal point of U.S. foreign policy toward Latin America, a major supplier. Funding for drug eradication and interdiction as well as crop substitution was tripled under Ronald Reagan, and spending on the "supply side" offensive increased by multiples of ten under Bill Clinton. Not surprisingly, George W. Bush has stepped up the effort. Every political or commercial improvement in the relationship between Washington and its southern neighbors happens as a reward for each country's effort against coca growing and drug trafficking. Equally, failure of "source" countries to cooperate means they are subject to economic penalties. Nothing illustrates better the entanglement of commercial and political issues with the war on drugs than the fact that the Andean Trade Preference Act (ATPA) exempting a few Andean countries' exports from tariffs, a cornerstone of Washington's relations with those countries, was renewed in 2002 as the Andean Trade Preference and Drug Enforcement Act

(ATPADEA). Every official speech, every high-level visit, every agreement signed by a representative of the U.S. government, stressed the issue.

The drug war pivoted on repression, not only at home but also at the source (by 2003, the Drug Enforcement Adminstration employed more than nine thousand people!). Half of the cocaine consumed in the United States was produced in Colombia, and coca leaves were grown in Peru and Bolivia (and later in Colombia). The policy of repression meant reducing supply with military force aimed at crop plantations and refining facilities just as much as at smuggling circuits. Creating incentives for peasants to produce alternative crops was part of the strategy. The responsibility fell on Latin American military and law enforcement units; the money, equipment, and training—and, above all, the relentless political pressure—were essentially provided by Washington. The United States went to war by proxy against a profitable business that was impossible to halt. The senseless war against the laws of supply and demand raised prices artificially, and therefore the profits and power of drug smugglers.

Not surprisingly, in the late 1980s the drug trade became intertwined with terrorist insurgency in Colombia through the activities of three groups: FARC (Fuerzas Armadas Revolucionarias de Colombia, Colombian Revolutionary Armed Forces), ELN (Ejército de Liberación Nacional, National Liberation Army), and the right-wing paramilitary AUC (Autodefensas Unidas de Colombia, United Self-Defense Forces of Colombia). Between 50 and 60 percent of their income was drug related, and they engaged in everything from coca leaf and opium cultivation to processing and distributing cocaine and heroin. They imported the raw material from Peru and Bolivia for a while, then started taxing and protecting coca and opium poppy cultivation inside Colombia. Terrorist groups grossing hundreds of millions of dollars each year from the drug business were soon as much a part of the "drug problem" as were the various cartels based in Colombia, with ramifications in other countries, including Mexico (drawn into the conflict because the drug war managed to divert the point of entry from Florida to California and Texas), the immediate neighbor of the United States. Colombia's social fabric and institutional structure were torn apart and remain in shambles to this day.

Drug-financed terrorist groups achieved such control of villages and towns across Colombia in the 1990s that a survey showed that 57 percent of heads of households had used, or knew people who had used, the informal dispute resolution mechanisms offered by neighborhood councils under control of the FARC; 35 percent of them attested to participating in communal public works coordinated by the FARC. The problem got worse with every new government and policy. Nothing had worked in the 1980s—not extradition of drug lords to the United States or, later, various negotiations between the government and the drug-financed insurgents thanks to which two smaller groups laid down their weapons in 1990. Nothing was working now either. In desperation, the government ceded 16,000 square miles of territory to the FARC between 1998 and 2001 as an incentive to negotiate peace, at the same time that the armed forces were beefed up in part with money from the United States. The terrorists and the drug lords were as powerful as ever.

Since drug-related finance was the decisive element behind the insurgents' forever-growing power and infrastructure, the drug war, constant even when the authorities were negotiating with terrorist groups, must bear no small responsibility for failure to stem the advance of terrorism and for the institutional and moral devastation that, as a result of violence and corruption brought forth by the illegal organizations, Colombians and neighboring Andean countries suffered year after year.

In 1998, the Colombian government announced the $7 billion Plan Colombia, ostensibly to revive the peace process and stimulate the economy as well as to reduce the supply of drugs. But this last component was truly the essence of the plan. The United States committed $1.3 billion, a good portion of which was earmarked for training and equipping Colombian antidrug units with Black Hawk and Huey helicopters, in addition to updating interdiction aircrafts. The helicopters could not be used against the terrorists, only against drug-related activities, a mystifying policy since Plan Colombia was a mobilization against the perverse institutional and economic effects of the combined, deeply related onslaught of drugs and terrorism. Colombia became the third-largest recipient of U.S. military assistance in the world.

Under the plan, drug-producing regions would be reclaimed by the government with the use of military force, potent chemicals would annihilate coca leaves and poppy fields, and laboratories and transport facilities would be destroyed. Impoverished, violent Colombia suddenly found itself engaged in a national strategy aimed at reducing the supply of drugs to the United States. Much of Colombia's resources and time were devoted to the cause in order to maintain good diplomatic relations with Washington.

Between 1999 and 2001, thousands of acres of coca leaves were sprayed from the air. Out of a total of 400,000 acres of coca plantations, between one-quarter and one-third were eradicated. The result? Legal crops and the neighboring population were affected, protests ensued, and coca bushes moved to neighboring Peru, even to Bolivia, and after a while they sprang back in Colombia. In fact, coca cultivation in the Andean region experienced a 21 percent increase during Plan Colombia's first fiscal year. It is therefore no surprise that the supply of cocaine in the United States did not diminish and that prices did not increase (apart from the fact that from time to time cocaine gains or loses ground vis-à-vis other drugs in the United States, and that other regions, especially Europe, also keep up international demand).

Despite spending more than $25 billion during the 1990s on fighting the drug war overseas, the U.S. government concluded that Plan Colombia's failure was a problem of scope. Therefore, the government appropriated another $1.5 billion in 2002 to go toward Colombia's drug war. This time U.S.-funded helicopters were allowed in combat against terrorist insurgents. Again, a reduction in Colombia's crop of coca by an estimated 15 percent was matched by an increase in Peru and Bolivia, according to both the U.S. Drug Enforcement Administration and the UN's Office for Drug Control. Within Colombia's borders the virtual eradication of coca from Putumayo coincided with an increase in output in Guaviare and a proliferation of smaller plots. Consequently, the supply—the main target of the drug war—did not diminish. As Steven Wisotsky has said, "If the cocaine industry commissioned a consultant to design a mechanism to ensure its profitability, it could not have done better than the war on drugs: just enough pressure to inflate prices, but not enough to keep its produce from the market."

The war on terrorism after the 9/11 attacks on the United States made it possible to widen the scope of military involvement in

Colombia by expanding the Pentagon's Miami-based Southern Command, which now sought to engage Andean countries much more forcefully in a regional security strategy and beef up its bases from Central America to the Amazon jungle. The new, wider focus made it easier for the United States to assist Colombia in its efforts to protect the Caño Limón–Covenas oil pipeline in a country where it is estimated that only one-fifth of oil fields have been explored and where American and Canadian firms compete with European firms in the search for that coveted resource. Drugs, however, were still the main objective, since Colombian terrorism is overwhelmingly dependent on that illegal business for funding. In that sense, the misguided drug war was the war on terrorism's worst enemy in the region. As Plan Colombia expanded, the Colombian drug-financed terrorist organizations, benefiting from high prices and uninterrupted supply resulting from the erroneous strategy, were crossing into Peru via the Putumayo River, into Ecuador at Sucumbíos, into Venezuela at Zulia, Táchira, and Apure, and into Brazil's Amazon region. The United States found itself conditioning relations with the affected countries—already devoting much time and resources toward goals other than development—on the establishment of more military bases and cooperation.

Plan Colombia did not fail. What failed is the three-pronged strategy of the drug war: interdiction, eradication, and crop substitution. Bolivia experienced a similar disaster in 1998, when the United States "urged" that country to put into practice the Dignity Plan in the Chapare region. The Bolivian military uprooted thousands of acres of coca plantations, and by 2001, coca leaf was reduced from close to 100,000 acres to 7,000 acres (another 24,000 acres were legally grown in other parts of the country). Tens of thousands of families lost their livelihood overnight, unable to sell for a profit the pineapples and bananas with which they attempted to replace coca bushes worth $400 million. The result was revolt—violent clashes with the police and many casualties.

The Bolivian authorities sent an expeditionary force of veteran soldiers trained and paid by the U.S. government. As could be expected, this force soon stood accused of atrocious human rights violations. Is it any wonder that Evo Morales, the son of Andean shepherds and a firebrand anti-American demagogue, almost made it to the presidency by defending the right to grow coca leaves and denounce Yankee bullies?

What could the United States show in return? The supply of cocaine into the American market did not diminish, and street prices remained the same. The consequences of this policy went beyond riots and outbursts of anger, and the emergence of a powerful, radical left-wing demagogue. The cause of free markets was in question, in part because the United States promised access to the U.S. market for Andean products while coca was being eradicated but did not deliver on time and without heavy conditions. The U.S. government's actions, particularly domestic agricultural subsidies that total $50 billion—or 21 percent of the farming industry's income—so contradicted promises of free trade that many Bolivians lashed out against the very idea of free trade, urged on by agitators who found in the devastating results of the drug war a perfect pretext for America bashing. The irony was that, while the country was busy protesting, coca cultivation was back: 95 percent of bushes being eradicated in 2002 were recently planted (by 2003, ten thousand new acres of illegal coca had popped up, according to the U.S. government). The fall of President Gonzalo Sánchez de Lozada in 2003, ostensibly due to a gas project that triggered popular upheaval and saw Evo Morales again in the streets, owed much to the drug conflict.

The case of Peru is just as telling. In the 1990s, deciding that the authoritarian policies of Alberto Fujimori and his dark prince, Vladimiro Montesinos, were necessary to combat terrorism and drugs, Washington accepted that the rule of law, freedom of the press, and other minutiae could be sidestepped. More than $110 million from U.S. taxpayers poured in. For a while, incentives given to peasants for crop substitution reduced coca growing by 60 percent. But those plantations ended up in Colombia. A few years later, with Peru deep in recession, its dictatorship's grip slackening, and the United States helping drive plantations from Colombia, coca returned with a vengeance. As in the case of Plan Colombia, Washington attributed the failure to insufficient resources. In 2002, the amount of U.S. taxpayers' money devoted to coca eradication in Peru tripled. By then, amid official U.S. complaints against Peru, peasants were ripping out coffee plants, cacao trees, and other crops, and replacing them with coca, three times as profitable. With the Maoist Shining Path making a comeback, drug lords started once again to pay terrorists for protection, and with that same money the terrorists bought their food from peasants. As in Bolivia, anti-American sentiment began to surface again in 2003; mobilizations were met with bloody repression in the Apurímac and Ene valleys and other regions of Peru's interior.

America's drug war has in no way advanced the cause of free markets and the rule of law. It is, in effect, a policy that thrives on repression and the suffocation of supply by engaging underdeveloped countries in a forceful reallocation of resources, the commitment of political capital, and the cession of civilian power to their military establishments, and it has been counterproductive, hurting individual rights and further weakening institutional safeguards against intrusive government. Just as interventionism and condescension, the two poles between which U.S. policy toward Latin America has oscillated, have caused resentment, the drug war has pushed the United States and Latin America as far apart as ever.

Free Trade—But Not Too Much

The United States and other developed nations have traded at an impressive pace since the end of World War II. Trade has grown at a faster rate than production and has practically come to define the era. Globalization, the buzzword of the early twenty-first century, rests in no small part on the expanded opportunities of international exchange. The political and moral force of free trade is such that even the nationalist left and the nationalist right pay lip service to it. Politicians never say that they are against free trade. If they are, they tend to argue that a trading partner is cheating by dumping products on the market with the help of direct or indirect subsidies, that sanitary standards of incoming products are poor, that labor conditions in the exporting nation are so ignominious that the product on offer is disqualified, or that labor is so cheap overseas that companies have unfair cost advantages.

These arguments constitute a pretext for impeding trade. What is symptomatic of the moral force achieved by free trade is that pretexts need to be invoked at all. Equally telling is the fact that the opponents of globalization do not necessarily condemn free trade. Oftentimes they do the opposite, by savaging developed countries for playing double standards with their numerous trade barriers.

While trade has grown at an astonishing rate in the West since World War II, it has not grown as much as it should have worldwide. Underdeveloped nations were by no means the only ones practicing economic nationalism and, strictly speaking, there has been no free trade. From the very beginning, commerce was marred by exceptions. The United States protected agriculture no less than the Europeans did. Policies designed to stimulate foreign economies—whether preferential trade or most-favored-nation status—excluded or limited key products. They went from agricultural imports to textiles and apparel, but other types of products, such as steel, were also restricted directly or indirectly.

Through target prices, deficiency payments, and price supports, the United States generates an overproduction of cotton, grains, sugar, oilseeds, and other farm products. Import quotas on raw sugar not only limit the amount that can be exported to the United States but also have the effect of depressing the world market price. Although some Latin American countries benefit from import quota rents because they sell for higher prices in the United States, restrictions on trade gravely affect the economies of the hemisphere. Safeguard quotas on textiles and clothing have been particularly hurtful for Andean nations—the very ones that were supposed to replace coca with other types of exports—as well as for Caribbean and Central American nations. Additional obstacles hindering Latin American trade derive from consumer and environmental protections; they include sanitary regulations on plant products and marketing orders that require incoming products to match the quality or size of domestic orders. In a sense, the United States has gone astray from the good old days at the closing of the eighteenth century, when George Washington was able to say in his Farewell Address that commercial policy "should hold an equal and impartial hand; neither seeking nor granting exclusive favors or preferences; consulting the natural course of things; diffusing and diversifying by gentle means the streams of commerce, but forcing nothing."

As in the case of the drug war, American barriers have left advocates of liberal capitalism in Latin America at a disadvantage in the face of anticapitalist trends. During the 2002 presidential contest in Brazil, Luiz Inácio "Lula" da Silva condemned the Free Trade Area of the Americas, a hemisphere-wide market being negotiated since 1998, on the forceful pretext that antidumping measures and farm subsidies would render "free trade" meaningless. Brazil faces tariffs on its exports of sugar (it is the world's largest producer), textiles, tobacco, and ethanol, and, in its capacity as the world's leading producer of orange juice, is particularly sensitive to high tariffs. Objections against trade would not disappear if the United States did away with protectionism; in the final analysis, free trade is good even if embraced unilaterally (in fact that is not the case, because critics of U.S. protectionism also practice their own forms of protectionism). But if the United States is to promote free-market capitalism in Latin America, it needs to start practicing what it preaches. By doing so, it will help to promote the values of freedom. Thomas Paine might have been talking about U.S. relations with Latin America instead of Europe when he stated that "commerce" would secure for America the "peace and friendship" of the region and that "her trade will always be her protection." This statement rings as true as ever in the context of hemispheric relations.

It has become so fashionable to talk about the Information Age and globalization that we often forget how far we are from a world in which goods, capital, and people can travel unimpeded. In the last decades of the twentieth century, protectionism became a particularly poignant emblem of the paradoxical nature of public policy in the capitalist world (it is only fitting that the war on terrorism should have restricted the flow of people, capital, and goods into the United States in recent years even further). Impeding free trade has been yet another, deeply wounding, attack against the values that the United States and Western Europe were supposedly promoting in the corporatist and state-mercantilist underdeveloped countries that so mirror the distant past of today's leading nations (Western Europe's obsession against genetically modified food, incidentally, will hurt Argentina and Brazil, both recent producers of these crops). In the tale of Latin America's perpetual corporatism, mercantilism, enthronement of privilege, wealth transfer, and political law, the leading nations of the world have played their part too.

PART II

What Succeeded

4

What Could Have Been

It is easy to forget that, mutatis mutandis, the consistent features of Latin America's political and economic system were at one point also distinctly present in the societies that make up what is known today as the developed world. The rich capitalist democracies did not go from the Dark Ages to civilization in one giant leap. They evolved, and what Latin America has mirrored from colonial times to the end of the twentieth century is a very particular moment of that long evolution, which started almost invisibly after the tenth century, continued through the late Middle Ages and the birth of the nation-state, and went on into the early modern era. There was a period in western Europe between the sixteenth and seventeenth centuries when fierce negotiations, power struggles fought with bare knuckles, took place as different groups of people exercising what might be called entrepreneurial leadership lobbied to extract various sets of property rights and freedoms from the political authorities. What turned out to be decisive for the rise of capitalism was that those struggles gradually and painfully enfranchised more and more people, securing rights and freedoms for all. The culture that emerged from the new benefits of institutional change ultimately reinforced and perpetuated those arrangements. It is also true that they were facilitated through cultural changes spurred by visionary leaders. The influence of ideas in the development of the market-based system is no less powerful than that of entrepreneurs seeking benefits from the small opportunities opening before their eyes.

In any case, before universal individual rights were secured and before private arrangements came to be sanctioned, rather than hindered, by government, Europe appeared to be a chaotic and unjust society full of second-class citizens. There was corporatism on a grand scale, state mercantilism of the nastier sort, obscene privilege, exploitative bottom-up wealth transfer, and political law that confused the law with the government.

What sets Latin America apart from other regions is that the similar state of affairs in emerging capitalist countries was transitory, a long bridge going from medieval servitude to modern freedom (though modernity also brought about the Leviathan state, so the progress that ensued must ultimately be qualified). Things were moving, in the leading nations, toward the generalization of the particular, toward the unceasing extension to new groups of people of those freedoms that singular groups were able to obtain in their confrontation with the authorities. As happens in all historic evolutions, the path was not smooth, and there were many difficulties along the way, but the direction of the movement was unequivocal. In Latin America, that evolution never really took place. What evolved was the world around, from which Latin America received technological innovations and other forms of global updating, so that at the end of the 1980s these countries looked different from the way they did in the nineteenth century and in the centuries before. The essential features of Latin America's institutional arrangements did not vary as they did in Europe's mercantilist era, nor were they transitory, evolutionary traits on the road to development. Europe's mercantilist phase was a long moment in a linear trajectory; Latin America's was, throughout its colonial and republican eras, circular. There was no evolution, and no involution for that matter; rather, a whirlwind of a movement gyrating around a static center.

It is convenient, then, to pause before assessing Latin America's attempt at capitalist reform in the 1990s and leave things for a while as they were at the end of the 1980s in order to digress briefly and trace the evolution of those key capitalist institutions, and of that leading actor, the individual, who created today's developed nations. In looking at them, we must ask, What is it about those countries' capitalism that was never quite mirrored in Latin America? The answer to that question will clarify what went wrong in Latin America, but, more important, it will shed light on what took place during the 1990s and will help us understand how viable deliberate capitalist reform is in a place where capitalism never evolved.

The Politics of Capitalism

Successful capitalist nations have in common that, at a certain moment, the political authorities, be it by convenience, weakness, or under the influence of force, began to respect private arrangements. Governments accepted the facts of daily life, the comings and goings of people seeking to do business, whether in agriculture, trade, or industry. The rest, including the Industrial Revolution, was the consequence of the ruling class and its political institutions having accepted, through legal sanctions, the private transactions of the people, making possible a consistent increase in investment per capita (the reason why the British population doubled during the Industrial Revolution). It was a bottom-up surge of private realities that, after long, arduous evolution, turned into policy by governments usually desperate to obtain revenue.

This process has an institutional interpretation and a cultural one. Both reinforce each other even if their respective proponents do not necessarily say so.

The institutional case goes somewhat like this. Douglass North and Robert Paul Thomas, for instance, have described with insight how population growth in Europe during the tenth century set off a gradual pattern, lasting three centuries, during which the scarcity of land and its diminishing output led to servants struggling with feudal lords for private ownership and, for others, to migration toward virgin territories in the northwest. Private property, specialization, and particularly trade, together with private systems of dispute adjudication, were the offspring of such events, with Venice, Flanders, and other places emerging as early hotbeds of capitalism. The system that prevailed in most of Europe was still "medieval": Nathan Rosenberg and L. E. Birdzell have shown how political and economic authority was still combined in the same institutions—the manor in the country, the guilds in the towns. In fact, the East, under the Saracen civilization that stretched as far as the Mediterranean, was a much freer world, and Venice's flowering owed much to its vibrant exchange with it. But the "medieval" arrangements were clearly coming under increasing pressure by the individual reactions to land scarcity and output decline, and to opportunity opening up in virgin lands.

Precisely because institutions did not evolve quickly or extensively enough under new population conditions, by the fourteenth century there was famine. The decline in population strengthened the servant vis-à-vis the lord because labor became more valuable and the fall in land rents diminished feudal dues. The peasants became more assertive, pressing for ownership and asking to pay with crops or even money instead of labor. As a result, the feudal system declined, and private property, trade, and the money economy gained ground. The process coincided with—and helped accelerate—the development of the nation-state, since feudal lords and tiny kingdoms were not able to provide the kind of services such social changes required. Justice and protection, traditionally provided by the lord of the manor, could now be sought from the state. The different parties—landowners in the country, traders in the cities—began to negotiate with the government.

This is when representative bodies, political assemblies representing those who produced wealth, began to play a significant role. Negotiations between the government (in most cases the king) and the assemblies gradually led to legal sanctioning of the myriad private arrangements and contracts involved in the process. Along the way, the governments offered limited property rights and exclusive privileges. In England and the Netherlands, the movement was toward full, universal rights; in France, toward a much less healthy mixture of mercantilism and property rights; and in Spain and Portugal, the countries that conquered Latin America, toward a system bearing against the individual. Those struggling for property rights or political freedom were not champions of liberty. They were oftentimes nobles or the producing and propertied elites wanting to secure their personal interests. The space that opened up for the individual as a result of the tension between personal interest and central authority (or even "corrupt" political transactions that go as far back as Henry III confirming to the barons the provisions of Magna Carta in exchange for money) ultimately proved beneficial for society as a whole, and mitigated the power of the nation-state.

The population increase during the sixteenth century caused a rise in agricultural prices and land rent, and gave the final impetus to private ownership of the land and market transactions in agriculture.

Similarly trade, greatly animated in the cities by the influx of new products from the New World, brought an array of institutional arrangements devised to reduce financial risk and civil liability. As was the case in the countryside, these capitalist developments taking place in daily life sought to avoid official interference and to obtain legal guarantees. The state was the inevitable counterpart, so wealth creators and government were locked in political battle for long periods of time. The government wanted fiscal revenue, and the producers wanted property rights (everything from patent and intellectual copyright laws to measures legitimizing joint-stock companies and bills of exchange). Such is the institutionalist perspective on how capitalism made its way in the West. But there is a cultural perspective too.

In this cultural perspective, institutional changes followed an opening of the mind. The remote origins of the concept of a government of laws as opposed to a government of men are to be found in ancient Greece, among statesmen like Solon and Pericles, or philosophers like Aristotle, and at the time of the Roman republic, among orators like Cicero. (An ancient Chinese tradition also exists, much less known in the West.) That concept, with some medieval exceptions such as the Saracen culture, Venice, and, later, some Spanish scholastics, died down until it resurfaced in seventeenth- and eighteenth-century Britain with lawyers and intellectuals taking a look at history. David Hume attributes the decline of the feudal order in England both to the effects of the Norman Conquest, with the king and his descendants gradually weakening the power of the barons over those below them, and to the growing consciousness on the part of certain elites regarding the rule of law. He dates the origin of this second factor to the discovery of Justinian's codes of law in the twelfth century: from then on, ecclesiastics began to see the advantages of civil law in the protection of their considerable properties from kings and barons. The codes themselves did not produce cultural change, but they gave great impulse to the value of law over the feudal arrangements that up to then had provided security at the expense of the individual. In this view, then, the institutional and political factors combined themselves with cultural factors—an awakening of many minds—to tear the fabric of feudalism. In more general terms, it is also possible, as Albert Nock argued, that the spirit of individualism was a by-product of the continental revival of learning. If it was not, strictly speaking, a by-product of the Renaissance, it certainly represented, in the context of the cultural revolution of the time, an awakening of minds.

Another decisive cultural influence on the rise of capitalism came from Martin Luther's challenge against the Catholic church and papal authority, based on principles such as the separation of the secular and the temporal realms, individual responsibility before God over the heads of the priests, and the questioning of hierarchic authority. His vision created the basis for the Reformation. Had such heresies been expressed in other times, they would not have found so many political allies in northern Europe, including Germany and England, where the authorities resented papal power. And the French and Dutch Huguenots, a variant of the same phenomenon, also left their mark on the sixteenth century with their cries for freedom of conscience in the civil wars of their time. Institutions, politics, and culture all moved in the direction of the individual, although not necessarily in the direction of tolerance (Puritan fanaticism was a child of the Reformation too). Such is, very succinctly, the cultural view.

Whatever the relative emphasis one chooses to place on institutional and cultural factors, individual freedom gathered pace in northern Europe while Mediterranean countries preserved more centralized, state-mercantilist systems. In France and, even more so, in Spain and Portugal, the centralist monarchy took power away from the assemblies and installed systems of taxation designed to promote guild monopolies and privileged corporations. In the Netherlands, on the other hand, the dukes of Burgundy slashed restrictive practices and consolidated political institutions—the Great Council, the Supreme Court of Appeal, the Estates-General—designed to protect the interests of the individual against the temptations of intrusive government. This happened as the English Parliament was limiting the powers of the Crown, paving the way for what would become the Industrial Revolution, an unplanned, wholly spontaneous child of capitalist evolution under political arrangements mostly honoring the private rewards of personal initiative, creativity, and enterprise.

Again, the ideas of great intellectual leaders—from John Locke to Adam Smith—grew from what was happening in the world around them and simultaneously helped shape the values of freedom in the minds of powerful elites. John Locke's ideas about "the law of nature" (whose remote origins can be traced back as far as the Greek Stoics), for instance, were part of that cultural advance: they constituted a theoretical formulation that built on previous philosophy—translating it, as did Hugo Grotius, into natural rights—and sought to persuade through argument that the word "natural" should not be taken literally; the origin of liberty is not so much in nature as in the cultural evolution of humans.

This is not to say that England or any other European country was a wholly open society. The sort of commentary that France and England inspired in Thomas Jefferson during the 1780s, when he was the American ambassador in Paris and was able to travel in Europe, gives an idea of how in the Old World, allowing for acute differences of degree from one country to another, wealth remained tightly concentrated, the class system continued to limit opportunity and property, and obstacles to trade across the Atlantic were abundant. The situation was much worse in France than in England. After a year in Paris, Jefferson wrote to an American correspondent, "The property [i.e., the land] of this country is absolutely concentrated in a very few hands, having revenues of from half a million guineas a year downward." And he went on to say, "Whenever there is in any country uncultivated lands and unemployed poor, it is clear that the laws of property have been so far extended as to violate natural rights."

In England, property rights were in better shape, but from Jefferson's point of view, the elites were still restricting access by the masses. After a diplomatic mission to London, Jefferson observed, "The aristocracy of England, which comprehends the nobility, the wealthy commoners, the high grades of priesthood and the officers of government, have the laws and government in their hands [and] have so managed them as to reduce the eleemosynary class, or paupers, below the means of supporting life, even by labor." Bearing in mind the varying grades of individual freedom from America to England to prerevolutionary France at the end of the eighteenth century, the tendency of the Western world was geared toward free-market capitalism. Freedom in the New World promoted freedom in the Old World, as it did in the mid-nineteenth century when the British repealed their protectionist navigation laws in the face of American free trade.

The social institutions that we associate with free-market capitalism, from property to merchant courts, from common law to the use of money, were born out of the free intercourse of people making private decisions and contracting with each other, not out of government policies. Even the capitalist corporation, which is essentially a web of contracts among people vested with property rights and dreams of creative endeavor and progress, was not a cold, politically engineered design but a spontaneous, deeply humane institutional development born out of the convenience of reducing transaction costs by integrating activities.

Latin America, meanwhile, under the influence of Iberia and of its own tradition, had instituted similar government structures and institutions that mercantilist Europe gradually abandoned. The static nature of its institutions, their failure to evolve, preserved the heart of sixteenth- and seventeenth-century European corporatism and mercantilism even as the next centuries brought many changes to its facade. Latin America today is in many ways a twenty-first-century snapshot of Western capitalism suddenly stopped halfway into its formation, right in the middle of that labyrinthine tangle made of exclusive bargains struck between the privileged corporations and the political authorities, before individual rights flowed from that struggle.

Capitalism and the Law

If Latin America's political and economic system has traditionally consisted of corporatism, state mercantilism, privilege, and wealth transfer, it is because of its fifth salient characteristic: political law. Legislation (also called positive law), the enactment and enforcement of mandatory rules by the state, has been used by governments, colonial and republican, democratic and dictatorial, socialist and right-wing, seeking to dictate human conduct. Latin America's political tradition has effaced the line separating the will of the ruler from the law and confused the role of government in constitutional law with the role of the law in private life. Sometimes with the best of intentions, more often with darker purposes, those in power dictated the rules of the game according to their whims, with no regard to custom and human practice, trapping individuals in a web of contradictory, arbitrary, and unpredictable mandates that made it impossible even to understand the law. The government meddled, through positive law and political control of the courts, in every aspect of social life, including the most private civil business. In so doing, it disregarded one of the pillars of free society, the preeminence of the law over the will of government.

Bruno Leoni has written persuasively about the evolution of private law and its impact on economic development. In Roman times, the government, whether republican or imperial, did not meddle much in civil law, which was based on the private claims adjudicated by jurisconsults. Justinian's Corpus Juris Civilis, or body of law, codified Roman jurisprudence long after the fall of Rome, but it was so respectful of case-by-case experience and devoid of positive statutory mandates that, when it was discovered in western Europe in the Middle Ages, it became a porous, flexible reference, not a set of alien rules imposing themselves on new, ever-changing realities (it did, however, lay the foundations for future, more intrusive forms of codification). English common law evolved through the very process of dealing with real human affairs.

In England and the Netherlands, the law evolved with capitalism, as market decisions and human interaction became more complex. Governments and legislative assemblies dealt with constitutional questions and criminal law, but civil law, even when formally codified, was a gradual, bottom-to-top process of daily acts of jurisprudence according to daily transactions and disputes. As the English historian Lytton Strachey wrote, "The English Constitution—that indescribable entity— is a living thing, growing with the growth of men, and assuming ever-varying forms in accordance with the subtle and complex laws of human character."

Positive law—what this book calls political law, particularly after the French Revolution and the enactment of Napoleon's codes—spilled some of its statutory, interventionist influence across the freer European nations, including England, where Parliament started to meddle more and more, but the spirit of the law as an entity above political power continued to foster capitalist development. French rationalism, which considered all legal arrangements of the old order to be emanations of monarchic absolutism and therefore enthroned positive or political law, did have a more pernicious effect in other places, including Latin America, where the Napoleonic codes were imported and it was thought that republican political institutions were the best engineers of justice, both in its traditional sense and its new, "social" dimension. Latin America did not import from continental Europe those features that helped limit the legislative powers of government in the nineteenth century (the Conseil d'État in France and effective judicial review in Germany).

Government was so far removed from the early evolution of the law, and its absence from the process was so vital to the growth of capitalism, that mercantile law or the "law merchant" was for centuries a private affair, first in Europe and then in the United States (in medieval Iceland, victims had a transferable property right allowing them to sell their right to prosecute a case of any nature). The law merchant was born in the fairs and markets of the new cities as a system of private courts and arbitrators that adjudicated disputes in a quick, efficient manner, and, although it was adopted in the fourteenth century by the common law courts, it continued to exist as a parallel form of private justice until the seventeenth century. International mercantile law, for its part, never ceased to exist.

In the United States, the law merchant existed from the beginning. During the seventeenth and eighteenth centuries, private arbitration was practically the sole system of civil dispute adjudication. Common law, which was in essence the recognition of a long tradition of dispute adjudication according to precedent, not mandate, by state courts, eventually developed into the system of justice, but as late as 1872 a California law stated that individuals were free to choose any type of court they wished. Private arbitration resurged in nineteenth-century England as the Civil War in the United States disrupted trade, particularly of cotton, across the Atlantic and contracts were affected. The influence of mercantile law was such that almost all professions, not only merchants, used private courts and arbitrators. Even today, international mercantile disputes are solved without the intervention of national state courts. Indeed, arbitration and "for-profit" courts, the product of a thousand-year tradition, are once again gaining ground in the United States.

It follows that, if the law was a major factor in the success of capitalism, adequate juridical systems and institutions are a prerequisite for development in any nation and at any point in time. Rich Western nations would not have seen capitalism blossom without the right kind of juridical tradition. Those nations that have prospered most are still the ones in which appropriate juridical institutions encourage free market capitalism. Gerald W. Scully has shown that countries with efficient and market-friendly juridical institutions grow three times as much as those without them (in those countries, the proportion of the public budget devoted to the judiciary is smaller than in Latin America). Indeed, some have argued, among them Edgardo Buscaglia and William Ratliff, that transaction costs arising out of differences in legal rules and juridical systems between countries that engage in commerce with one another should be considered nontariff barriers to trade.

The absence of appropriate legal institutions, or, to be more precise, of political arrangements sensitive to the best legal traditions of capitalism, made real, sustained development impossible in Latin America during the nineteenth and twentieth centuries. The relationship between political and legal institutions in Latin America has been the exact opposite of that which exists in the West—never mind that over time political law has intruded more and more in people's freedoms in developed countries. Almost everywhere you look in recent times you see evidence of this. Two examples illustrate how far the law in Latin America is from the concerns of individuals. In Argentina, during Carlos Menem's presidency in the 1990s, citizens began to rebel against the bombardment of regulations emanating from authorities. They turned to the courts, seeking compensation from the government. Anticipating what might happen, the government passed a law protecting itself from making actual payments, limiting sanctions won by litigants to simple declarations of intent. In five years, court orders mandating compensation from the authorities equaled one-third of Argentina's public expenditure. Positive or political law, which those regulations that originated the problem were born of, was compounded by an ineffective justice system in the face of political power. Meanwhile, in Peru, the failure of judicial institutions is such that in recent decades, as part of the wider phenomenon of the underground economy, there has emerged a sort of informal justice system whereby neighborhood organizations in the shantytowns adjudicate disputes over land or resolve divorce filings, transport unions arbitrate claims among their members, and street vendors appeal to their trade organizations in order to seek damages from injuring parties. This private justice born on the margins of state justice amounts to a sort of civil disobedience against the Peruvian institutions of law.

The close connection between law and political economy means that in Latin America, contrary to what once existed in the developed world, the law has been a decisive factor in the birth, development, and consolidation of the statist political economy.

Capitalism in the United States

Few things are more traumatic for an underdeveloped nation than living next door to a prosperous country that started from a position of disadvantage. That is the complex of Latin American countries with regard to the United States, a country with no great ancient history, colonized by Europeans one hundred years later than its neighbors, that at the turn of the twenty-first century had achieved eight to nine times their per capita income. The great success of American capitalism stems from the same factors that brought prosperity to western Europe, except that the United States maintained for decades many of the tenets of limited government while some nations failed to do so.

What might have seemed from a late-seventeenth-century perspective an inferiority on the part of early American settlements vis-à-vis Latin America's massive colonial structure, namely small-scale systems of self-government with people who had fled religious persecution, was in fact the seed of capitalism in North America. Of course, there were Pilgrims in the early part of the seventeenth century who were inspired by collectivist agrarian utopias, but starvation and the fight for survival gave rise to private plots and individual or family ownership. The settlers did not arrive as Spanish-style conquistadores but aboard trading companies' ships, and from very early on their relationship to government was removed from notions of divine right (which is not to say the trading companies did not hold the colonies under bondage and that colonists did not exterminate natives in some areas).

Soon one word, "property," came to define everything North American colonizers struggled for. In the absence of strong political establishments, colonizers and immigrants did not have to force the law and official institutions to adapt to their bottom-up, emerging society based on enterprise and commerce—the type of process we saw happening in some parts of Europe. Instead, their official institutions and laws flowed from their grassroots activities (of which the New England town meeting was a symbol) and therefore closely reflected their liberties. They wrestled with British colonial governors and restrictions (in parts not controlled by France or Spain), and there was considerable state mercantilism in the relationship between the elites and the political machinery in different states in the form of land grants and other favors. But the culture of local self-government and other decentralized practices made the situation in no way comparable to the Iberian structure prevailing in the rest of the hemisphere.

When, in the following century, George III attempted to tighten the screws on the thirteen colonies—that is, to expropriate the wealth of American individuals through taxation and tariffs that limited freedoms—they rebelled. At that very moment Latin America was undergoing reform of the wrong kind under the inspiration of both Charles III, the Spanish monarch, and the Portuguese prime minister, the Marquis of Pombal, who further centralized government, consolidated the bureaucracy, and encouraged a system of limited property rights.

After the revolution, the general tendency of the American government, despite interventionist spasms, was to respect the economic rights of the individual. As a recent book has noted, property rights in the United States have gone through various key moments: the extralegal private arrangements of early squatters who used various ingenuous devices ("tomahawk rights," "cabin rights," "corn rights") for representing ownership and transferring titles; the abolition by Thomas Jefferson, in Virginia, of impediments to selling property outside of the family; government recognition of the right to land arising from improvements made to it; the 1866 legislation legitimizing the private contracts of miners and the right of gold rush pioneers to purchase mines they had worked in. Terry Anderson and Peter Hill have studied how nineteenth-century expansion into the western territories involved a multitude of private contracts through which people defined and protected their rights to land they acquired and worked on, and how squatters formed voluntary associations in order to register land claims and enforce the title of members. When the government auctioned much of the land, in practice it simply recognized squatters who settled before the auction and who invoked the Preemption Act of 1830, which protected first possession rights. Later on, the homesteading policy of the 1860s conditioned titles on occupiers having made investments in their property, but the institutions of power still legitimized the freedom of individuals. (One must not overlook the many injustices committed in the tortuous process of establishing a system of property rights in the West and the Southwest, especially the various subterfuges with which American settlers, through the use of either the courts or government agencies, dispossessed previous settlers, including Spanish Americans, whose customary and institutional arrangements gave them little protection against newcomers.)

The path followed by property rights in the United States mirrored the process that we saw earlier in Europe with governments acknowledging the spontaneous contracts made by individuals and respecting, through political institutions, the multiple private arrangements of society in order to honor the economic rights of citizens. While this was happening in the United States, Latin American elites, having recently won independence from Spain and Portugal, were instituting firewalls around their exclusive rights and denying the masses access to ownership.

During the nineteenth century, both the United States and certain western European nations kept trading and manufacturing largely as autonomous spheres in which government did not meddle. The peace that reigned in Europe between 1815 and 1914, and the spectacular success of the United States during that century, owe everything to those freedoms, underpinned by the firm protection of individual rights (though women and many minority groups, of course, were excluded for a shamefully long time). Under such arrangements, the civilizing influence of commerce prompted Richard Cobden to say, "Not a bale of merchandise leaves our shores, but it bears the seeds of intelligence and fruitful thought to the members of some less enlightened community." Latin American society, on the other hand, which to no small extent participated in international trade and the globalization of capital before economic nationalism crept into its institutions in the 1920s, was unable to reap the benefits of that intense exchange because of its corporatist, state-mercantilist, privilege-ridden, wealth-transferring structure enabled by political law.

It would be wrong to conclude that in nineteenth-century America there was no room for compassion and that profit was the sole motivation of human action. In fact, research has rediscovered the history of civic associations, fraternal orders, friendly societies, and religious groups in nineteenth-century America and Britain that provided the safety nets we tend to associate with governments today: medical care, unemployment insurance, education, and even law and order. Other "public goods," such as turnpikes, also resulted from people cooperating with one another on a private basis. It is hardly surprising, then, that thousands of residential community and condominium associations have taken over a number of neighborhood and local services in the last two decades.

The economic freedoms of the United States through much of the nineteenth century had two consequences that Latin America must bear in mind. The first was the formidable accumulation of capital that transformed the United States, by the end of the nineteenth century, into the world's strongest economy. The Protestant work ethic, which encouraged saving money and investing in developing production, influenced the process. Latin America's political and economic institutions, and the accompanying culture of immediate gain on the part of those with access to wealth in a context they knew to be unstable, never permitted similar levels of capital formation. The second consequence is perhaps more crucial: free-market capitalism was so deeply rooted in the United States that when government began to gnaw at the foundations of economic freedom in the late nineteenth century and after World War I, the damage was not nearly as profound as seen in Latin America after economic nationalism replaced what free trade there was, consolidating a long-embedded system that was not conducive to a free society. In the United States, it limited, without destroying, a set of institutions that, despite an accumulation of political interferences, had made the country resilient enough to continue to encourage capital formation.

War has usually sparked off interventionism in the United States.

The Civil War fostered spasms of interventionism in both the North and the South that had lasting effects in particular areas of the economy. After World War I, but particularly since the 1930s, the government began to adopt policies that reduced the sphere of liberty in order to promote "social justice," and the concept of judicial review whereby the courts were supposed to uphold the law in the face of intrusive legislation was eroded. The dimensions of this phenomenon did not rival western Europe's Bismarckian welfare state—that nineteenth-century creation that, to this day, absorbs half the wealth produced by most European countries—or Latin America's mercantilist populism. They did, however, indicate that even in free societies the impulses of intrusive government are alive. After World War II, but especially since the 1960s, a succession of government programs has taken a toll on American taxpayers and put in place considerable wealth transfer mechanisms. But when this trend started, America was already a dominant superpower. When Latin America justifies its statist policies by pointing to the fact that the United States has also relied on big government in the last half century, it misses the point.

Jeffrey Rogers Hummel has aptly described how the Civil War increased the levels of taxation in the United States beyond those in most other nations at the time and how public borrowing skyrocketed because fiscal revenues covered only one-fifth of expenses. America went from having an unregulated monetary system with no central bank to the Legal Tender Act. The government printed fiat money—"greenbacks"—not backed by specie, and Californians refused to accept paper money and continued to use gold. Internal tariffs shot up, purporting to protect industry, the Department of Agriculture saw the light in 1862, the government started to dictate the prices at which it purchased supplies and to limit the acreage of cotton and tobacco, and state-run companies appeared in the South.

The next phase of interventionism arose out of World War I, as Robert Higgs has shown, with public spending—that is, the size of government—rising from 7 percent to 21 percent of the gross national product. The GNP went back to prewar levels in the early 1920s and rose to 15 percent during the New Deal era, which brought a number of changes—in labor-management relations, welfare programs, federal regulations—that became engraved in America's economy. The result was a long way from nineteenth-century capitalism, but it was still way ahead of underdeveloped nations, where the problem went far beyond high levels of government spending and regulation to include the absence of the rule of law and very basic individual rights protection, as well as the absence of separation between state and government.

After the Korean War, the size of the U.S. government was the equivalent of over one-fifth of GNP. In the 1960s, 1970s, and 1980s, due to government transfer payments, including Social Security, it went up to 38 percent, and it has remained at around one-third of the total size of the economy ever since. Again, after centuries of high capital formation under a climate of incentives for private enterprise in general, this very unhealthy increase in interventionism has not been able to unseat the United States from world supremacy or to destroy the capitalist engine driving the country forward. The equivalent increase in intrusive government in an underdeveloped nation would have caused much more harm.

5

The Liberal Tradition

Just as one can speak of an anticapitalist or illiberal tradition in Latin America, which has ruled through the twists and turns of precolonial, colonial, and republican times, it is possible to speak of a capitalist or liberal tradition that has left a trail of inspiring episodes through the centuries. It might seem exaggerated to speak of a "tradition" when the history of liberty in Latin America seems to spell no more than a list of moments, exceptional talents, minority groups, or passing institutions that never crystallized into the liberation of the individual. But it would be wrong to judge the liberal ideal from the point of view of its failure to establish itself as the governing principle. There is indeed a tradition, if loose and not always assumed as such by the spirits informing it, that indicates there was nothing predetermined about the triumph of oppression. Indeed, it exposes the factors, like culture, brandished by those who think freedom is a luxury underdeveloped countries cannot afford.

From the days when Indians in Central America and Mexico used cacao seeds as money in order to facilitate exchange to the present-day informal economy, the nature and instinct of the "Latin American species" are no different from those of the rest of the human species. There is nothing whatever to suggest that the native cultures, either in their precolonial or mestizo forms, could not have responded creatively and successfully to the incentives of liberty had they been given the chance. After all, they were able to produce, under collectivism and even totalitarianism, awesome public works (or wonderful private violations). Culture is as much influenced by institutions as institutions are influenced by culture, and it varies from community to community for myriad different reasons. But all cultures share a certain common nature that has proved to be responsive to liberty in very different sorts of environments. In any case, the predominant culture in Latin America is overwhelmingly "Western" (although not in the Anglo-Protestant but in the Ibero-Catholic sense) and, as we have seen, the contribution of "Western" ideas and decision makers to Latin America's underdevelopment has been and continues to be notable. It is not native culture that stands in the way of common sense.

It would be risky to deny that, in Latin America as in other parts of the world, collectivism has been a widely accepted ethos, not simply the artificial creation of a handful of tyrants who imposed it on freedom-loving victims. After so many millennia of collectivism and its proven endurance even in the most advanced societies, it is safe to say that there is a part of human nature that fears freedom. Latin Americans have been no exception. But the lessons of universal history also indicate that all types of societies respond well and immediately to freedom once they experience it, and that people resist, sometimes at the cost of their own lives, attempts to take it away from them. The hidden capitalist or liberal tradition of Latin America reminds us that things could have been, and could still be, different.

No successful Latin American reform can be undertaken without an awareness of the intermittent signals liberty has sent over the centuries in its own lands, the vanquished history time has so vindicated. It goes as far back as family units working their own land and exchanging goods in the ancient Americas to the Jesuits of the school of Salamanca that discovered the monetary causes of inflation or the subjective nature of value at the very time when Spain and Portugal colonized Latin America in the sixteenth century, and from them to the informal economy as the contemporary and inventive response to the state's illegitimacy. In between, the mid-sixteenth-century rebellion of Gonzalo Pizarro; the 1812 liberal constitution of Cádiz, Spain; the ideas that inspired the independence struggle; the brilliant Argentinean three-quarter century that flowed from Juan Bautista Alberdi's vision (and that of others, like Domingo Faustino Sarmiento); and the post–World War II intellectuals who went against the current are some of the traces left by the Latin American tradition of the individual.

The Individual Sparkle in the Collectivist Night

Trade was important in all three of the great pre-Columbian civilizations—the Incas, Aztecs, and Mayas—even though communications were limited by the fact that they had no draft or pack animals and had not discovered the wheel (the Mayas used it only in toys). Once powerful bureaucracies were established, trade was used by the state for its own purposes, and mercantile private initiative was curtailed, but commerce was a tradition.

Before the consolidation of Tenochtitlán in the heart of Mexico as the center of the Aztec Empire, that city-state shared regional preeminence with Tlatelolco. And whereas Tenochtitlán focused on the values of war, Tlatelolco was an entirely mercantile enterprise. Tenochtitlán was jealous of the merchants of Tlatelolco, who traded in valuable commodities. Through commercial activity, a class of merchants and entrepreneurs came to constitute a sort of "integrating element" once political consolidation took place and the empire was ruled from its center at Tenochtitlán, with trade continuing to be a feature of daily life. The *pochtecas* specialized in long-distance trade and supervised markets in the Valley of Mexico. There was an abundance of plants and animals to feed the Mexicas of the capital, but most trade took place with the surrounding areas, with marine products (the city was built on a huge lagoon) being exchanged for wood and stone. Although the empire was essentially divided between the ruling class and the great mass of common people who labored on the land, there were some ten thousand merchants, constituting in many ways a social class of their own. Under the heavy weight of state controls (a limitation that seems to have existed in various grades since the birth of civilization), these people nonetheless maintained a culture of exchange, a type of relationship in which mutual benefit, not vertical authority and servile obedience, was the guiding principle. The state intervened more directly in long-distance trade, which was treaty-based and from which competition was excluded, but spy traders went into foreign markets to buy and sell more freely and competitively; in the home marketplaces, on the other hand, "everyone with a few cacao beans in his pocket was welcome." Thanks to this mercantile activity, the concept of money (of a term of reference against which the values of different things could be measured) was very much alive, albeit in a primitive sense, through the use of cacao, gold and zinc, and other mediums of exchange. The bustling activity of merchants was sufficiently appreciated by the state to be honored with a distinct place in the emperor's legal code. Significantly, merchants even had special law courts.

Among the Mayas, whose civilization flourished in the Yucatán peninsula and the surrounding areas, trade was also a remarkable cultural feature. Long before the Classic period of Maya civilization, which began in the third century A.D., trade was a mainstay at locations such as Chiapa de Corzo, Abaj Takalik, El Baúl, and Chalchuapa. Later, trade developed so much that communities on the coast were fed not by the agricultural lands in their immediate vicinity but by the interior hinterlands, where they obtained food but also textiles and other goods. Trade played an important role in creating the loose, confederate organization of the Maya culture, in which there was no permanent political center but rather a system of city-states among which hegemonic influence shifted, Tikal being the best known. When the Europeans arrived, there was no longer a Maya polity, but the descendants of that civilization were well acquainted with the notion of exchange.

The Incas, for their part, also knew the benefits of trade, although once the empire came into being, they went a long way toward eliminating it. Important cultures had surfaced in what is today known as Peru long before the Incas. The Tiahuanaco culture, born around A.D. 500 in the mountains of southern Peru, traded with villages on the coast and even with Central America. It was only under the Inca Empire, the period in which Spain came in contact with that part of the world, that trade become a marginal activity and was limited to superfluous goods. Before the empire came into being, when the Inca kingdom was but one among many others, trade continued to be a part of life in the Andes. Women in particular engaged in trade, and their presence in the market was particularly visible. And it is ironic that the Incas' decisions were often announced in the marketplace.

Numerous notarial records of early colonial times show Indians actively engaging in contracts with Spanish dealers, and testimonies given by Indians in local Peruvian communities to Spanish inspectors in the sixteenth century speak of trade. Notarial records show *kurakas* (local chiefs) establishing contracts with Spanish colonials whereby they provided labor in exchange for a fee using traditional social customs that had been in place long before the Europeans arrived. The *kuraka* received raw cotton from the Spaniards and distributed it to the Indians under his jurisdiction. The Indians delivered the finished cloth to the *kuraka*, who in turn sold it to the Spaniards for cash payment. By the mid-sixteenth century, the Indians were already diverting part of their labor, apart from that required of them by the authorities, for the production of goods for the Spanish market. By the eighteenth century, not only *kurakas* but also the wealthier members of Indian society traded their possessions in the Spanish markets for goods they then sold to fellow Indians. An entire class of merchants called *principales* stocked the shops with European commodities bought from Spanish merchants. The greatest Indian rebel against Spanish rule, José Gabriel Tupac Amaru, a *kuraka*, obtained much revenue from trading in quicksilver and other merchandise in Lima, the mining region of Potosí, and other Andean towns. Although the incorporation of Indians into the Spanish market owes much to the dislocation of traditional social norms imposed by colonial taxes and expropriation of land, the immediate response of Indian society after the conquest and the subsequent adaptation to limited opportunities attest to their own trading traditions.

Aside from trade, there was another important way the individual spirit breathed life into the ancient Andes. Between the time of the Tiahuanaco culture's decline and the emergence of the Inca Empire, there was a political eclipse during which the people of the Andes returned to their small, family- and land-based clans (the emergence of small despotic kingdoms notwithstanding). Each ayllu consisted of an agrarian community of one or more families claiming to descend from some remote ancestor who was considered a divinity. Among these primitive people there was an outstanding element of private property. The families owned the land, which was distributed by the chief. The houses in which they lived, like their orchards, belonged to them, and so did their tools. Although the chief, the *kuraka*, was an authority wielding power over the community, he had obligations, the protection of private property being paramount. Inevitably under such a system, differences in wealth developed between the ayllu communities, so extreme that they eventually led to conflict and war. The *kuraka* supervised and represented the kindred members of his community, and the Indians, in exchange for favors and labor they were not automatically obliged to supply, received certain services from him, such as the settling of disputes, the enforcement of claims by the weaker members, and the conduct of rituals. Evidence of many disputes between *kurakas* and their local kinsmen indicates how strongly the members of the community felt about the authority invading their sphere.

Craftsmanship was another way individuality cut through the veil of that very oppressive world. Craftsmen and artisans, although part of the downtrodden laboring class, enjoyed a measure of freedom to engrave their personality, their view of the surrounding world, and their imagination on their work. Much of what they did was mechanical and routine. A simple look at what has survived, however, indicates not only skill but also something much more important: unique, nontransferable features that can derive only from individual souls at work. Ironic souls at that, because their craft, a shy but unequivocal cry of individuality, was almost entirely for the benefit of a system designed to stifle the individual.

Anyone who visits a market fair of the Indian communities of the Andes, the south of Mexico, or Guatemala will detect a powerful commercial spirit among peoples in many ways remote from the mainstream Western culture. Although in altered form, the ayllu is still alive today, and one has only to see how peasants have parceled out 60 percent of the land collectivized by agrarian reform in Peru to recognize the heritage of ancient times, when the communities used to parcel out the land among the families and individuals who subsequently became owners of it. Not to mention the arts of pottery and weaving, which Indians practice today with as much creativity as centuries ago and try to place in the local or international market. So, among the Indians who came to be organized in vast empires under the Aztecs and the Incas, and in powerful city-states in the case of the Mayas, the spirit of the individual and of voluntary cooperation among individuals and families was part of life, however much counterbalanced by certain collective customs and communal hierarchies.

The fact that imperial power did much to coerce that spirit into subservience does not erase its existence from the cultural heritage. The individual sparkle never quite died in the collectivist night.

Rebels and Cassocks

From the very beginning, the conquest of South America was marked by tensions over property and autonomy between the conquerors and the Spanish monarchy in whose name they appropriated vast empires. The outcome of the conflict was defined very early on, when the independent-minded and ambitious first wave of conquistadores put up a fierce but ultimately unsuccessful fight against the metropolitan power in defense of two principles: government by consent and private property. The fact that they were themselves authoritarian with regard to the native population and that the kind of property they defended included serfs laboring on their estates from whom they exacted large tributes does not detract from the point that among the shapers of Latin America's decisive formative period, principles of limited government emerged under the leadership of significant players. They were defeated, but they constitute a precedent of some importance. Chief among the rebels was Gonzalo Pizarro, the brother and political heir of Francisco Pizarro.

In the mid-1540s, the Spanish monarchy established viceroyalties in the New World in order to consolidate its direct control over the colonies and passed laws limiting the estates of the conquistadores. The ensuing conflict in Peru saw the emergence of a powerful, ideologically motivated movement led by Gonzalo Pizarro but also including major intellectual voices ready to invoke doctrines of government by consent and private property in order to justify their sedition against absolutism. The rebels based a good part of their claims on St. Thomas Aquinas's natural law doctrine and the medieval Spanish legal codes known as Las Siete Partidas, which echoed Justinian's codification of Roman jurisprudence. Monarchical absolutism in Europe had swept away notions that obedience was conditional on the laws respecting natural law, serving the public good, or enjoying the consent of the people, but the moral and intellectual force of such principles was still enough to send shivers down the king's spine. Gonzalo Pizarro's men were well aware of the commotion provoked by the local communities that had revolted against taxes and other limitations of their freedoms in Castile. And even within the realm of rigid scholastic doctrine, the kind that had moved from the original teachings of Aquinas to the justification of absolutism under God's law, there were legal and moral voices in Spain seeking to put government under the rule of higher principles. The reaction of the king to the rebellion in South America was aimed therefore at preventing further cracks in the edifice of absolutism as much as retaining control of the colonies.

In documents such as Representación de Huamanga, the manifesto of the rebellion, letters to the king, and other writings, Gonzalo and his men spelled out the idea that defending property and questioning laws that had been passed without consultation was not tantamount to disloyalty. In warning that they would "obey but not comply" with the laws, they expressed their respect for the institution of the king and sought to avoid opening themselves to the accusation of high treason, but they also resorted to the maximum form of civic virtue: the defense of moral principle against government. The rebels who met cruel deaths (and inflicted some too) were early sparks of the individualist spirit in Latin America. They also followed, whether consciously or not, a tradition vested in the local villages of Spain that resisted the king's authority and in the Saracens, who had ruled Iberia with a liberal hand and whose scientific energy and enterprise still influenced that part of the world when the unified Christian monarchy undertook the conquest of the Americas.

A much more systematic and profound contribution to the individual spirit in the sixteenth century, however, came in the form of the School of Salamanca, a group of Jesuit and Dominican scholars who are today considered forerunners of the much better-known intellectual currents that make up the philosophical foundation of the free society, from the Scottish Enlightenment and the French physiocrats of the eighteenth century to the Manchester School of the nineteenth century and the Austrian School of both the nineteenth and twentieth centuries. Scholastics did not renege on the Hapsburg monarchy or question the divine nature of the ruler; indeed, they provided the theological justification of both. But those associated with the School of Salamanca (some of them did not actually study or teach at that university) introduced common sense and reason into the theological perspective on worldly matters and dared argue with many of the misconceptions that underpinned official thinking in everything from the value of goods to the role of money and taxation. They based their beliefs on natural law as developed by Thomas Aquinas a few centuries before (which was, as we have seen, a double-edged sword).

Their teachings went largely unheeded in Spain and therefore in Latin America, where in practice scholasticism meant nothing more than the theological justification of the oppressive colonial system. One wonders what might have become of Latin America had the teachings and writings of the School of Salamanca been followed. The first scholars "to grasp the role of commerce and trade in bringing about an interdependent world based upon law and consent" remind us that very different kinds of choices could have been made and that lack of reasonable ideas was not to blame for the type of colonial society that Latin America has been unable to shed.

The greatest contribution lay in discovering the subjective nature of value, under which no good exchanged in the market has an intrinsic, objective value that can be determined by an authority. Value, as Diego de Covarrubias y Leyva, Luis Saravia de la Calle, Jerónimo Castillo de Bovadilla, and others stated, has to do with each individual's "esteem." The only way to establish the "just price"—a medieval obsession—is to let supply and demand do their work. Prices, under such a view, are not determined by costs, which are prices in themselves (including wages), but by the wishes of the public in a competitive exchange environment. "Only God" knows what the "just price" is.

Alejandro Chafuén has aptly described many other contributions to the capitalist ethos by the School of Salamanca. Francisco de Vitoria, preeminent among the scholars, denounced the slavery of Indians as running contrary to natural law; Domingo de Soto and Tomás de Mercado criticized common ownership; Juan de Mariana justified killing tyrants because they violated law and consent, and he asked for moderate taxes as well as a reduction of public spending; Martín de Azpilcueta, Luis de Molina, and Diego de Covarrubias y Leyva understood the monetary causes of inflation, a major topic at a time when Latin American bullion was affecting prices and debasement of the currency was a frequent government ploy to expropriate the wealth of the king's subjects; finally, Fray Felipe de la Cruz and others, while not going as far as accepting the concept of interest, justified the discounting of bills of exchange. The Jesuits even saw some sense in Copernicus's findings and tried to reconcile the scientific description of the universe with their Christian conception of it.

These crucial observations speak of an old tradition of capitalist thought in the Spanish world of which Latin America was a part. It was eclipsed by the dominant spirit of the Counter-Reformation, which turned the valuable economic lessons of the scholastics into academic speculation while reserving real policy for everything they so lucidly attacked. The fact that they were themselves part of the scholastic foundation of the Spanish state meant they were not heretics, and their acceptance of the divine nature of the king counterbalanced their efforts to base the rule of government in law and consent. History paid more attention to the kind of rigidity and sophistry that scholastics of the Counter-Reformation—like Francisco Suarez, the foremost interpreter of Thomist thought—expressed and that policy actually practiced than to the revolutionary discoveries of many of these social scientists *avant la lettre*. Nevertheless, their teachings are there, eager to be unearthed from oblivion or ignorance.

Liberals (Sort Of)

We have seen how liberalism concealed conservative power structures in the nineteenth century and how the ideas of the European (and American) Enlightenment that so influenced the leaders of the independence movement translated into new forms of authoritarianism and exclusion. But the independence movement bore genuine expressions of liberty.

Free trade was one of them. As early as the mid-eighteenth century, Venezuelan merchants declared armed revolt against the Guipúzcoa company, created to ensure that Venezuela traded with imperial markets and eliminated commercial exchange with foreign powers. By the latter part of the eighteenth century, free trade was a rallying cry of early independence sentiment around the region. Strong reaction against the Spanish monopoly was coupled with the aspiration to trade with England, France, Holland, and others.

Additional forms of government impediment to free enterprise were also scrutinized. The ideas of Rousseau and other collectivists were not the only influence on Latin Americans. The French physiocrats, with their message of minimal government direction and their belief that progress came from freedom of individuals to multiply the resources of nature, also made a strong impact. Calls for abolishing taxes and duties were no less powerful than the defense of free trade.

Last but not least, civic engagement at the municipal level was critical. While policy was not dictated at the local level, the municipalities were focal points of citizen discussion and participation. These and other sorts of civic associations, including religious groups, especially Masonic clubs, took active roles in creating local networks for the independence struggle. They constituted an embryonic form of civil society. Independence, in no small way their child, eventually suffocated them.

These three features—free trade, minimal taxation, and grassroots association—could have been developed by more apt and visionary leaders into very different types of societies from those that emerged from the new republics.

The independence movement was a complex mix of liberal and conservative tendencies. The 1812 constitution, signed under Napoleon's occupation by Spanish politicians and a number of Latin American delegates in the Spanish city of Cádiz, became a symbol of liberalism, a label used, it seems, on that occasion for the first time ever. Although, after Napoleon's expulsion from Spain and Portugal, Latin American Creoles reacted against Spanish and Portuguese liberalism, giving powerful impetus to the independence movement in the name of traditional values, many of those taking part in the mobilization against colonial rule acted on the spirit and the principles of that liberal document.

Thus, two contradictory forces were present at the birth of the Latin American republics. Tragically, these contradictions lived within the leaders themselves. The fact that the result of their actions was so disappointing has obscured many of the right instincts they held alongside their monarchical and aristocratic temptations in some cases, and in others their collectivist, Rousseau-inspired view of government as the embodiment of the "general will" of the people. Francisco de Miranda, the precursor of Venezuela's independence, was shocked at the end of the eighteenth century to find so many merchants and blacksmiths in the Massachusetts Assembly and wondered how democracy could function under such uncultured leadership. But that aristocratic penchant coexisted with his fervor for the Founding Fathers of the United States. Argentina's Mariano Moreno and Manuel Belgrano devoted much of their political acumen to breaking the Spanish hold on Buenos Aires's trade and promoting free exchange. Two Mexican priests, Miguel Hidalgo and Jose María Morelos, the legendary precursors of independence, led peasant and mestizo armies in the hope of giving the excluded masses participation in the republican institutions they were seeking to bring about and of abolishing slavery, monopolies, taxation of Indians, and other forms of discrimination against the underprivileged. In Colombia, Francisco de Paula Santander got out of his military uniform and decided to become a civilian ruler, symbolizing the obedience of men of arms to civil institutions.

Hidalgo and Morelos were not, strictly speaking, liberal leaders with a vision of limited government and individual liberty in all spheres. But if wider representation and recognition of enterprising actors in society, free trade and minimal duties, mestizo legitimacy at the heart of the republic, and the expulsion of military values from political institutions had been predominant in independent Latin America, the statism that also informed their actions, and those of many others, might have been greatly attenuated. The echo of their better musings is not entirely dead.

Amid the chaos and the furor of Latin America's nineteenth century, two stories speak to us of a certain type of civilization. One was Argentina's relatively limited government under its 1853 constitution, which presided over some seven decades of expansion. The other was Chile's stability, brought about not by tyrannical imposition but by an exercise in political and juridical moderation on the part of its leading class.

Juan Bautista Alberdi, a leading figure in the remarkable Argentinean "generation of 1837," has been forgotten amid the more colorful, larger-than-life despots of his time. His book *Bases y puntos de partida para la organización de la República Argentina*, published in 1852, served as the foundation for the constitution of 1853. It reflected to a large extent his belief, influenced by the American Revolution and the U.S. Constitution, that the essential role of government was to protect life and property, that federalism was the best possible compromise between central and local government, and that free trade was the engine of real progress. He was obsessed both with encouraging European immigration and with the works of Adam Smith, David Hume, the French physiocrats, and *The Federalist Papers* (his weakness for British utilitarians did not essentially alter his liberal persuasion). With the various limitations in a country where the native population was brutally displaced, Argentina managed to narrow the scope of its government's powers and remove obstacles to capitalist endeavor and voluntary association in such a way that it soon attained impressive levels of development. Commercial banks, for instance, were allowed to issue their own notes in the 1880s, something unthinkable today.

During the latter part of the nineteenth century, due to constitutional reform and, doubtless, to the cultural influx of many European immigrants, Argentina experienced the second-highest rate of economic growth and enjoyed the greatest rate of foreign investment per capita in the world. From 1892 to 1913, the wages and income in real terms for rural and industrial workers were higher than those of Switzerland, Germany, and France. In 1910, the volume of Argentina's exports was greater than that of Canada and Australia. By the 1920s, its economy was well ahead of those of many western European nations, and a solid middle class constituted the backbone of society. In 1928, its GDP per capita was the twelfth greatest in the world (it was, however, less than half that of the United States). Its cultural achievements were no less admired than its economic progress. Later events, coupled with a sharp rise in populism, led Argentina down a drastically different path, which indicates that, despite the important inroads that capitalism made in that country, the phenomenon was not deep enough to become part of the cultural legacy transmitted from generation to generation. The gap between "European" Buenos Aires and the criollo interior never really closed. In the 1940s, with economic nationalism, a good part of the interior moved to the periphery of the capital, what is known as Greater Buenos Aires. By then, the rules of the game were a long way from Alberdi's vision. Although authoritarianism had been present and political participation had been restricted under the 1853 rules of the game, the visionary "generation of 1837" has to be credited with influencing the political atmosphere and shaping events in a manner that seems exotic from the point of view of the rest of the region.

The case of Chile was remarkably different. The contribution of its leaders lay not in presiding over a period of growth through private enterprise but in moderating the relationship between the institutions of power and the population by providing the state with some predictable, stable qualities that surpassed the will of those who exercised government and tolerated in citizens a sense of the juridical. A conservative, oligarchic rule persisted, but of a much less authoritarian disposition than in other parts and with a sense of the superiority of laws over politicians. Chile learned to respect institutions and the instruments of the law in deeper ways than other Latin American nations, where clear lines of demarcation were never set between the permanent, neutral functions of authority and contingent, intrusive power politics. Aside from the political figures who shaped the nation, among them Diego Portales, the influence of Andrés Bello deserves special attention. Bello, a Venezuelan who spent a large part of his life in Chile, developed Latin America's foremost codes of civil law and wrote authoritative volumes on criminal and international law, as well as studies of grammar. Legal codes certainly did not turn out to be a blessing for Latin America once they became the instruments of legislative intervention around the region, but Bello's approach was based on the belief that law and not political whim should be the governing principle. Both he and Chile's military hero, Bernardo O'Higgins, were influenced by Francisco de Miranda, the Anglophile precursor of South America's independence, whom they met in London. The British penchant for common sense, moderate discourse, and civility played a part in shaping Chile's early republic by inspiring in the leaders responsible for molding the conservative Chilean institutions a moderating sense of the state as "form" as opposed to purely action. Chile's oligarchy was in that sense more civilized than those in the rest of Latin America. Another important factor was the penetration of the landholding class by mercantile groups partly composed of Basques, providing the elite with a spectrum of moderately diverse economic interest and infusing it with an entrepreneurial culture. Later developments in the tumultuous twentieth century make it difficult to think of Chile as a stable, law-abiding country. But perhaps Chile's contemporary progress owes more to a culture that survived those political and economic upheavals than one would expect.

The Survivors

For those who believe in liberty, no contemporary Latin American phenomenon is more powerful than the informal or underground economy. Much has been written about it and plenty of praise has been heaped on it, but its lessons are yet to be heeded by public policy. It should really be called the survival economy because it includes millions of people around the world who carve out an existence for themselves outside of the law simply because doing business through the regular process—from obtaining licenses and incorporating a small firm to complying with local and central government regulations—is expensive, time-consuming, and often downright impossible. Furthermore, the legal economy offers no guarantees to those who, having accepted the onerous rules of the game, are not close to the political machinery that decides the fate of any enterprise.

It is estimated that the informal economy is worth around $5 trillion worldwide, that is, half the size of the U.S. economy. Although all nations have an informal economy, in rich countries it represents an average of 15 percent of all the goods and services provided, whereas in underdeveloped countries it represents at least one-third of total economic output. Since informality means lack of secure property rights and powerful enforcement mechanisms, insecurity and risk are very high. With insufficient capacity to save, no access to formal credit, insurance, and other institutions associated with the legal economy, productivity is very low. It is a labor-intensive, not a capital-intensive, world in which the costs of illegality—from very high interest rates on informal credit and insurance to the absence of tort law—make it very hard to develop. Although at least one-third of the entire economic output comes from informal activities, in most underdeveloped countries the proportion of workers involved in providing informal goods and services is much larger than a third of the total active population. It means quite simply the survival of the poor.

Housing, transport, manufacturing, retail commerce (both through street vending and in illegal markets or shopping centers), and other activities to which informal producers devote their time represent about 60 percent of man-hours worked in Peru. Informal employment accounts for more than 50 percent of the working population in Mexico and 40 percent of wage earners in Argentina, and involves more Brazilians than the combined number of people in the public sector and in formal industry in that country. Every year Peruvians looking for a place to settle invade about four hundred square miles of land. The overwhelming majority of new houses are built without the mandatory municipal license. Needless to say, only five of the forty-two municipal districts that make up Lima have an updated census of housing property. The percentage of construction that is not officially recorded is equally stunning.

Brazil's Amazon region involves some two million square miles, government land that has been opened to private settlement and claim not unlike what happened on America's western frontier. Families have taken possession of plots of land, negotiated informal arrangements, and tried to fend off squatting by people who invaded land already claimed. The lack of a speedy, flexible, and adequate system of recognition and enforcement by the authorities, however, has forced many settlers to operate outside of the law on a permanent basis. Under such a system, the further outside the political process people are, the more precarious their arrangements. But life does not stop. The poor make do any way they can.

These are just a few examples in a region where the size of the informal economy is such that it has created not only a parallel economy but also a sort of parallel culture (in Chile, by contrast, the informal economy represents just under one-fifth of the total size of the economy).

The informal economy has been the response of the poor to the illegitimacy of the state. In the process of surviving outside of the law in the urban centers to which they migrated from the countryside or in the capital cities to which they migrated from the provincial towns, they had not only to do business but, more generally, to live under spontaneously generated institutions designed to cover the most basic needs, from putting a roof over one's head to protecting one's meager belongings. Those institutions flowed from the customs of the poor. Isaiah Berlin had an eye on the past but was inadvertently anticipating this contemporary urban phenomenon of the underdeveloped world when he chose to refer to this quote by Giambattista Vico: "To each stage of social change there corresponds its own type of law, government, religion, art, myth, language, manners." The proliferation of evangelical cults, the growth of mestizo artistic movements, the emergence of idiosyncratic modes of expression, the invention of particular symbols taken out of everyday life, and other symptoms speak to us of a cultural transformation beyond the purely economic dimension. It began in the middle of the twentieth century, but its implications, a direct response to the system that shut out the poor, did not grip Latin America until much later.

By the 1980s and 1990s, it became fashionable to say that the informal economy was not simply a spectacle of land invasions, violent disputes among shantytown neighbors, dirty street vending, rash driving in unsafe public transport vehicles, and disloyal tax evasion by millions of people, but also a potential powerhouse of development. Latin America discovered in amazement (or was it horror?) that the poor, just like the rest, actually like to own property, produce goods and services privately, exchange them by contract rather than command, and enjoy the fruits of their hard labor. Every politician and commentator praised the inventiveness, entrepreneurial spirit, productive potential, survival instincts, organizational skills, and cultural achievements of the "informals," as they began to call the poor. They were unaware of the fact that the underground economy had been noticed in other parts of the poor world long before and that it had been lauded as the social cushion preventing revolution in other regions. American anthropologist William Mangin had extracted the right conclusions regarding this phenomenon two decades before, based on extensive and pathbreaking research of squatter settlements conducted in Peru and other places in the 1950s and 1960s. Had Latin America heeded his pioneering work (together with that of British anthropologist John Turner), those countries might have become prosperous by now. As early as 1971, anthropologist Keith Hart delivered a paper in which he spoke of the informal economy in some African nations as "a means of salvation" allowing people "denied success by the formal opportunity structure" to "increase their incomes." Even before that time, studies had been conducted in Latin American urban squatter settlements by both Latin American and U.S. researchers, with results that allowed scholars in the mid-1970s to identify rules and norms arising out of informal arrangements in areas such as housing, credit, public works, and dispute adjudication, and providing a certain security, justice, and organization to urban dwellers, who, despite their functioning outside of the formal law, became more or less integrated with the rest of society.

There is nothing particularly new in the current informal economy: the rise of the West in centuries past took place in exactly the same way, with millions of people producing and exchanging goods and services under spontaneous rules of the game that developed according to expanding needs. In her famous book *The Discovery of Freedom*, Rose Wilder Lane attributes to "smuggling and graft" the survival of trade under "planned economies" for six thousand years and celebrates the intense illegal commerce in which colonial America engaged under English rule. Much of the trade conducted by Americans under colonial rule before the revolution was also illegal, as was the case with colonial trade in Latin America, where other violations, such as urban squatting, were present as early as the sixteenth century.

In recent times, ironically, as government grew in the developed world and unemployment became a fixture, the underground economy became prominent in rich countries. Because it evaded taxes and regulations, it was illegal, but the ends that people pursued were perfectly legitimate. Some of the most important economic achievements of our time, such as the semiconductor industry, were closely connected to the underground economy in the United States. In the 1970s, many of the companies associated with the rise of what came to be known as Silicon Valley subcontracted home-based labor that evaded government regulations and taxes. The computer industry later encouraged a decentralized type of work relationship that made it easier to hire home-based labor that could go undetected by the authorities and thus soften the unemployment caused by government policies. As happens in poor countries (on a very different scale), the informal economy has many indirect connections to the formal economy, and they go beyond the hiring of illegal immigrants without paying Social Security taxes. Other developed nations, such as Italy, have been known for their extensive underground economies, which have helped ameliorate the disasters brought about by their corrupt and meddling politicians.

Unlike what happens in Latin America, in rich countries the official institutions adapted to the masses centuries ago, allowing capitalism to take off. Institutions work as a system of incentives and disincentives. Informal activity in the developed world is nowadays a marginal phenomenon, however significant in times of recession. The institutions still make it more costly to break the law than to abide by it. In Latin America, despite ritual gestures in favor of the informal economy—such as distributing property titles or deeds that signify "ownership" but not real, fungible property in practice—the legal country continues to exclude the other by imposing barrier after barrier against entry. A recent study demonstrates how little has been solved by the government distribution of titles among 1.2 million squatter homes in Peru between 1995 and 2001. The policy did not allow the poor to turn their dormant assets into active capital through access to credit, although it did encourage some of the beneficiaries to spend more time working outside of their homes because of the greater security of ownership. However, the rise in hours of work among the beneficiaries represents a very small percentage of the national work hours. Distributing titles in an environment where not even the written constitution is taken seriously is like placing a cello between the knees of a handcuffed musician. Without repealing the mountain of norms responsible for the black market, distributing ownership papers amounts to attacking merely a symptom.

It is estimated that the worldwide value of savings among the poor is forty times all the foreign aid distributed since 1945, yet the potential of the informal economy cannot be realized until the survival economy is allowed the right of citizenship. Without real property rights, there are no long-term decisions: entrepreneurs are not able to capitalize the present value of future expected profits (which is done by discounting the interest rates into the present values of those future profits). Prosperity still eludes Latin America because an economy in which most people do business illegally with a third of the productivity of those who belong to the formal club is condemned to low rates of real growth, a widening wealth divide, and social resentment.

This state of affairs is bad for everyone. The legal enterprises cannot grow and pay high salaries to more people so that they can buy goods and services from midsize and small companies, and these in turn, because of a depressed market, are obliged to sell their products to public employees (the reason why so many informal vendors cluster around state buildings waiting to attract customers). In Peru, for instance, only 2 percent of all private companies are legal, and they produce 60 percent of the wealth, while the other 98 percent of all enterprises, being illegal, produce little.

Because Latin American nations simply have not opened up the exclusive world of the law to the informal economy, the poor, over whose heads the reform years passed like Andean condors, seem not to have become Adam Smith's creators of wealth and prosperity, after all. The passion for the "informals" has therefore subsided in the official discourse of Latin America. But they are as strong an inspiration as ever for anyone convinced that what stands between survival and prosperity is not innate incapacity on the part of ordinary citizens or metaphysical fatality.

A double legacy, then, permits one to look at the history of liberty in Latin American as no barren land. One is academic and intellectual. It goes all the way from the School of Salamanca at the time when Latin America was a colony of Iberia to the handful of Latin American intellectuals who set out as early as the 1970s to debunk contemporary myths, among them Carlos Rangel in Venezuela and the pioneers of the Francisco Marroquín University in Guatemala, who have since inspired a growing list of writers and academic centers. The other legacy is practical. It has very ancient roots, traceable even under the suffocating states of the pre-Columbian world, in the customary behavior of native inhabitants seeking to obtain from nature and from social cooperation of various kinds the basics for subsistence. This legacy continues to stare one in the eye wherever one goes in Latin America. It is the daily struggle of ordinary men and women who survive through clandestine property and enterprise.

PART III

Reform

6

When Things Looked Right, They Were Wrong

There is one final element that must be discussed before we can address the so-called capitalist reforms of the 1990s and their devastating effects on the region. In Latin America's recent and distant past there is more than the piecemeal, geological formation of layer after layer of statism. There is also a long list of attempts at reform, a body of evidence showing that, throughout Latin America's history, individuals and groups, whether in or out of power, attempted to alter the way government was organized and the manner in which power related to the individual.

Although there were successes along the way, they were short-lived and, in the final analysis, unable to produce the desired effects. Inadequate reform has plagued the region no less than its corporatist, state-mercantilist, privilege-ridden, wealth-transferring tradition under political law. Liberal or capitalist reform never managed to produce societies based on liberty or a truly capitalist system of human endeavor. The reasons are as telling about Latin America's underdevelopment as about the need to learn from those mistakes.

It is misleading to separate political and economic reform; the relationship between the two is umbilical, as we have seen in the course of capitalist development in rich countries just as much as in underdevelopment in poor ones. The reason is not a mystery: the economy is human action under a set of rules, and those rules, good or bad, are the stuff of politics. But, for the sake of argument, one can distinguish, in the history of attempts by Latin Americans to carve a little star in the thick night of oppression, some "political" and some "economic."

The effort to reduce the power of the church in the nineteenth century was more "political" than "economic," although it was ultimately an assault on the concentration of power and, insofar as the economy responds to the incentives and impediments arising out of the organization of power, it had an economic dimension. The fever of "positivism" that gripped some Latin American countries at the end of the nineteenth century and the beginning of the twentieth was more "economic" than "political" in that its obsession was investment and the creation of the economic infrastructure of modernity, but politics cannot be left out since the rules that governed this economic machinery were firmly in the hands of the state. Something similar can be said of the export boom in the first decades of the twentieth century.

In any case, the so-called capitalist reforms of the 1990s have a long genealogy behind them. Many of those precedents in export-led, capital investment–rich political economy that failed to deliver free-market capitalism contain some of the germs of what happened in the 1990s. Had those responsible for reform considered the history of pseudocapitalism in the region, things might have turned out differently.

A Conservative Is a Liberal in Office

History has attributed the observation "There is nothing quite so much like a conservative as a liberal in office" to the Viscount of Albuquerque, who lived in Brazil in the nineteenth century. This paradox fits the description of almost every movement bent on reform of the status quo in the last two centuries. Even before exercising power, liberal or progressive struggles to cut through the cobweb of traditional, oligarchic, authoritarian institutions ultimately betrayed a thinly veiled attachment to new forms of corporatism, mercantilism, privilege, wealth transfer, and political law.

The very feat of independence was, in many ways, a reactionary effort despite the Enlightenment rhetoric that presided over it. When Napoleon invaded Spain and put his younger brother on the throne of Ferdinand VII, traditionalists in Spain resisted French dominance. Creole traditionalists echoed them in the colonies. Although Napoleon was the heir to the French Revolution and therefore in theory the standard-bearer of liberalism against reactionary Spain, the resistance against the invasion inspired liberal ideals on both sides of the Atlantic, triggering the movement for independence in the colonies and encouraging a culture of local, community-based activity in Latin America, and was ultimately responsible for the 1812 liberal constitution, signed by some Latin American delegates in Cádiz together with their Spanish colleagues. And yet events unfolded in such a way that what seemed liberal turned conservative. Ferdinand VII came back after Napoleon's fall, did away with the 1812 constitution, and restored despotism, only to be forced to accept liberalism in 1820 and tolerate anticlerical leaders in government who opposed any autonomy in the colonies—a move that only inflamed calls for Latin American independence, led by members of the elite, many of whom were conservatives who had experienced some self-government and were not prepared to accept metropolitan despotism. Both liberals and conservatives participated in the wars of independence, and the fashionable ideas of the Enlightenment were the powerful driving force behind the action. But independence, purportedly a liberal undertaking, was from the very beginning tainted with a conservative sense of attachment to particular privileges enjoyed by the elite.

A succession of caudillos—a tradition with some Spanish Visigothic flavor to it—ensued, a number of whom called themselves liberals, others conservatives, some centralists, others federalists, but all of whom were authoritarian and showed little interest in breaking with privilege. Liberals were Rousseau-type liberals, with their centralist, organic, hierarchic idea of power. Under liberal no less than under conservative governments, women could exercise property rights only through their men and did not enjoy basic civil rights, including the right to vote or hold public office. Liberals and conservatives saw the government as the great arbiter of opportunity. Both sides understood that through the exercise of political power one could have access to jobs and to private property. Government was the vehicle of social mobility. The ideological inclination of liberals did not translate into less patronage and economic favoritism than took place under conservatives.

Throughout Latin America, nineteenth-century liberals were most concerned with reforming the church—or, rather, the exorbitant power of the church, particularly its hold on land, education, and marriage. The church was then one of the pillars of the corporatist, state-mercantilist, privilege-ridden, wealth-transferring system under political law. Any attempt at empowering the individual—removing barriers to property, social mobility, personal initiative—necessarily meant divesting that all-pervading and intrusive institution married to the state of some of its powers. Benito Juárez, a Mexican symbol of liberalism, engaged in precisely such a reform in the late 1850s. Liberals began by restricting ecclesiastic and military privileges in matters deemed "civilian." In 1856, the Lerdo Law required all "corporations" to sell their lands. That general term was actually aimed at the church, which was ordered to put its most valuable and productive land on the market. The 1857 constitution confirmed the reforms and took them one step further by secularizing education. The war that followed saw the liberal movement triumph in its drive to end church control over cemeteries and civil marriage, and to separate it from the state. In the spirit of enhancing the role of the individual over the corporation, confradias (lay brotherhoods) were replaced by *mayordomías*, the emphasis being on the individual *mayordomo*.

The impetus to modernize Mexico, however, was neutered by the same liberals who enacted reform (matters were not very different in other countries, including Chile, after the entailed estate was suppressed). What good was it to divest the church of its highly concentrated ownership of land if the same laws forced Indian communities to get rid of their property, thereby creating other enclaves of privilege through the transfer of vast amounts of land to a handful of hacendados or big Creole landowners? What good was it to impose legal restrictions on the military if the use of force—the military component of political power—was the fundamental source of legitimacy for liberals struggling to retain government and combat enemies? And what good was it to divest private corporations of some of their prerogatives if the state was to become involved, through wealth transfer and political interference, in activities that created new forms of discrimination?

The intentions, the ideological genuineness, and the intellectual acumen of the reformers were not to blame. As has always been the case throughout the region, reformers often mistook symptoms for causes. The church was not the real enemy; the culprits were concentration of power, stratified or exclusive property rights, the state as the enforcer of a particular creed, and the law as an extension and not as a limit of government. Reformers tried to remove particular institutions and individuals from positions of authority but failed to change the nature of authority itself. The result was a slightly less brutal form of wealth concentration, hierarchic imposition, and discriminatory rules.

After independence, the various economies of Latin America underwent a period of stagnation. The devastation of the war and the effects of the ensuing political instability and of the absence of Spanish trade forced the region into mere economic subsistence. But one of the driving forces of the independence movement had been the thirst for open commerce and global investment, both of which were held back, it was believed, by the anachronism of the colonial regime. In fact, Mexico opened its borders to all foreign goods at a uniform tariff of 25 percent as early as 1821. Once the disruptive aftermath of the wars for independence ended, Latin America felt the symptoms of economic liberalization. Most countries engaged in economic reform, aggressively promoting foreign investment, raising capital abroad, and trading with Europe and, to a lesser extent, with the United States. The railways and steam engine navigation, riding on the back of foreign capital, reduced the cost of transport and opened markets beyond the usual trading ports. Settlers moved into open spaces, bringing remote areas into the world economy. Reformers were convinced that Latin America was the land of the future.

But once again reformers mistook symptoms for causes; through the machinery of government, Latin American countries were concentrating property, political power, and economic opportunity in the hands of the landed elite. Naturally, economic growth had a spillover effect on other people, but the grip of the elite on politics and therefore on economic rights ensured that progress was superficial, benefiting the top layer of society and ultimately widening the gap between the theoretical and the real republic, which should have begun to be filled by a middle class. Reformers had believed that the problem was Spain, and once commerce opened up to other partners—the British, the Germans, the Americans—prosperity would occur. They had believed that the problem was having only one market for Latin America's primary products, and once other markets were available, the region would take off. They had believed that the lack of industry was due to the absence of foreign investment, and once capital from abroad became available, capitalism would prosper. They were right only to an extent. In fact, trade, investment, and access to capital had not been the causes of western European and American capitalism. They had been the symptoms and consequences of institutional frameworks within which economic activity, the contract society, had not remained in the hands of a few powerful people but had expanded to the masses. In the absence of that framework, investment and trade could not bring liberal capitalism to entire nations.

Latin America's economic landscape changed when the continent experienced globalization in the last half of the nineteenth century. But prosperity is not the right word to describe what happened. It was a funnel economy, with a wide end where wealth was accumulated on behalf of the modern global oligarchy and a narrow end where the majority was left out. Free-market capitalism did not describe the new Latin America. In the country, there were self-sufficient manors and heavily concentrated estates for export crops. In the towns were the officials and absentee landowners, and merchants and artisans working for them. The town, as Stanislav Andreski wrote, had a "parasitic" relationship to the village: it consumed agricultural products without producing and supplying almost anything in return.

Two countries, Brazil and Chile, emerged as oases of stability in the nineteenth century. They are often held up as examples of political and economic progress interrupted by later events but that constitute a reference for reform that seeks a stable, predictable environment in which investors can prosper. A closer look suggests that the evaluation is far-fetched, and some of the antecedents of misguided reform can be found in both countries (especially Brazil), even though political stability benefited certain sectors of the economy.

Brazil's independence was peaceful and civilized. Fleeing from Napoleon's invading troops, the Portuguese king moved to Brazil. The royal family settled in, and once the king returned to Portugal, the independence movement ensued. One of the king's sons was proclaimed emperor of Brazil as Pedro I. Under Pedro II, who succeeded his father in 1831, the country achieved political stability until the fall of the monarchy in 1889. The planters constituted the mainstay of the Crown, which presided over the second-largest slave economy in the New World, just behind that of the American South (by the time the slave trade ended, five million slaves had been sold to Brazil). Imperial centralism kept the territory together amid regional forces that would otherwise have caused disintegration. The different regions were not federal entities competing for investment but local coalitions competing for money and political patronage, through a parliament that did not watch over unbiased rules of the game but, instead, reflected the fragmentary framework of property rights and the wealth-transferring structure of the state. Brazil might not have gone through the equivalent of the American Civil War, but its stable environment was much less conducive to capitalism than that of the United States, despite territorial expansion and the devastating consequences of the war between the North and the South. Again, the value of stability that some Latin Americans view as a panacea against underdevelopment can be misleading. The stability of authoritarian order and exclusive business interests might stimulate growth in certain pockets of the economy but, as was the case in nineteenth-century Brazil, it does not generate liberal capitalism.

The 1880s brought some reforms, such as deregulation in capital markets and, in 1888, the formal abolition of slavery. But reform once again acted as a vehicle for the rearrangement and realignment of vested interests. The elite hacendados no longer admired the monarchy; the republic they brought about, however, with the help of many progressive intellectuals, became a fig leaf attempting to conceal the persistence of traditional bastions of power. The landed oligarchy and the military—Brazil's supreme institution—dominated the political game for the next forty years.

Chile's stability in the nineteenth century was more productive than Brazil's, but, as in Brazil, the gap between the oligarchy and the rest of society was great. By 1830, the conservative landowning elite, under the influence of Diego Portales, was able to mold the republican state. The military was subordinated to civilian authorities, and the constitution that emerged lasted until the early part of the twentieth century. The fact that Chile had not been a viceroyalty and had stayed at the margins of the Spanish edifice meant that the republic was less suffocated by its colonial heritage. Immigration, particularly Basque, brought entrepreneurial acumen to the leading echelons of the economy. Ethnic and racial homogeneity reduced social tensions next door in Peru. Stability helped develop the Chilean state, and by the end of the century Chile defeated Peru, the seat of the former South American Spanish empire, and its ally Bolivia in the War of the Pacific, thereby incorporating nitrate into its economy to the great benefit of the state budget, which was able to live off that primary product without needing to levy high taxes on producers.

But stability did not mean a predictable set of neutral rules governing individual initiative, safeguarding contracts, and respecting freedom. On the contrary, it meant a conservative environment in which a global entrepreneurial elite was able to put together a state that embodied national interests and encouraged investment and development among privileged property owners. That type of stability, as was the case in Brazil, paved the way for economic instability in the twentieth century, when the legitimacy of the conservative state came into question by an underrepresented society. The heart of the oligarchic republic was then torn open, and the results were messy. Chile joined its unstable Latin American neighbors, and an open, capitalist society had still not been born.

Been There, Done That

Between the last quarter of the nineteenth century and the first quarter of the twentieth, progress took hold in Latin America. An observer who witnessed the rush toward capitalism would be amazed by that feverish antecedent of Latin American globalization. In retrospect, one can identify a two-phased phenomenon, not necessarily planned that way or neatly sequential.

First came the explosion of positivism followed by the export boom. Positivism was the name given to French social scientist Auguste Comte's idea that progress was a deliberate, rational process whereby central authorities, identifying the inexorable, historic laws that govern societies, accelerated development through social engineering. The government was morally responsible for bringing about progress, but for that purpose it relied heavily on private enterprise and kept fiscal numbers in order. While positivism had only a mild impact on the United States, particularly in the South due to its racist history, in Latin America, governments, intellectuals, and business elites became obsessed with it.

Tied to this dynamic was the "export or die" mentality that both fueled and was fed by the boom of primary exports and the development of industries revolving around them. The whole period, from the positivism of the late 1800s to the export drive of the early 1900s, was the greatest attempt at capitalist development prior to the one that took the region by storm in the 1990s. It spanned many years and its intensity was awesome. Any capitalist revolution at the end of the twentieth century and the turn of the twenty-first would have done well to heed the lessons of that period.

It is not surprising that positivism, an offspring of the Enlightenment that drew inspiration from Charles Darwin, Herbert Spencer, and James Mill, took root so firmly in Latin America. After many decades of stagnation and political instability following the wars for independence, here was the philosophy that held progress to be a scientific phenomenon. It was to be explored by observation, hypothesis, and experimentation, and, once it was identified, progress could be accelerated through the organic forces of society under the direction of the state, the supreme guarantor of order, a prime condition for development. Private investment, particularly foreign investment, was crucial, which meant that the public purse must be tightly managed to ensure an orderly state of affairs. The new commercial groups could find accommodation among the oligarchy's old boys' club. But the state played a leading role; in fact, it was the engine of progress, and it relied on heavy involvement in infrastructure works, promoting education, and cultivating a cozy relationship with the business elite. Prosperity would come through legislation, but its tool would be capitalist private enterprise and government would be its legislative and political engineer.

The late part of the nineteenth century and the early years of the twentieth century saw many symbols of positivism in the region: Mexico's Porfirio Díaz between 1876 and 1910, Brazil's waning monarchy in the 1870s and 1890s and its nascent republic thereafter, and Venezuela's Juan Vicente Gomez. In Uruguay, José Batlle y Ordoñez, the founder of the Latin American welfare state, also fit the bill, but he exercised his power more modestly than did his counterparts. For the rest, positivism spelled high degrees of centralized political control and authoritarianism. One of positivism's leading intellectual figures in Latin America, Laureano Vallenilla, staunchly defended the idea of "democratic Caesarism"—that is, of quasi-dictatorial power—as a condition for material progress, the god on whose altar all other considerations must be sacrificed.

For positivists, the centralization of political power and the subordination of political institutions to particular interests was not an obstacle to but rather a condition for the creation of wealth. Without economic growth, political democracy was a sham. Porfirio Díaz, therefore, established a political dictatorship that respected private enterprise. Foreign investment tripled, exports grew 6.1 percent a year, some industries flourished, and railroads and highways crisscrossed the country. The material signs of progress—a positivist, futuristic emblem—were all there, just as in Brazil, where the idea of economic progress stimulated the struggle for the emancipation of slaves and the demise of the monarchy, or, a few years later, in Venezuela, where foreign investors, many of them American, could not stop drilling oil from the blessed subsoil.

But despite impressive growth, some industrial expansion, rising exports, abundant foreign investment, and political and fiscal stability, capitalism and prosperity did not flourish in those years. The very fact that these positivist years were followed by economic nationalism testifies to their basic failure and speaks directly to the nature of development—the quintessential difference between the exterior manifestations of prosperity and the real cause of the wealth of nations.

Positivism's crucial flaws, which would haunt Latin America again once economic nationalism collapsed and the pendulum swung back to private enterprise and open borders, are no mystery. Its first mistake was conceiving of development as a deliberate national achievement, not as the natural consequence of individual human action pursuing independent objectives. The distinction is not academic. Because politicians thought that progress could be engineered from the upper echelons of government, the emphasis was not on the rules protecting the contract society but on legislation designed to speed the "scientific" force of material advance. It was believed, even as private property was respected, that legislation alone could have positive effects on the economy. Top-to-bottom political decisions, not institutional arrangements arising from voluntary cooperation, were the source of economic incentive.

That fundamental premise was ultimately incompatible with the market economy even as private businesspeople and private enterprise enjoyed overwhelming government support. Political incentives passed through legislation translated into commercial codes, mining codes, subsidies, and tariffs aimed at helping those activities deemed of paramount importance for material development, at the expense of activities deemed less significant. As has always been the case, fiscal necessity was a decisive criterion for granting privileges. Díaz allowed bankers to write banking laws that hindered entry into the system. Obligingly, the beneficiaries provided the government with credit lines. Domestic investors seeking to expand into new industries bought government protection by subscribing to its bond issues. The result was the perpetuation of Latin America's old system.

The second basic flaw, closely connected to the first, was the idea that freedom could be treated as a set of compartments and not as a whole. Political and economic freedom were separated in the belief that vertical political authority could spur the type of stability, protection, and stimulus that chaotic and fragile democratic institutions could not. This outlook presumed a false dichotomy. The real choice was not between stable dictatorship and unruly democracy, but between a political system, whether democratic or dictatorial, that did not protect individual rights and one that did. The false dichotomy presiding over government action marred progress during the positivist years, yet it also compromised the future because dictatorships were followed by democracy, but not by the rule of law.

Positivism's third flaw, derived from the previous two, was the idea that development was attached to certain outward signs, particular machines, specific industries, strategic sectors, and chosen elites, rather than to a general environment. Consequently, resources were deployed—and arbitrarily allocated—toward desired targets through various incentives. The result was a very notable development of particular sectors—transport infrastructure being the major one—that were so splendidly visible as to convince the leaders that progress was materializing. Fragmentary property rights can certainly concentrate investment and therefore develop particular areas of the economy, but they hinder the sustained growth of the rest of society and ultimately even compromise the capacity of those privileged industries to survive once the government can no longer guarantee its support. It was precisely this positivist mentality that pushed Díaz in Mexico to direct investment toward oil and the expropriation of peasant village lands purportedly to secure an adequate supply of land, water, and labor for development. Had the effort gone toward respecting all property rights, Mexican agriculture might have produced stunning results. Powerful agriculture is one of the elements that served the development of industry in the rich capitalist nations. But the history of capitalism shows that the process must be spontaneous, the unintended result of millions of individual minds and hearts pursuing private goals through a market-based allocation of resources and dissemination of information. The web of general development is made of a multitude of tiny threads—including those peasants Díaz sacrificed for his big positivist plan. The positivist experience shows that targeted development results in integral underdevelopment.

Riding on the heels of positivism came the export boom of the early twentieth century. Once again, Latin America seemed to be the promised land. Europeans and Americans wanted to invest in and trade with the continent. For centuries, Latin America had exported precious metals. Before the railroad, the only other important export was sugar, produced in the Caribbean islands and northeastern Brazil. In the last decades of the nineteenth century, guano and nitrates became Peru's export jewels, then Chile defeated Peru and Bolivia in war and took control of nitrates. Brazil started to export coffee, Argentina experienced a veritable leap forward with its supply of meat and cereals, while the Caribbean countries concentrated on tropical fruit. A few decades later, oil fueled Mexico and Venezuela's entry into the world markets. As would happen at the end of the twentieth century, foreign investors rushed into Latin America looking for a stake in the export economy, the nascent transport industry, and banking. Shortly thereafter, Peru diversified its export base to include cotton, sugar, and copper; Colombia began to export coffee; and Bolivia sold a wealth of tin. By the late 1920s, primary products and raw materials gave Latin America a nearly 10 percent share in world trade. This "open" pattern lasted until 1930, when economic nationalism, which had made its first inroads during World War I, took possession of the Latin American soul.

But a closer look reveals that the government and the parasitic elite were playing as predatory a role as ever in the era of "free trade" and the export boom. There was high protection against imports, the net result constituting a form of tax burden on the export economy. Land and labor policies conferred arbitrary grants to cronies at the expense of the poor, and restricted mobility. Many areas of the economy were sacrificed, under the zero-sum mentality, in order to subsidize transportation and education. Except for Colombia, where small and midsized companies flourished, the state made every effort to discourage the dissemination of property and enterprise among the destitute. Numerous regulations destined to "manage" the supply of export products in order to sustain prices limited the freedom of producers. In Cuba, where sugar had flourished thanks to thousands of private contracts closely reflecting the customs and uses of individuals and allowed for minimal transaction costs, the government imposed quotas and production restrictions, eventually affecting the country's world market share.

The export boom showed an abundance of natural resources can be a mixed blessing and sometimes a curse. The economies were dependent on volatile commodity prices. There tended to be insufficient diversification, and the "Dutch disease" haunted the republics, with money that came in from the export proceeds raising prices of nontradable domestic goods and causing an appreciation of the real exchange, therefore working against manufacturing, whose capacity to adjust was limited in the face of high business costs due to government intervention. Much more significantly, the export boom injected life into the traditional government-individual relations. Instead of bringing about prosperity for large sectors of the population (with the exception of Argentina, where liberal capitalism made greater inroads and bred a high degree of development), the export era consolidated the predatory institutions and the divide between the oligarchy and the masses. The expansion of certain crops and industries might have brought new faces into the oligarchy with commercial interests enlarging a privileged caste previously monopolized by landowners, but the touchstone of the system remained: economic success and failure were more than ever tied to the political network.

Capitalism and the Boots

The reforms of the 1990s have one more precedent—the South American military dictatorships of the 1960s and 1970s. Those exercises in political oppression were by no means exceptional in the history of the region. But the failure of economic nationalism gave them, by contrast, such prestige that many conservatives and even libertarians have pointed to them as examples of free-market reform and excused the absence of political freedoms as the necessary price for opening trade, promoting investment, selling state companies, keeping wages in check, and encouraging private enterprise. These dictatorial experiments did in fact try to revert to some aspects of economic nationalism, still the dominant feature of the region's political economy at the time, but that philosophy so pervaded the establishment that even the "capitalist" military regimes were unable to shake off its premises. In any event, the governments in power after the fall of the military dictatorships that ostensibly produced capitalism resumed many of the old policies.

Those dictatorships—in Brazil, Argentina, and Uruguay—that sought to combine political authoritarianism with "free markets" were children of a long tradition of delusion, a new attempt at doing what Latin America had tried in the nineteenth and early twentieth centuries before economic nationalism set in. The results were, as always, impressive on the outside, in some cases with high growth rates caused by targeted investment and an increase in commerce, but frustrating deep down because no profound variation took place in the way society was organized, or in the way incentives affected individual choice and institutions accommodated private initiative. The original sin conditioned those reforms, as it had previous attempts at capitalism, resulting in even greater concentration of wealth.

Brazil's military took over in the 1960s and determined that the country would achieve greatness through government action. The effort was directed toward investment in infrastructure—dams, highways, and hydroelectric plants—as well as in light and heavy industry, with the purpose of replacing traditional commodities with manufactured goods as the country's major contributions to the world market. Public investment was used directly to promote sectors' transport equipment and other industries, and active alliances were established on the part of the political authorities with particular labor and business interests. At the same time, three successive finance ministers, Roberto Campos, Delfim Nieto, and Mario Henrique Simonsen, lifted many trade barriers and encouraged foreign capital inflows, while the regime suppressed powerful workers' unions and reined in government employees. Brazil's "miracle" achieved high growth rates between the mid-1960s and 1980. By the mid-1970s, industrial goods constituted almost a third of all exports, which was not bad for a country known until then for its sugar, coffee, and bananas. The trend continued in the 1980s, under democracy, so that by the early 1990s industry constituted 38 percent of Brazil's GDP.

Argentina also experienced a so-called free-market dictatorship between 1966 and 1973, when some tariff barriers were dropped, cutbacks were applied in the public sector, a tight lid was placed on wages, and some state companies were sold, while all-out war was waged against left-wing insurrection. Uruguay, for its part, went through creeping authoritarianism in the 1960s, and by 1973 all pretense of civilian rule was abandoned with the military takeover and reform similar to that undertaken in Argentina.

A number of elements attest to the weaknesses of those "miracles." Capital inflows, which fed strong local currencies, cheapened imports and made exports more expensive. This resulted in an increase in imports as well as the servicing of the debt, leading to an important outflow of foreign exchange. Governments, rather than letting the currencies depreciate according to market forces so that they would reflect and therefore "correct" the imbalances, maintained high exchange rates. Consumption outgrew investment, and in the absence of structural reform, with taxes rising in order to keep up with high public expenses, local industries had a hard time competing with imports. Financing government-created deficits, sustaining huge consumption levels, and being uncompetitive were not grave problems while foreign capital continued to come in. But once it stopped, especially with short-term capital going back out, recession set in and the real economy was exposed. It became clear that the winners had been those businesses that received government support. Almost everyone else—that is, consumers as well as the many producers who had not been blessed by government favoritism—was left out in the cold. It also became evident that the government, while reducing its scope in some areas, had actually grown. Nothing attests more powerfully to the deceitful nature of the "capitalist" dictatorship than the fact that, for all its encouragement of private enterprise, it believed that progress was a government program. Multiple government actions, including many surviving tariffs and import licenses, had even perpetuated old rent-seeking habits.

Statistical growth—that old Latin American curse—was significant in Brazil. But high growth rates were also present under policies of economic nationalism in many countries. In any case, three-quarters of the total gain in income was absorbed by the richest 10 percent of the Brazilian population: the concentration, not the dispersion, of wealth was the reality behind statistical growth. By the early 1990s, the per capita income of many states in northeastern Brazil was $2,900, half the national average, whereas in the more advanced regions it was three times that average. Argentina's "capitalist" dictatorship managed a less spectacular 3.4 percent rate of economic growth and Uruguay not even half that figure.

As had happened in the late nineteenth century and the early twentieth century, under the military rule of the 1960s and 1970s free-market capitalism was not exactly the name of the game. It could be said that pseudocapitalist reform has consolidated, not attenuated, traditional flaws. When things look right but are in fact wrong, the result can be worse than when they are obviously wrong.

7

The Fever of Change

Reform takes place when the vested interests supporting the status quo come under attack by other interests seeking to survive at their expense once the government, because of fiscal disarray or political illegitimacy, is no longer in a position to guarantee either party the "parasitic" rewards of that very status quo. Revolution is that same process taken one step further, in the absence of political mechanisms able to peacefully resolve the conflict. Of course, appearances do not necessarily betray the naked power game. It may be that the reformists are not entirely hypocritical about the ideals they profess to embody, and it may also be that the constituencies behind them—or behind revolutionary vanguards when revolution is involved—and those simply struggling for change without being organically associated with the leading groups really want change as a matter of universal principle. But any institutional change that takes a society from one form of predation to another through reform or revolution, even if the new rules benefit more people and eliminate many of the evils of the old rules, ultimately translates as the successful attempt of groups vested with particular interests to replace the old ones (or to continue, by adapting to the new times, to concentrate opportunity and profit in their hands). The alternative scenario, in which reform or revolution produces decisive movement toward the rule of law, and power is disseminated among numerous groups whose prosperity is by no means a previously determined outcome, is also possible. In that case, paradoxical good comes from the power conflict between interest groups: the hopes of the principled constituents—and their better leaders—become realized. As we have seen, the reforms undertaken at various times in Latin America during two centuries of republican life belong squarely in the first category. They amounted mostly to traumatic reshuffling of political and economic power. Were the reforms of the 1990s any different?

In order to answer that question, we must look at what was done.

The Mutiny of the Elites

Fiscal collapse, monetary chaos, and productive stagnation brought about by economic nationalism as the state lost legitimacy, and at a time when foreign lending and aid were no longer available, paved the way for Latin American reform. The various coalitions that had a vested interest in economic nationalism came into conflict. In Chile in the 1970s, Mexico in the 1980s, and Argentina and Peru in the 1990s, the central conflict was between those directly dependent on money for their survival and those whose stake in the system, while also constituting a form of wealth transfer, related to other types of government action, especially protectionism, rather than fiscal handouts.

Those who depended on government spending were seriously harmed by the financial calamity that resulted from socialist policies, populism, and what Venezuelan writer Carlos Rangel called "Third World ideology." Large deficits, restricted access to foreign credit, and high inflation are a lethal combination for those who live off the government. The logic of the statist system, once the financial position of the state is eroded and the currency is debased, is to push for further intervention, that is, for nationalization of industry and finance. From Salvador Allende in Chile to Alan García in Peru, and from López Portillo in Mexico to Raul Alfonsín in Argentina, the governments that preceded reform were forced by fiscal and monetary collapse to listen to the radical groups pushing the government to expropriate wealth from the private economy. The degrees of interventionism differed across Latin America, Chile's Allende being the most radical and Argentina's Alfonsín the mildest, but the tendency was unequivocal. Not surprisingly, other factions of the system, in this case private interests, reacted. These industrial and financial groups had a stake in the mercantilist environment and were dependent on state protection, but any move on the part of the state to appropriate wealth was really a threat aimed at them. They were the only successful private interests in countries where "private enterprise" meant little more than a bunch of privileged groups owing their high returns to government favoritism. In many cases, the reaction was against not potential but actual state takeover—Chile, Mexico, and Peru went ahead with nationalization of key sectors, including banking.

The reaction was no longer a purely conservative defense of the status quo. It could not be: the position of the threatened or affected parties had also been seriously eroded by fiscal and monetary chaos, and, in any event, the move on the part of radical statists created an unavoidable power struggle and made change inevitable—a scenario that guaranteed an overhaul of the political and economic map and, paradoxically, a reduction of rents on *both* sides. By turning on one another, in the form of intellectual attacks on economic nationalism and of popular upheaval, the elites opened the way for reform.

The confrontation took the form of ideological revision of a kind not seen since the emergence of economic nationalism and included political events as diverse as Augusto Pinochet's military coup in Chile, Alberto Fujimori's victory in Peru, the remaking of Carlos Menem's Justicialista Party (Perón's old party) in Argentina, the split of the PRI dictatorship into conservative and reformist factions in Mexico, and the reinvention of Fernando Henrique Cardoso, a luminary of the "dependency theory" in the 1970s, who became president of Brazil in the 1990s and abandoned every economic idea he had previously defended.

The United States quickly backed the reformist reaction against statism without regard to the ethical nature of the new regimes, or to their origin and methods. Thus, Mexico's PRI dictatorship and Fujimori's autocracy, both very corrupt systems, received the type of backing that Pinochet's military government had enjoyed in its day. What was not socialist had to be capitalist. Indeed, it looked capitalist, and if it was capitalist, it was "one of us." Latin America became one of the main laboratories for what was termed the "Washington Consensus," a set of policies backed by multilateral bodies and think tanks, and centered on fiscal discipline, economic liberalization, and privatization. The world community at large, not only the United States, became enamored with Latin America. It was now the place to invest in, to trade with, to engage in political partnership, to exhibit as the epitome of "emerging markets." Its leaders' faces were splashed across glossy financial magazines in the United States, Europe, and Asia; they were rapturously applauded on Wall Street, in London, and in Hong Kong; and they toured the planet, taking part in splendid road shows vaunting their achievements.

So what was it all about?

Turning the Tide

Reform varied considerably from one place to the next. In Mexico, economic reform shadowed the gradual decline of the PRI dictatorship, from Carlos Salinas's fraudulent victory in 1988, a watershed in government-opposition dynamics, to Ernesto Zedillo's impeccable handing of power, for the first time in many decades, to a non-PRI president-elect, Vicente Fox, in 2000. In Peru, reform came by way of a dictatorship led by a civilian president who won a free and fair election but, using Shining Path's terrorist onslaught as a pretext, staged a coup from power. In Chile, although the main thrust of reform took place under the "Chicago boys" of the Pinochet regime, the socialist and Christian-democratic Concertación Democrática coalition preserved the legacy and expanded parts of it after democracy was recovered in 1989. In El Salvador, reform coincided with the end of the civil war and dissolved after the collapse of the Soviet bloc, which had supported and inspired the left-wing insurgency.

Differences were not limited to the varying political contexts: the intensity and depth of reform were not the same in every country. In general, it can be said that reform was most profound in those countries that had performed poorly in the 1950–80 period and less profound in those where previous performance did not seem to warrant an urgent need for radical change. Chile, Argentina, and Peru, in South America, and El Salvador and the Dominican Republic, in Central America and the Caribbean, were the leading reformists. Mexico, in North America, was equally, if not more, audacious in many areas, but more modest in others, as was the case with Bolivia and Uruguay, in South America. Brazil took a long time to warm up to reform and never went beyond moderate transformations, although the sheer size of the country, and therefore of its economy, tends to render its belated changes a larger profile. Colombia, which had experienced consistent economic growth until left-wing terrorism aided by drug money declared war on the country, was modest in its reforms. So were Venezuela, where abundant oil revenues tended to lull impetus for anything too radical, and Ecuador, where oil and a not too dismal macroeconomic performance in previous years also worked as a disincentive. The government of Paraguay, in perpetual political chaos, appeared not to have much time to consider reform. El Salvador's neighbors in Central America joined the feast with less passion, because the weight of economic nationalism was somewhat less oppressive. Among the Central America laggards, Costa Rica and Guatemala embraced reform to the greatest extent.

Reform in the 1990s took place in two not always neatly differentiated stages. "Fiscal and monetary stabilization" is the phrase used by international bureaucrats and academics to refer to the set of measures aimed at ending inflation and restoring sound housekeeping. The second phase is often referred to as "structural" or "second-generation reform," meaning tax, trade, financial, investment, and labor reform, as well as privatization and the switch from pay-as-you-go pension schemes to private-account retirements.

Bringing down inflation—the first stage of reform—amounted to pulling the economy back down. The Latin American economies had behaved for far too long as if there were no connection between the volume of money that was printed and the volume of goods and services produced, nor between the amount of money governments spent and the amount of taxes they collected. Aside from any other consideration, restoring proportionality between the monetary mass and national production and reducing government bills in order to lower the pressure on the central bank were acts of economic honesty and an admission of deceit. Ever since the 1930s, when the gold standard was dropped, monetary policy had been at the mercy of political fiction producing abundant fiat money as if it constituted real wealth. Without resorting to the gold standard, many governments pegged their monetary policies to reality. In 1991, Argentina actually pegged the currency to another "standard," in this case the dollar, by establishing a currency board that tied the volume of local pesos to the amount of foreign reserves, but other countries, such as Brazil in the mid-1990s, preferred simply to opt for monetary restraint. El Salvador and Ecuador actually adopted the dollar as their currency.

All governments attacked the two most important causes of fiscal deficit: subsidies to producers or consumers, and state companies that employed thousands of workers and whose real balance sheets were often in the red. For a long time Latin America lived under the illusion that the resources acquired by the government in order to employ people and subsidize the economy did not come out of the pockets of ordinary citizens. In Brazil, 70 percent of the government's revenue covered the federal payroll, and 90 percent of the budget in the twenty-six states (not counting the federal district) was devoted to the same purpose. The situation was not much different elsewhere. Citizens in developed countries, even those that sustain large welfare states, are conscious of the fact that public spending is paid for with the wealth produced by their efforts. In Latin America, few people pay direct taxes, and the causality that relates the government's expenditure to society's wealth had for a long time been lost in the minds of most ordinary citizens. The reduction of public spending in Chile, Mexico, Argentina, Brazil, Peru, Bolivia, and other countries, which included layoffs and salary cuts or ceilings, seemed like more than an act of fiscal prudence: it looked like a backlash against the rapacious nature of government.

"Shock therapy" policies involved lifting controls and therefore led to traumatic realignments of prices. In Mexico and Peru, letting fuel and food prices float freely provoked spectacular one-time rises. But the benefits were soon felt. The reduction of inflation (in Chile, Bolivia, Peru, and Argentina, it was actually hyperinflation) benefited both consumers and producers after the initial one-off "shock." By 1996, thanks to monetary restraint and a fiscal prudence that reduced two-digit deficits to single digits, average inflation across the region was 17.7 percent. In many countries, including Brazil and those that had suffered hyperinflation, it was below 10 percent, in line with international standards.

But monetary and fiscal stabilization was only the beginning. Tax reform was a natural first step of structural change. Income taxes were lowered for all categories. Mexico and Argentina reduced their top marginal tax rates to 35 percent and 40 percent respectively, Colombia to 35 percent, Brazil to 28 percent. Minimum taxable income was fixed at such levels that a large part of the population—70 percent of the labor force in the case of Chile—became exempt from taxation altogether. Corporate taxes were set at a regional average of 35 percent, and some countries, including Peru, did away with capital gains taxes. Tax systems were simplified, as in Chile, where similar types of income were taxed at similar rates (which brought evasion down close to the standard of developed countries). Only Bolivia dared to instate an almost flat income tax. In general, the tendency was to reduce the burden of taxation on income and concentrate on consumption. Multiple sales taxes were dropped in favor of uniform value-added taxes in most countries, although many products were exempt.

Commercial policy reversed decades of import substitution. Modern-day trumpets of Jericho brought down tariffs and other types of barriers, eliminated quota restrictions and import licenses, limited or did away with state trading agencies, and removed export taxes in most countries. Argentina's maximum tariff level went from 55 percent in 1985 to 22 percent in 1992, Brazil's from 105 to 65 percent, Chile's from 20 to 11 percent, Mexico's from 100 to 20 percent, and Peru's from 120 to 15 percent. Although the average tariff for the region—15 percent, later reduced to 13.7 percent—was still higher than the 4 percent average in the United States (where some sectors were under heavy protection), tariff reduction was considerable. The policy stayed the course even when exchange rates, which ceased to be political instruments to artificially promote exports, were high and made imports cheaper. It was thought that reducing some of the burdens on private enterprise, such as taxes and labor-related costs, was a better way to promote exports than debasing the currency.

Against what economic nationalism used to maintain, in some countries the opening of trade helped develop local industry in ways import substitution had been unable to. By the end of the 1990s, almost 85 percent of Mexico's exports consisted of manufactures, twice the figure of the mid-1980s. Oil and other mineral exports, which represented 50 percent of Mexico's commercial offer to the world in the 1980s, accounted for only 11 percent of the country's exports by the end of the 1990s (although the budget was still heavily dependent on oil revenues). Countries with less access to the U.S. market were not as successful in developing local manufactures and selling them abroad; nonetheless, reform brought down the proportion of primary products to 40 percent of total Latin American exports.

Trade with the rest of the world was aggressively expanded. Exchange among Latin American countries, until then negligible, came to comprise nearly a quarter of the region's total commerce. Brazil, for instance, became the principal market for Argentina's products, and a substantial proportion of Brazilian sales abroad were directed toward the countries of MERCOSUR, the South American common market born in 1991 with Brazil, Argentina, Uruguay, and Paraguay as partners. (Chile and Bolivia become associates later, making the combined GDP of MERCOSUR countries over $1 trillion; negotiations for a trade agreement with five Andean countries started in mid-2003 even as one of them, Peru, also became an associate member.)

Free trade policies also extended the commercial exchange between Latin America and Europe, Asia, and, in particular, the United States. By 1997, nearly 20 percent of U.S. exports were destined for Latin America—the United States was exporting more goods to Brazil than to China, more to Argentina than to Russia, more to Chile than to India, and twice as much to Central America and the Caribbean as to eastern Europe. In turn, Latin American exports to the United States more than doubled in the 1990s, whereas Asia and Europe increased their exports to the U.S. market by no more than 10 percent. During the reform years, the exports of the region's seven biggest economies experienced an 80 percent growth and, lo and behold, Mexico, Argentina, Chile, Colombia, and the Central American countries were able to increase their share of foreign markets.

Of the more than twenty bilateral and regional commercial agreements signed during the reform years, the North American Free Trade Agreement (NAFTA) is the best known and had the greatest impact. It did not promote proper free trade, because people were excluded from the liberties conferred on goods and capital movements, and even these were subject to limits and exceptions in a text, not poetically enthralling, that included thousands of pages of preamble and twenty-two chapters, with in some cases an extremely long calendar for the adoption of the new measures. But it made things "freer" than before. Mexico's President Carlos Salinas clearly saw it as a way to lock in some of the changes made to the economy and to send positive signals to investors. Before NAFTA, U.S. tariffs on Mexican imports were 5 percent on average, but high nontariff barriers were aimed against fruits, vegetables, sugar, textiles, and apparel. Mexican tariffs, in turn, were above 10 percent, and a number of U.S. goods, including cars and auto parts, were subject to impossible nontariff barriers (usually the worst type of barriers). After NAFTA, trade flourished between the two countries. In fact, by the late 1990s, total trade among the United States, Canada, and Mexico amounted to $490 billion, half their commercial exchange with the world. By 2003, it was close to $600 billion.

The scheme, more contagious than cholera (which had resurfaced at the time!), served as a catalyst for a number of other trade agreements, for instance between Canada and Chile, between Canada and Costa Rica, and between Mexico and a number of Latin American nations, including Chile. Other agreements were later negotiated between Latin American countries, such as Mexico and Chile, and the European Union. There was even a trade deal between Chile and South Korea. Some countries adopted NAFTA-type rules in an effort to make themselves more attractive to the business community without striking formal trade deals. Canada and Chile went beyond NAFTA rules and established a 35 percent minimum local content in the auto sector, as opposed to 60 percent. The commercial accord with Chile allowed Canada better access than the United States, which still faced 11 percent tariffs, to that small market. The free trade agreement between the United States and Chile announced at the end of 2002—after "fast-track" authority was arduously obtained by the White House from a reluctant Congress—now makes up for that disadvantage. In 2003, the United States and Central America, an elephant and an ant, also pursued a (much-conditioned) free trade agreement. At the end of the year, the United States announced that negotiations toward FTAs with Colombia, Peru, Ecuador, and Bolivia would start in 2004.

Negotiations for the Free Trade Area of the Americas (FTAA)—involving 800 million people and $3.4 trillion in trade—began very slowly. They did not seriously get under way until 2002, by which time enthusiasm for free trade had subsided in much of the region. By 2003, Brazil was governed by a labor party with serious misgivings about further opening its economic borders in light of persistent U.S. protectionism (the pretext) and bent on counterbalancing U.S. hegemony (the hidden agenda) with some sort of South American free trade zone built around the strong partnership between Brazil and Argentina and including a possible monetary union between these two and perhaps other MERCOSUR countries. Nonetheless, negotiations took place between the United States and Latin America toward a hemispheric free trade zone, inspired by NAFTA and the many commercial agreements of the reform era. If we consider the fact that these discussions were held at the same time that the Doha Round of world trade talks occurred, what emerges is a truly labyrinthine web of government negotiations, all of them producing their own political bodies and separate arrangements for a purpose that ultimately should have little to do with governments: the free exchange of goods and services among people of various nations. But one thing about commercial reform is certain: Latin America had a new appetite for commerce.

Financial liberalization was another feat of Latin America's reformist decade. Bank reserve ratios were reduced and minimal capital requirements established (international guidelines, such as the Basle Accord, were taken into account), although a number of retail lending constraints remained; curbs on interest rates were removed. Some countries were so audacious in embracing deregulation that they surpassed Chile, the model nation for many of these changes but still sore from its financial crisis of the early 1980s and therefore inclined to maintain a few restrictive norms (a reserve requirement was maintained until 1998 for short-term capital inflows and subsequently the government has reserved the right to impose controls of up to a year that do not substantially impede financial transfers). Mexico, Argentina, and Peru opened their markets significantly and capital was quite free to move. Others followed suit.

Restrictions on foreign investment were removed from Mexico to Patagonia. Even Mexico under the PRI allowed foreigners to obtain 100 percent ownership in financial services, communications, building and construction, agriculture and livestock, magazine and newspapers, air travel, and other major sectors of the economy. In part thanks to NAFTA and the acceleration of reform after the peso crisis of 1994–95, U.S. direct investment in Mexico amounted to $3 billion per year, slightly less than half of total direct investment inflows into the country. Many U.S. companies facing competition from Asian imports reduced their production costs by opening production facilities across the border. More than half of Mexico's exports to the United States originated from multinational investors.

The response of foreign investors was overwhelmingly positive across the region. By the mid-1990s, annual capital inflows into Latin America totaled 5 percent of GDP, half in direct investment and half in indirect portfolio investment; in 1996, net direct foreign investment alone amounted to more than $35 billion, and by 1999 it amounted to almost $80 billion, more than 80 percent going to the largest three economies. In the period between 1993 and 1996, direct investment by U.S. companies in Latin America increased by 40 percent, to a cumulative $144 billion, 18 percent of total U.S. direct foreign investment abroad. More than half of U.S. involvement in Latin America's economy resided in the financial sector and 28 percent in industry, but in Brazil, where U.S. investment saw a 55 percent increase between 1993 and 1996, the percentage going to industry was considerably higher. Investors couldn't get enough of Latin America: during the 1990s, nearly $400 billion of capital rushed into a region from where money had been escaping frantically in the previous years, like its emigrants, aboard anything that floated. In the active second half of the decade, Brazil, Argentina, Mexico, and Chile were the principal recipients of direct foreign investment.

Labor regulations were reformed, reducing hiring costs, making it easier to fire workers, and limiting collective bargaining by trade (as opposed to by company) in an effort to break the stranglehold of Marxist unions on production. This area of reform, however, varied widely from country to country and in general did not go as far as other reforms. Brazil, Colombia, and Nicaragua emerged with the most flexible labor laws, and Mexico, Bolivia, and El Salvador with the most rigid. In between, Peru tilted toward the first group, Argentina toward the second.

Monetary, fiscal, tax, trade, financial, investment, and labor reform brought growth to countries whose economies had been stagnant. In general, those countries where reform was widest and deepest, both in the effort to strangle inflation and in the wider sense of liberalization, were also the ones that grew at the fastest pace in the last decade of the twentieth century. Because these countries had been most affected by the devastation of economic nationalism, it is difficult to judge exactly how much of that expansion in output was due to the scope and nature of the reforms themselves and how much to the initial impulse that any body forcefully contained receives when it is suddenly given space to move. But since growth was sustained through much of the decade in those countries, reform was clearly a crucial factor in the rate of increase in production.

Chile has been called the model country for many of the reforms. But drawing parallels between Chile and the rest of Latin America is misleading, not only because its reforms started much earlier than elsewhere but also because they have been more sustained, and the savings and investment levels (between 25 and 27 percent of the GDP), as well as the productivity gains that have resulted from that consistency, put it well ahead of the region. It has not broken loose of underdevelopment yet, but a number of factors permitting (such as pending reforms), it is not inconceivable that it may do so in the next generation.

Chile, Argentina, Peru, Bolivia, the Dominican Republic, and El Salvador all experienced major reform and boasted significant macroeconomic statistics in the 1990s, at least compared to their immediate prereform years. Annual economic growth measured in terms of GDP in the decade reached 6 percent in Chile, 5.2 in the Dominican Republic, 4.7 in Peru, 4.6 in Argentina, and 3.8 in Bolivia. The only other countries that match those growth rates for the same period without having engaged in equally far-reaching reforms are those Central American nations where the weight of economic nationalism was less suffocating than in the rest of the region. Brazil, Mexico, Uruguay, and Venezuela, where reform was not as profound because the preceding crisis was not as acute, had slower growth. Of the four, Mexico, where reform went furthest, shows the greatest rate of expansion, immediately followed by Uruguay. Colombia, where economic nationalism did not take root as deeply as in surrounding nations and where there had been growth during the 1980s when neighboring countries were stagnant, maintained a steady but moderate economic performance in the 1990s.

There was an increase in the rate of capital formation in all of these countries, including slow reformers, but only Chile and Costa Rica did significantly better in this respect than in the 1950–80 period (Bolivia and Colombia also increased their rates but less substantially). As for the rest, the ranking order relating to growth in production can be misleading because certain countries, like Colombia, have developed systems better geared toward capital accumulation and therefore obtain more significant results than countries like Argentina or Peru where the particular circumstances of the critical starting point of reform account for better output growth figures. However, it is still the case that, regarding capital formation in years of strong performance, for instance between 1995 and 1997, those countries where reform was boldest, such as Chile, Peru, and Bolivia, show more impressive variations than the others.

The Fever of Privatization

The magnitude of the transformations that took place in Latin America should not be underestimated. The reforms helped move the region from a nationalistic to a global economy, from an import-substituting to an exporting trade pattern, from governments that produced and consumed too much to ones that retreated from direct intervention in various areas of economic and social life. The reforms were significant because the starting point was the mammoth twentieth-century state. Many of the reforms reinstituted what existed before economic nationalism (allowing for all the changes that took place in the world in five decades). In that sense, reform was not without precedent, or, to be more exact, the destination port of that reform was not new territory for Latin America. What was new was the fact that reform of this scope had to be implemented at all, because Latin America had no prior experience in repealing fifty years of state control over the economy and society.

Without a doubt, privatization was the jewel of reform. It became the symbol of the era, above monetary, fiscal, tax, trade, financial, investment, and labor reform. It was unique in that Latin America, indeed the rest of the world, had not dealt before with the challenge of dismounting such an edifice of state property and production, even if the result meant going back to a time when the state did not own as many companies, produce as many goods, trade as many commodities, and consume as many resources. Since privatization, and reform in general, was a new form of transition, even if the passage from state to private enterprise was not necessarily an unknown scenario for Latin America, many things could happen along the way to compound some of the flaws remaining from the region's history of private enterprise. Whether this happened would depend on how the process of privatizing the economy was undertaken, what type of institutional framework presided over the transition, and what kind of political system was in place during and after the change. So, as with the other reforms, let us see what was done before we examine, in the next chapter, the success or failure of privatization.

Chile privatized state companies as early as the 1970s, followed by Mexico in the 1980s, but the phenomenon acquired hemispheric proportions in the 1990s, when almost all the others, starting with Argentina and Peru and ending with Brazil, joined the feast. Three distinct phases or waves of privatization can be identified. The first phase encompassed industrial and commercial enterprises, many of which had been swallowed by governments at some point during the era of economic nationalism, while others were entirely products of the state. The second phase involved the service sector, including basic utilities such as energy, water, and telecommunications as well as financial entities, and infrastructure projects in areas such as transport. Removing money-losing enterprises from government ownership paved the way for private and foreign capital to upgrade technology and equipment, expand services, and streamline operations. Many of these large projects, from railroads to gas pipelines to energy grids, are international rather than purely national, following their natural constitution.

The third phase, by no means as boldly implemented as the previous two, transferred some of those social security provisions that remain sacred cows of the state in developed countries: pensions were widely privatized, and private retirement funds became major sources of savings and domestic investment, whereas in health and education greater competition and choice were only partially introduced in very few countries—Chile, as usual, led the way.

The three phases are not necessarily sequential, but they are distinct in that they constitute separate "families" of state entities transferred to private owners, each one involving different types of procedures or bearing particular features. In much of Latin America it is more accurate to speak of two rather than three phases, since the third is far from complete and in most cases has involved only pensions. In most countries where the state has divested itself of social security, it has not envisaged such policy as part of a wider scheme of devolving basic social services to the citizens but almost as the second-phase type of privatization of a financial service.

Chile undertook a vast program of privatization in the mid-1970s, long before Margaret Thatcher launched her program of divestitures against socialism in the United Kingdom. A number of factors made this possible, from Allende's dismal economic legacy to the fact that Pinochet's brutal dictatorship left the economy in the hands of a group of "Chicago boys" who probably didn't realize the consequences their decisions would have on the region in the coming years. In 1973, Chile's government controlled some 620 companies, many but not all of which had been taken over by Allende. Privatization started in 1974 when the government returned entities that had been expropriated: industrial and commercial companies first, then financial institutions. It continued with the sale of enterprises that had been in state hands since the 1960s. The recession of the early 1980s put a hold on this policy, but privatization was resumed in 1984, with industrial, commodities, and primary products corporations sold to private interests. Soon the number of state businesses had been reduced to fewer than seventy. Toward the end of Pinochet's rule, some of the big service companies, including electric utilities and telecommunications, were also transferred. By the end of the 1980s, some three-quarters of the government's entrepreneurial participation in Chile's GDP had been eliminated.

Mexico also engaged in privatization before the craze of the

1990s. In the early 1980s, the state owned just over twelve hundred companies. Miguel de la Madrid, who came to power in 1982, initiated the sale of government property. By 1988, when President Carlos Salinas announced further reform, some 765 companies had been transferred. The figure, however, is misleading because all of the enterprises combined did not account for more than 3 percent of government-related output. But the symbolism was powerful—Mexico had joined Chile, both under authoritarian governments, in creating a model for the rest of the region to follow. One-fifth of all privatizations that took place in the world during the 1980s occurred in Mexico.

The pattern in Mexico was similar to that in Chile, with industrial (food, drink, tobacco) and commercial (retail) enterprises sold first, then the service companies, starting with financial institutions and continuing with hotels and the smaller telecommunications concerns, and some commodity-related businesses such as sugar mills. In Chile, and later across the continent, the weightier entities, including the mammoth telecommunications concern, were left for the final stages. By 1991, halfway into Salinas's mandate, almost one thousand companies had been transferred for $38 billion.

The rest of the region followed Chile's and Mexico's lead and took up privatization with fervor in the 1990s. It was time to undo much of what had been done in the previous decades: production and commerce were best left to private enterprise. Through a combination of direct sale, auction, stock market offer, and long-term concession, with investment banks advising on minimum prices, the Latin American governments obtained substantial funds from local and especially foreign investors in the process of divesting themselves of many of those "strategic" concerns.

Argentina and Peru were next to engage in privatization, although Brazil, a relatively slower reformer but a much larger country and the world's eighth-largest economy, sold many companies for large sums of money and therefore, in absolute terms, became a leader in the pack.

Carlos Menem managed to sell off some four hundred companies in Argentina in three years (the figure includes the units into which many of the state corporations were broken up, a recurring pattern across the region). Unlike other Latin American countries, Argentina did not focus on industry and commerce first and then on the service sector. Everything that could be sold off was put on the market as soon as possible. As early as 1990, two symbols of state enterprise, the national airline and the telecommunications monopoly, were disposed of. By 1993, YPF (Yacimientos Petrolíferos Fiscales), the state gas and oil concern, was auctioned off for $3 billion; it was eventually taken over by Spain's Repsol for $13 billion. Export industries and consumer goods companies with large domestic market shares were particularly attractive to investors, but everything that could be sold, including big energy utilities that attracted Chilean capital, and some water and sanitation companies, went under the hammer (water services are the responsibility of municipalities; between 1991 and 1998, only 30 percent of the services were privatized).

Peru started to privatize in 1991, but the process did not gather momentum until the middle of the decade. In the first three years, some thirty enterprises were sold for a total of $2.5 billion. In 1994, twenty-nine companies were transferred for the equivalent of one-third of the government's revenue; twenty-eight were transacted the following year and another twenty-eight in 1996, this time for the equivalent of one-quarter of fiscal revenue. Divestitures slowed after 1997 because of the recession, but by the year 2000, almost two hundred entities had been privatized for just over $9 billion in Peru. Investors made future commitments for another $9 billion, although that figure also included projects not having to do with the actual transfer of state assets, like the exploitation of the Camisea natural gas reserve in the Andes, won by the Pluspetrol-Hunt-SK consortium made up of Argentinean, American, and Korean capital, and the exploitation of tens of thousands of square miles of the Biabo Cordillera Azul forest zone.

The most significant sales or concessions of the decade involved telecommunications (Empresa Nacional de Telecomunicaciones and Compañía Peruana de Teléfonos), power generation and distribution (Electroperú and Electrolima), railroads (Empresa Nacional de Ferrocarriles), ports (Empresa Nacional de Puertos), oil (Petroperú and Petromar), steel (SiderPerú), fishing (Pesca Perú), mining (Centromín and Tintaya), and banking (Banco Continental). Large state entities were broken up into different units and the assets sold separately, with a number of them remaining under government control. Only a few of the ports were given in concession.

Brazil got off to a slow start compared to its neighbors but made up for it in the second part of the decade, particularly between 1996 and 1998, with gigantic telecommunications, energy utilities, railroads, and financial companies being transferred for dozens of billions of dollars. By 2001, the Brazilian government had divested itself of 119 companies for a total of $67.9 billion in revenue and $18.1 billion of transfers in debt.

When Fernando Cardoso won the presidency in 1994, only 31 companies had been sold, although the list included the steel producer Companhia Siderúrgica Nacional, an emblem of Brazilian statism. Cardoso blew new life into privatization: by 1996 he had auctioned off another 20 entities, bringing the number of sales up until that point to more than 50, for almost $25 billion. In the next few years, another $40 billion was obtained through the sale of major concerns, starting with the mining company Vale do Rio Doce, the largest entity to be privatized in Latin America after it was acquired by a Brazilian corporation for $3.6 billion. But that sum seemed insignificant in 1998 when Telecommunicaçoes Brasileiras S.A. (Telebrás) was transferred for close to $19 billion to various local and foreign consortia.

Telebrás was an undercapitalized, bureaucratic $14-billion-a-year state enterprise whose twenty-eight operating subsidiaries employed ninety thousand people and provided terrible service: there were 15 million people on waiting lists for fixed lines and 5 million for cellular phones at the time. The government had a controlling stake with no more than 20 percent of the shares. Between 1995 and 1998, Telebrás was groomed for privatization, a process that involved splitting it into twelve units—three regular, fixed-line telecoms; eight cellular companies; and one long-distance carrier. The twelve units were sold in 1998 to Spanish, Portuguese, Canadian, American, Italian, and Brazilian corporations, with the biggest prizes, São Paulo's fixed and cellular-phone entities, going to Spain's Telefónica and Portugal's Telecom. The long-distance carrier, Embratel, was sold to the U.S. conglomerate MCI for $2.3 billion.

Many other significant privatizations took place in the second half of the decade despite the general loss of confidence in so-called emerging markets in the wake of Southeast Asia's collapse, which had serious consequences for Brazil. Major energy utilities, petrochemical plants, transport concerns, mining companies, and telecommunications entities were privatized. By 2001, the electricity sector accounted for 31 percent of the total value of auctions, the telecommunications sector for another 31 percent, followed by steel and mining with 8 percent each, and oil and gas with 7 percent.

Concessions were given in different public service areas for some $10 billion. Petróleo Brasileiro S.A. (Petrobrás) was not sold, but the government monopoly of the oil industry—worth more than $30 billion in the stock market—was broken. After four decades in which the state enterprise had been unable to satisfy domestic demand (one-third of Brazil's oil was still being imported), it was time to let private capital participate, mostly through joint ventures and concessions, in the business of producing and importing both oil and natural gas. In another decision charged with symbolism under the presidency of a former "dependency theory" intellectual, Brazil formally renounced dreams of self-sufficiency in energy, with its power grid being linked to Argentina's through a concession given to Exxon and a $2 billion gas pipeline joining Bolivia to São Paulo built with financial help from the World Bank.

Many countries privatized a large portion of their state companies. The Bolivian government earmarked some 175 enterprises for privatization and started the transfer in 1992. Under President Gonzalo Sánchez de Lozada, the process reached full speed in the mid-1990s, by which time companies representing 90 percent of the total value of available government assets were being auctioned off. Between 1995 and 1996, some $1.7 billion, the equivalent of around 25 percent of GDP, was generated by divestitures. The highlight was the transfer of the six monopolies accounting for 12.5 percent of the nation's GDP: Yacimientos Petrolíferos Fiscales de Bolivia (oil and gas), Empresa Nacional de Telecomunicaciones (telecommunications), Empresa Nacional de Electricidad (electricity), Empresa Metalúrgica Vinto (metallurgy), Lloyd Aéreo Boliviano (airline), and Empresa Nacional de Ferrocarriles (railroads). Because of the political sensitivity surrounding these state monopolies, the government devised a system of "capitalization" for them whereby private corporations were invited to establish joint ventures with different units into which they were broken up. State ownership and control was in effect diluted.

Colombia had been affected less by the entrepreneurial state than some of its neighbors. Privatization there did not reach the same dimensions as in other countries. It started with small manufacturing entities, continued with part of the telecommunications sector in 1992 through various backdoor mechanisms due to fierce public opposition, and reached its peak in 1996 and 1997 with the sale of utilities, especially in the electricity sector, as well as mines, banks, and insurance institutions, attracting capital from the United States, Spain, South Africa, Chile, and Venezuela. Significant concessions were granted in the air, sea, and river transport sectors from then on, as well as in the commodities business. The electricity sector represented more than half of all transfers.

Venezuela was particularly unstable in the 1990s, with military coups, ideological swings, and riots. Nonetheless, privatization was undertaken in the industrial and service sectors. By far the most important divestiture was that of Compañía Anómina Nacional Teléfonos de Venezuela (CANTV), which was partially sold in 1991, the rest of the government's shares being offered through the domestic and the New York stock exchanges in the late 1990s.

The trend was not lost on Central America and the Caribbean, either. El Salvador and the Dominican Republic put special emphasis on, and obtained their greatest revenue from, the transfer of electric utilities, while in Guatemala and Panama, telecommunications entities made the most impact. Even Cuba courted foreign capital, although full privatization did not take place. Foreign companies from some forty countries were instead invited to establish joint ventures with government enterprises: Spain concentrated on tourism; Canada on mining; Mexico on telecommunications, textiles, and concrete; and France, Sweden, and Britain on energy.

And, of course, Chile, the pioneer of privatization, and Mexico continued to transfer state assets during the 1990s. Chile's democratic government privatized little in the early 1990s, but in 1994, under Eduardo Frei, a new wave of transfers was set off. Private capital was invited to buy shares and manage a number of sewage and sanitation entities, while other types of companies, from mines to airlines to electric utilities, were sold and (timid) efforts were undertaken to open oil and mining to a limited degree of private participation. In Mexico, financial institutions made the bulk of new privatizations, while electric utilities remained largely untouched. Railroads were transferred, water and sanitation concessions were given, and many ports and cargo terminals were placed in private hands.

There was little privatization elsewhere. Ecuador's government attempted to privatize its telecommunications and public utilities, but negligible progress was made due to fierce political opposition and constant institutional chaos. Some concessions were given to foreign companies. Uruguay, where a referendum defeated the government's privatization proposal, managed to transfer some financial institutions but mostly shied away from the trend, as did Costa Rica; these two countries were credited with the greatest political stability and juridical reliability in the region. Paraguay, absorbed in violent political upheaval, did not even attempt to make divestiture. Haiti, torn by barbaric violence, insulated itself from the outside world.

The fever of privatization helped Latin America attract a massive influx of diversified foreign investment. By the end of the decade, multinational corporations had a 38.7 percent stake in the sales of the region's top five hundred companies. U.S. corporations were the most numerous, but many corporations from Germany (10.6 percent), Spain (10 percent), France (9.2 percent), and Italy (5 percent) were also involved. The combined European investments were greater than investments by U.S. corporations, whereas in the early 1990s American firms had had an eight-to-one lead over Europe. The Spanish "conquest" was particularly impressive. Telefónica and Iberia opened the way; the energy and power giants Repsol, Endesa, and Iberdrola dominated the middle of the decade; and starting in 1996, Banco Santander, Banco Bilbao Vizcaya, Banco Central Hispano, and other Spanish banks came to hold almost one-third of the assets of all foreign-owned financial institutions in the region, a larger share than the one enjoyed by U.S. interests.

The emergence of Latin American conglomerates investing across the region, brought about in no small measure by privatization, helped further diversify the source of foreign capital. Mexican, Brazilian, Argentinean, Chilean, and Venezuelan firms related to activities as diverse as electricity, the food industry, telecommunications, oil and gas, construction, information technology, real estate, banking, agribusiness, and mining fanned across Latin America to compete with U.S., Canadian, European, and Asian corporations.

The benefits of privatization were apparent from the beginning. Capital inflows raised investment levels; companies accustomed to losing money quickly became more productive and therefore profitable. With the exception of Colombia, Chile, and, to a lesser extent, Brazil, state corporations had been major sources of fiscal deficits before the 1990s. Profitability in the privatized firms grew by 51 percent in Argentina, 61 percent in Peru, 41 percent in Mexico, 8 percent in Chile and Brazil, 10 percent in Colombia, and 5 percent in Bolivia. Production in those companies rose between 25 and 50 percent (depending on the particular country involved), and productivity, measured in terms of sales per worker, shot up by 25 to 112 percent, with Chile, Mexico, and Peru registering improvements of more than 80 percent. Fewer than half, and sometimes not even a quarter, of the increases were a result of layoffs and downsizing, according to Mexican and Argentinean studies. The improvement in the quality of service was particularly acute in telecommunications, as waiting periods for new lines were reduced by at least 50 percent and household penetration grew or increased between 5 and 14 percent a year, even in rural areas. Service improved in other areas too. Before the privatization of water got under way in 1995, child mortality rates were falling at much the same pace in all municipalities in Argentina. Research has found that after 1995, the fall of baseline mortality accelerated by 4.5 to 10 percent in the municipalities where water was privatized.

By the year 2000, privatization was running out of steam, with a drop in government asset transfers of nearly 60 percent. There still remained a number of "untouchables," especially in Venezuela, Mexico, Brazil, and Ecuador, where selling powerful state-run oil and gas corporations and transferring rights to those sources of "national wealth" was out of the question, even if private capital was partially allowed to participate in business and establish joint ventures with the government. Electricity remains a sacred cow in Mexico, and the Peruvian government, still the owner of nearly forty entities, also maintains an important stake in power generation and transmission as well as ownership of the water company servicing the capital city (the water and sanitation utilities in the provinces are still in the hands of local government). Chile, surprisingly, has kept 40 percent of mining under government ownership, mainly through Corporación Nacional del Cobre (Codelco), its prized copper giant, which continues to provide a constitutionally mandated rent to the military establishment. And forest concessions, a highly controversial matter, are limited in the various countries where they exist.

Allowing for these considerable exceptions, and others, it is an indisputable fact that in the last decade no other part of the world, not even Central Europe, came down with the fever of privatization to the same degree as Latin America.

Rejuvenating Old Age

Having looked at monetary, fiscal, tax, trade, financial, investment, and labor reform, as well as the transfer of state assets, we come to pension reform, a type of privatization that would have been unthinkable in previous decades.

Chile pioneered pension reform in 1980 by radically changing its system. The law allowed workers to opt out of the government program and put money that would otherwise have gone toward the payroll tax into private retirement accounts. Those who opted out (which the majority eventually did) were required to place 10 percent of their salaries in personal accounts managed by the fund of their choice. Those people who already received state pensions would continue to do so, and those who had already made contributions to the pay-as-you-go system but opted out for a personal account received an interest-bearing "recognition bond." Certain regulations required the elderly to use pension funds that invested more heavily in fixed-income securities, while the younger generation could use pension funds that placed more money in stock.

The reform, which was extended to the government disability program, empowered workers by making them property owners; boosted savings and investment thanks to an accumulation of assets now totaling more than $40 billion, or 50 percent of the country's GDP; modernized capital and labor markets; and helped to give the country an average 7 percent annual rate of growth during most of the 1990s. The bankrupt system that forced each new generation, in a world of diminishing fertility rates and increasing life expectancy, to sustain its elders, and transferred wealth from the less well-off to the more well-off since the latter tend to start work later and live longer, was turned around so that retirement became a form of enterprise and of accumulating capital to benefit future generations.

The Chilean model gained global recognition and was imitated in many Latin American and Central European countries. The substantial hostility surrounding efforts to dismantle the welfare state, in the case of western Europe, and the Social Security system, in the case of the United States, has prevented its adoption in the developed world.

Seven Latin American nations privatized pensions. Brazil, which boasts a bankrupt pay-as-you-go pension program, avoided reform. With the exception of El Salvador, which adopted the Chilean model in 1998, all the countries introduced some variation. Bolivia eliminated the old state pension system altogether in 1997, but other nations lagged a few steps behind. Peru took up the scheme in 1993, allowing new entrants to opt for the pay-as-you-go program. Argentina underwent reform in 1994, maintaining a basic state pension for all. In the same year, Colombia left the door open for workers who opted for the private retirement account to return to the old system. Uruguay, the cradle of Latin America's welfare state, engaged in modest reform in 1996, keeping the old state system but allowing workers to divert part of their salary into private accounts. In 1997, Mexico established a two-tier system whereby workers in the private sector could opt for private pensions, receiving government contributions if they had already contributed to the old scheme, while state employees remained in the government program.

Staggering numbers of people were attracted by private pensions: 16 million in Mexico, 8 million in Argentina, 4 million in Colombia, 2.5 million in Peru, 1 million in El Salvador, half a million in Uruguay, half a million in Bolivia.

Private pension funds have accumulated a significant pool of capital: $20 billion in Argentina, $13 billion in Mexico, $3 billion in Colombia, $2.5 billion in Peru, $651 million in Uruguay, $575 million in Bolivia, $213 million in El Salvador. No capitalist exploiter has ever sucked as much blood out of his workers as these workers have sucked out of themselves.

The rest of Latin America was less willing to follow in Chile's footsteps in privatizing health insurance, which allowed workers to opt out of the government scheme as long as they devoted a minimum 7 percent of their salary to private insurers. The fever of privatization had some limits after all.

8

The Capitalist Mirage

In forsaking economic nationalism, it is beyond dispute that Latin America has undergone an epoch-making set of changes. But in judging them, the essential question to ask is this: Did monetary, fiscal, tax, trade, finance, investment, and labor reform, together with the privatization of state enterprises and pensions, attack the tradition that has haunted Latin America through ancient, colonial, and republican times, that subsoil running below every early attempt to build something worthy on these lands? Did those reforms alter the relationship between the institutions of power and the individual, or did they constitute a reshuffling of elites, ideologies, and economic models within that incarcerating matrix that has molded every previous experiment in Latin American liberation? We have seen that it is possible to have democracy without political freedom and a privately run economy without economic freedom, or, as Pascal Salin has written, that "a market economy can exist even in collectivist societies," while true liberty demands "property rights and the freedom of contract." Was this, then, a capitalist revolution or a capitalist mirage?

Defenders of privatization, and of the free-market economy in general, have overlooked the difference between the creation of an open society and the transition to an open society. In advocating reform, they unconsciously assumed that liberal capitalism would be created from nothing. On discovering that the space is neither empty nor virgin and that within it the existing elements undermine, exhaust, or devour the new, Latin America is confronted with a lesson that is nearly as important as the free society itself. The route by which it is reached, the transition—the process wherein government should yield to individuals by forsaking corporatism, state mercantilism, privilege, wealth transfer, and political law—can easily give way to a subtle, almost as injurious type of interference from the authorities. Despite the state's apparent withdrawal, political power allied with special interests can still impose numerous constraints on society. The fact that the transition to private enterprise creates new opportunities for predation is a perverse irony of statism—the injustices arising from the transition would not be an issue in the absence of statism in the first place.

Roger Douglas, one of the heroes of New Zealand's transition, has made two points that Latin American reformists largely missed. First, the essence of structural reform is the abolishment of privilege, something that is very difficult to achieve because "quite often the costs can be seen because they're concentrated, while the benefits are often widely dispersed." Therefore, the pressure from interest groups, whether local or foreign, seeking to avoid the abolition of their privileges, or to obtain new ones, tends to exceed the pressure from society as a whole, the overall beneficiary of reform. If we consider the fact that the majority of people living in underdeveloped countries are primarily concerned with survival and subsistence, the advantage enjoyed by interest groups is greater there than in prosperous environments. George Reisman has made a similar point by noting that because a subsidy is much greater per beneficiary than the cost of that subsidy for each taxpayer, lobbyists push hard, whereas taxpayers do not. The point is only partially relevant in Latin America, where few people pay direct taxes, but there are many other ways that wealth-transfer mechanisms enjoy the advantage of cost dispersion among their many victims.

Douglas's second observation on transition pertains to the simultaneity of the various reforms, for him an essential condition for success: "Do not try to advance a step at a time . . . move in quantum leaps." The economy consists of a network of connections; there is no point in eliminating export subsidies if transport tariffs and regulations are maintained, and shipping port and services are not privatized. What good are fiscal gains if, instead of reducing taxes or the debt, the government dedicates these gains to exorbitant expenditures that create a sustained fiscal commitment? What good is it to reduce the number of government employees if anticapitalist labor legislation prevents the market from reabsorbing those very workers? What long-term benefit can be obtained from opening the doors to foreign investors while preventing the rule of law from taking root and therefore limiting the capacity of millions of individuals, especially the poor, to form and accumulate capital over a long, sustained period of time, including those occasions when foreign investors leave? What use is guaranteeing property rights to a bunch of colossal private corporations if small and medium-size businesses, which in all capitalist countries are the main creators of jobs, do not enjoy similar guarantees on the part of the legal system?

If reform does not consist of a systematic, all-encompassing assault on the myriad mechanisms through which power allocates opportunity and vests particular individuals and groups with rights the rest of society is barred from, the transition can end up replacing one form of corporatism, state mercantilism, privilege, wealth transfer, and political law with another. In that case, what occurs is a transition from state to private ownership, but not from underdevelopment to liberal capitalism.

Economic collapse and the crisis of state legitimacy, as we have seen, paved the way for change in Latin America. Fiscal calamity, historically a cause of political and economic transformations in many parts of the world, was a crucial factor. In this case, it limited the governments' vision of the real stuff of underdevelopment, which is not simply a matter of who owned the assets, just as it is not simply a matter of finding the right tax policy or deciding how low tariffs should come down. Those might be essential adjustments in countries where the foundations of liberal capitalism, of a free society, are already in place but where interventionism has crept in over the years. Latin America lacked the institutional foundations of development, a more profound matter than specific public policies. But governments were desperate to attack their insolvency problems, so the transition to a free economy was much less important than obtaining resources and ridding themselves of certain costs. This paramount concern also meant that governments would have a stake in the new structure of economic power because the old elites who were unable to sustain economic nationalism had to be replaced by new elites (called "capitalist" or "neoliberal") able to restore the fiscal strength of the state through their taxes and their credit.

From Monopoly to Monopoly

The failure of privatization deftly illustrates the fundamental flaw of Latin American reforms. Governments were obsessed with obtaining cash from sales or reducing obligations through debt and equity swaps. They therefore acted as if government assets really belonged to the government and not to the workers who had mixed their labor with them—if we are to apply the homesteading principle—or, more widely, to everyone who had been forced to sustain their existence. Had governments been aware of this fundamental philosophical question, they would have transferred assets to the workers and, when that was not applicable, to all citizens, letting them, as shareholders, decide whom to sell them to in a market transaction free of government intervention. Many investors would still have bet their money on those resources, with the obvious rewards for the workers-turned-capitalists as well as society at large, and without the profoundly negative baggage that resulted from the type of privatization that actually took place. Some workers might have decided not to sell the assets and, instead, tried to manage their companies themselves in a competitive environment. Undoubtedly, some companies would have been liquidated, but the alternative, transferring the cost of their artificial existence to society, was far worse. Recently 8 million people became shareholders in Spain through privatization. Nothing of the sort happened in Latin America.

Argentina justified the concession of its mail service (it was reversed years later) because it was the only way to balance the budget; in the late 1990s, Colombia insisted that selling seven utilities and public service companies was the only way to balance the books; Venezuela stated that privatization was necessary to pay off the government debt and passed laws to accomplish that; Mexico and Peru made it clear that privatization was the only avenue left to acquire the money needed to sustain social aid.

To begin with, these objectives were not even met. Deficits grew, as in Argentina, where President Menem left office with a $10 billion deficit; the overall debt in Latin America shot to a historic $600 billion (Brazil's public debt in 2002 was four times its export earnings), and Peru's $2 billion fund to alleviate poverty as well as Mexico's some 250,000 committees into which poor people were organized under the Programa Nacional de Solidaridad mainly served to establish efficient machines of political patronage and strengthen local and village government bureaucracies that managed their own public works budgets. The result was a fascinating paradox: after divesting itself of many money-losing companies, the Latin American state continued to absorb a similar share of the people's wealth.

The fundamental point, however, is not that the goals of privatization were not met. There was a crucial problem with the goals themselves, which goes a long way toward explaining why privatization did not signify a transition to a free society. If the governments' primary concern about state enterprises was the fiscal burden they constituted, and if selling assets was mainly an opportunity to obtain new resources, then privatization was a statist policy. Through privatization, the government, acting as an interest group (one that made the rules and decisions), sought its own benefits. The fact that some of those benefits (which by nature were temporary since one cannot privatize state assets twice) were then redistributed to the poor only made matters worse. A new form of dependency was created, and once the flow of money from privatization stopped, those who had become "entitled" to it took to the streets. Taxes eventually had to be raised; in 2003 Peru's general sales tax was raised to 19 percent and the government created a new tax on bank transactions.

Historically, all governments that set out to obtain resources allied themselves with private interests able to produce the resources from which their cut could be drawn—the stuff of mercantilism. No government whose primary concern is its own subsistence works under the principle that a free society will eventually produce the necessary means for the preservation of the political structure presiding over it. What tends to happen instead, and certainly was the case in Latin America, is that government allies itself with private interests able to provide necessary income. Because alliance between government and private interests in the reform years hinged on the transfer of assets to private parties, that is, on privatization, the process has been mistakenly understood as "capitalist reform."

Privatization installed a new class of elites, made up of local and foreign interests, in the place of the old ruling class under economic nationalism. In every country, through the granting of monopolies, the passing of discriminatory regulations, or the use of subsidies, the government facilitated the creation of new groups that came to dominate the economy. In some cases, the statist groups reengineered themselves; in others, new groups displaced the elites of economic nationalism; but in all cases some form of "crony capitalism" existed.

The intensity of crony capitalism varies from country to country, but the most powerful interests in every nation's economy were, in one way or another, government beneficiaries. There took place what many decades ago Andreski had called "a parasitic involution of capitalism," defined as a "tendency to seek profits and alter market conditions by political means in the widest sense of the word." Had this not been a major factor in the loss of legitimacy of the old republic?

The transition from economic nationalism to "capitalism" affected ownership but not the treatment of property rights in Latin America. Ownership changed hands while property rights remained in the hands of government. Indeed, the very role of government as the entity selling state enterprises to private bidders strengthened the idea that property rights are government concessions, prizes that political power concedes in return for something else, much like in the old days when the authorities granted land in newly conquered territories to people chosen because of special services they had delivered to the Crown or for their ability to pay taxes. Privatization exalted the notion that property is a political concession, not a higher or universal law that empowers individuals, beyond the government's power, so it can be the object of contract and exchange.

The confusion was exacerbated by the fact that free-market advocates the world over saluted Latin American privatization as the harbinger of a free society. Murray Rothbard was thinking about them ahead of time when, a quarter of a century ago, he criticized free-market "utilitarians," who are supposed to be skeptical of the virtues of government intervention because they "are so content to leave the fundamental underpinning of the market process, the definition of property rights and the allocation of property titles, wholly in the hands of government." Privatization was a welcome abjuration of government involvement in production and commerce (with many exceptions), but it was not an abjuration of the idea of government as the source of property rights to serve its own purposes. An exercise in vesting particular groups with property rights and titles, privatization molded economic power according to the government's criteria, that is to say, according to its needs and ambitions. Rather than the decentralization of power throughout society and the reduction of political authority, what took place was a rotation of power around the axis of government. Admittedly, when state enterprises are sold to the highest bidder, what we have is a form of arbitrary allocation of property rights. But if that is done in the absence of other reforms aimed precisely at placing property rights over and above the will of government, then liberal capitalism will not occur. It is worse when the actual transfer of state property is carried through so as to reinforce the interventionist and authoritarian role of the government in the allocation of property rights. This is where the transfer of monopolies comes into play.

Privatization exposed monopolies as government creations, belying the proposition long held in Latin America that they are "capitalist" evils. In order to raise the price of assets and make it attractive for powerful corporations to participate in the process, most of the telecommunications and electric utility divestitures took the form of monopoly transfers. Exclusive rights were also given in other auctions. Various telecommunications monopolies were granted to the CARSO group in Mexico, to Telefónica in Peru, and to Telefónica and an alliance of France Télécom and Stet in Argentina, where the market was segmented into different geographical areas. In Venezuela, the government and the state telecom company, CANTV, renegotiated the contract prior to privatization to ensure a monopoly in a number of services. Electricity monopolies were ceded in Peru, Venezuela, Bolivia, the Dominican Republic, and even Chile (where transmission and distribution were the object of exclusive rights and where generation became a duopoly activity with much vertical integration, with the result that one company, Enersis, came to control assets in generation, transmission, and distribution); regional gas monopolies were established in Argentina; banks were turned into an oligopoly in Mexico, with barriers to entry including specific limits to foreign participation and with the government guaranteeing deposits and acting as a lender of last resort; the railroad system was sold as a monopoly in Bolivia; each route in Buenos Aires's private transport system was exploited by one company (not to mention existing regional truck-transport monopolies that continued to exist in many countries, supported by powerful unions); the Peruvian national airline, Aeroperú, was sold to Aeroméxico with exclusive international routes.

In many cases, monopolies were established with five- and ten-year time limits but, either through direct extensions or subtle new regulations, exclusive rights were in place for much longer. The control of networks enjoyed by the privatized utilities companies was a substantial advantage over potential new entrants (although technology has found ways of circumventing such networks, erroneously called "natural monopolies," both in telecommunications and electricity, but the precondition for such technology to translate into competition is freedom of entry). Not surprisingly, huge profits were reaped (Mexico's Telmex recovered its initial investment in two years), prices skyrocketed (Peru's telephone rates quadrupled in the first few years; Argentina's experienced a marked yearly rise), and the quality of service, although far superior to what existed before privatization, became a matter of vociferous debate across the region. As could be expected, corruption scandals related to these "crony" privatizations shook the hemisphere from Mexico to Argentina (sales of state assets were least corrupt in Chile and Brazil). More important, new pockets of economic power, through alliances of domestic and foreign interests, were formed, and governments passed laws that served the interests of those in power.

Apart from outright monopoly transfers, the authorities engineered the formation of new power groups through privatization, from government credit to tax breaks to official guarantees. Chile's Enersis electricity utility, the origin of which was the privatized Chilectra firm, was supported by government policy: the state bank lent money to the managers of Chilectra, who had been appointed by the authorities, so that they could acquire a 20 percent stake of the state enterprise. A few years later, the entity, Chile's main distribution firm, was a privately owned holding company worth $5 billion (eventually it was acquired by the Spanish power giant Endesa). The official who had originally appointed the managers of the state enterprise and facilitated their taking over the company from within in its transition to private ownership was hired by Enersis years later. Other Chilean interest groups that emerged from privatization of state concerns received tax benefits or indirect subsidies, and, more important, they owed a good part of their capacity to acquire state property to their government-anointed access to credit. The new business elite was to an extent the child of government, although Chile has moved further toward the creation of a competitive market economy than have its neighbors.

Brazil gave tax breaks to privatized corporations, particularly to telecommunications companies. Peru exempted many of the transferred assets, especially the big energy utilities, from income tax over a period of ten years. Mexico gave the oligopoly-controlled privatized banks deposit guarantees that ended up costing taxpayers $68 billion when irresponsible managers brought about a banking collapse. Under privatization, expanded credit was a key instrument of government favors to private interests all over Latin America, raising liabilities in the banking system and causing many a crisis, not unlike the effects provoked by unhealthy credit in Asia in the second half of the 1990s; Mexico's FOBAPROA case was the most notorious. Indemnities worth billions of dollars were also granted to the beneficiaries of road concessions.

Perfectly conscious of his role as midwife to the new Mexican elite (and in encouraging the expansion of old ones), President Salinas famously met with the nation's most prominent businessmen during the 1994 campaign to request hundreds of millions needed to reelect the PRI. In Argentina, ten interest groups control most of the economy. Many of them, such as Techint, Pérez Companc, Macri, and Citicorp Equity Investment, aligned themselves with foreign interests, which guaranteed them access to fresh capital through the stock and bond markets, and offered them in return cozy access to the privatized entities, including concessions or public works contracts. In general, the most attractive sectors of the privatized economy, such as banking, energy, and telecommunications, have been dominated by foreign interests allied with smaller local interests, helped along by government favors in the form of monopoly concessions (or vertical integration in the energy and electricity business), tax exemptions, discriminatory regulation, and expanded credit.

Privatization resulted not only in a reshuffling of elite groups but also greater efficiency and better quality of service. In addition, it rid the government of a fiscal burden. The uncompetitive nature of the process increased opportunities for regulation and juridical instability too. Because many of the privatized utilities affect the daily lives of the masses, once state enterprises were transferred, individuals became more aware of government interference. Paradoxically, while governments bestowed privileges on private owners, they also saw the political need to establish regulations in order to ensure that prices and rates of products and services did not skyrocket. Even the Chilean government periodically regulates electricity rates and introduces new constraints, and the Peruvian government, like much of the region, uses special regulatory bodies to interfere in the telephone, electricity, transport, and copyright markets. Those regulatory bodies were, in effect, new forms of state companies—an ironic outcome for a process whose supposed aim was to eliminate government entities. The system used to this day is price-cap regulation, as in the United Kingdom, rather than rate-of-return regulation, as in the United States, but there are major differences with Britain: Latin American regulatory bodies are government instruments, and utility norms are very specific and written into all manner of legal documents. The government has, in effect, found a new way to prevent consumers from dictating what to sell, how much, and at what price.

The origin of the problem is, of course, that governments have created private monopolies in those areas. It is a common flaw: even in the United Kingdom, privatization involved duopolies (in telecommunications and electricity generation) and monopolies (in electricity distribution, gas, and water), which created the need for regulatory bodies in order to do the job that competition would have done itself. The result was much legal wrangling and consumer dissatisfaction. Had there been no government-induced monopolies (more competition was eventually introduced), regulations would have been unnecessary because the competitive process would have served the consumers more effectively; private contracts do a better job than regulators, who by definition are not in a position to calculate the costs of the companies involved and the prices they should charge for their services. But the lessons of the British experience were entirely lost on Latin America. By trying to limit the devastating effects of their own policies on consumers by barring entry to new participants openly or hypocritically, Latin American governments set price caps and ceilings for services. Naturally, they have not managed to bring prices and rates as low as they would have had there been greater competition, so the political gain from their intervention has been minimal.

Private monopolies enjoyed enough power to influence the nature of the regulations, and the interdependence between them and the various governments was such that both had an interest in reaching compromises. As Arthur Seldon has observed, "regulation invariably ends by favoring the regulated industries" and "the regulated capture the regulators." (That is a reason why in countries like the United States, abundant regulation, costing business up to $1 trillion a year, has come to interfere with people's lives in recent years, and there is a growing realization that the economy could become dangerously uncompetitive in the future. American politicians are finding that once regulations are in place, undoing them is a Herculean task.) But given the types of markets created by the very nature of monopoly transfers, the political cost of unhappy consumers made interventionist regulation unavoidable. These regulations succeeded in discouraging companies from making greater capital investments and offering better services or expanding their activities (except through new government-granted privileges). Many other previously established or newly created regulations, in everything from housing to the labor market, hurt producers during the reform years, affecting the amount and/or the quality of supply and therefore ultimately wounding consumers too. Resources were squandered by consumer-defense entities trying to deliver services that only competition could provide.

After a while, utilities got involved in bitter legal disputes with the authorities, using their lobbying power to press their case. One example of the chain of negative effects brought about by monopolies and subsequent regulatory intervention is the Dominican Republic, where the Spanish Unión Fenosa firm, which partially owned the privatized electricity concern, went from making lots of money to eventually demanding that the government subsidize the distributors Edenorte and Edesur because they were no longer profitable. The government shocked the nation by declaring that corruption had taken place in the transfer of the privatized stake to Unión Fenosa approved by the previous government, and it eventually took control of the entities. What started as a monopoly transfer and was compounded by regulatory interference thus became a source of political and juridical instability. Similar conflicts have arisen in Peru, where the electric utilities and the leading telephone company have been the object of denunciations, both for high rates and ethical issues, by politicians and commentators who do not identify the origin of the problem in the type of transfers undertaken by authorities who acted to strengthen the regulatory bodies. These regulatory bodies, themselves the consequence of monopoly privatization, unable to control prices effectively, are also the object of vituperation. Responding to pressure, they tend to penalize private companies rather than benefit consumers through the opening of competition.

Latin American regulators have not helped ordinary citizens because the evils of privilege are greater than the benefits of price caps and because through the mechanism of disincentives those regulations are forcing the owners of private companies to transfer costs to their clients, which in turn is creating political and juridical tensions between private enterprise and government. These tensions do not disrupt the new elite pattern—the result always leaves the leading corporations in an enviable position. The process, however, perpetuates an old tradition of institutional fragility, reinforces political power as the source of rights, and places the focus of wealth creation on the relationship between government and special interests. This does not imply, of course, that when oversight of a particular activity is transferred from administrative agencies to the courts, as happened in Chile with water rights in 1981, things immediately improve on all counts (Chile, on the other hand, now has near-universal water and sanitation coverage). The political norms that provide the legal framework, the influence of particular interests on the judiciary, and the lack of a tradition of free trade can all continue to conspire against a healthy market. But the regulatory agencies only create new problems. Working courts, not more bureaucracy, are the solution to these old problems.

Because government and private enterprise share common interests, these disputes eventually produce compromises, as in Peru, when an attempt was made to repeal the ten-year tax exemption the government had granted to the privatized electric utilities and, after much confrontation, the authorities finally allowed the arbitration mechanism to favor private companies in order to avoid greater ills (or when, in 2003, political pressure forced Telefónica to reduce its basic tariff by 31 percent, something that could have been done much more smoothly through competition). But the consequence, in the end, is the return of statism under popular pressure. In Argentina, the mess created by interventionist privatization ended up with President Kirchner announcing in 2004 the creation of a new public sector to ensure the adequate supply of natural gas!

At the turn of the new millennium, Mexico grappled with loss of investment and jobs as some three hundred manufacturing plants moved to China between 2001 and 2003, further illustrating the problems introduced by monopolies. Under the state monopoly, the cost of energy is 20 percent higher than in competing countries; under Telmex's protected position, increased communication costs and the restricted transport market mean that proximity to the United States is no longer a decisive advantage over Asia.

Not surprisingly, privatization was a missed chance to vest ordinary people with property ownership in Latin America. Despite its flaws, privatization in the United Kingdom created opportunities for millions of citizens to own shares, facilitating their access to capital and thereby giving them a stake in the wealth generated by the privatized companies. Some Central European countries, such as the Czech Republic, also recognized citizens' rights to acquire shares in privatized companies (banks later bought a large number of them from the public, however, and, as is the case in Germany and Japan, became important partners in the big corporations). In Latin America, no government made a comparable effort to use divestiture as an opportunity to facilitate property ownership among citizens who were actually the real "owners" of government assets either because they had mixed their labor with them or because, through taxes or the loss of capital imposed by the very existence of state-owned companies, they had been forced to sustain them. Chile managed to bring some one hundred thousand people into stock ownership and to sell four hundred thousand housing units to the less fortunate, by no means a small achievement, and Bolivia reserved a percentage of its six major concerns for the public by transferring new shares to the private pension system. Minor worker participation in the transfer of state property took place in Argentina in oil, telecommunications, and mail companies, and Peru set up a retirement fund with stocks owned by public-sector pensioners in privatized companies, Fondo Nacional de Ahorro Público (FONAHPU), originally worth $1.3 billion, but it mostly served to cover fiscal deficits. These and similar cases did not have a major impact on increasing property ownership in the region. Except in Chile, the workers or pensioners "owning" the stock could not freely sell it.

The diffusion of power, the vesting of millions of people with capital by simply giving them the freedom to acquire it, was not an objective of Latin American privatization. Such an objective would have run contrary to the need to maximize immediate returns to the government in the form of revenue and credit from big corporations, banks, and private pension funds that bought government bonds. Of course, vesting particular individuals with capital from the top down, however widely, is a form of government intervention and, as such, unfair to those left out of the loop. The problem originates from the need to transfer state assets. Given that they will end up in private hands, opening ownership participation to workers who may face layoffs and to a wider public with little practical experience of the benefits of real liberal capitalism is a way of limiting the effects of government intervention inherent in the very act of privatizing state companies (not to mention the fact that employees and taxpayers acquire a certain right over a company that they have sustained). In any event, workers and ordinary citizens choose whether to participate or not, and the government's job is to allow them access to share ownership if they seek it.

The only effort to allow the masses access to capital was the privatization of pensions. But even as citizens recovered the right to enjoy the fruits of their labor, government pensions were maintained in most countries, at a cost by no means restricted to those burdened with the payroll taxes. Furthermore, pension reform itself was not saved from state mercantilism and crony capitalism: in many countries, private pension funds were forced to invest heavily in government bonds. This was a very old tradition of state concessions (limited property rights) in exchange for funding. In Mexico, the law stated that at least 64 percent of portfolios had to be in government bonds. By 2003, despite the withdrawal of the requirement, the different regulations ensured that nearly 90 percent of pension funds' money was invested in such instruments. In Argentina, pension funds were mainly invested in government bonds when the government defaulted on most of its $141 billion foreign debt at the end of 2001 and, after suspending payment of its domestic debt also, ended up devaluing its currency—thus expropriating the savings of the pensioners. In 2003, the government again penalized them by decreeing that only a small percentage of the bonds' face value would be honored.

One final objection to privatization is that the governments of Latin America shied away from allowing private property in sensitive areas, among them those relating to the environment. Political authorities have not yet understood that the best way to protect the environment is to have clearly defined property rights that create individual rather than diffuse responsibility. Individual responsibility is what competitive privatization really amounts to, since only the individual, who must assume the consequences of his actions, his mistakes, and his successes, is really responsible for an asset. Concessions such as the ones given in the Amazon forests are limited forms of property that create incentives for immediate exploitation as opposed to long-term preservation, something that hurts indigenous communities in particular. In parts of Brazil's 750,000-square-mile Amazon region, where settlements have taken place over the years, the government retains the right to redistribute land if the large holdings are not in production, an ambiguous situation that often allows for expropriation or the legitimization of violent squatting, just as small holdings with insecure titles are themselves victims of predatory activity by large companies. Investment, therefore, is limited.

Only Chile obtains most of its wood from new forest plantations. Other nations—from Brazil and Argentina to Uruguay, Peru, and Costa Rica—have belatedly and partially opened the way for such efforts, but even when they bear fruit, by the end of this decade most of the wood will still be extracted from original forests. Impediments to private initiative continue to take a toll on ecosystems.

Through crony capitalism, Latin American reform perpetuated the region's history of underdevelopment, its corporatism, state mercantilism, privilege, wealth transfer, and political as opposed to natural or universal law. New interests became the corporate partners of the state. Through various mercantilist mechanisms, the government allocated capital among private businesses. Opportunity was reserved for a chosen, privileged elite. As ever, the system produced rents, that is, predatory profits resulting from government intervention, not from the producers' ability to satisfy the consumers, and wealth was therefore redistributed from the bottom to the top. And, finally, in the process of dismounting statism, Latin American governments enthroned the statist malady par excellence: the subordination of the law to the empire of political power. Political law was the mechanism by which the new forms of corporatism, state mercantilism, privilege, and wealth transfer were engineered.

From Privilege to Privilege

Privatization was by no means the only vehicle through which the traditional system was reinforced by the transition that aimed to dismantle it. Every other reform—monetary, fiscal, tax, trade, financial, investment, and labor—carried implicit crony capitalism rules of the game by which the government, appearing to retreat, subtly or not so subtly vested favored interests with power at the expense of the less fortunate.

Monetary and fiscal reform reduced inflation and brought about stability. But the discretionary power of monetary authorities was and is used in multiple forms—for example, to attract foreign investors by means of an exchange rate that transfers the costs to other producers and high interest rates that burden borrowers. Mandatory fractional reserve levels were and are raised and lowered according to whether governments want to augment or reduce the money in circulation, and even though interest rate restrictions were lifted, the authorities continue to influence the price of money by manipulating the rates of their own monetary institutions or simply by borrowing. Even under a currency board policy, Argentina's central bank used its assets and reserves to neutralize or compensate for, as the case may be, foreign exchange coming in or going out.

Fiscal spending has increased everywhere (since the end of the decade, the entire region has had significant deficits), with particular sectors receiving subsidies that others have to pay. In the 1990s, deficits were lower than in the 1980s only because revenue was higher, not because the government understood its own predatory nature, the automatic impost its mere existence forces on society's productive capacity. Power devolved from the federal to the state governments in Brazil and Argentina, and overall spending increased dramatically. Argentina's federal transfers to the provinces rose by 33 percent between 1994 and 2000. The mess in the nation's accounts caused by high spending (including higher debt costs because of rising U.S. interest rates) eventually played a major role in bringing about default, the end of "convertibility" (the name given to the currency board, which was always less than orthodox), and the ensuing political chaos that toppled three governments in a row. Brazil's total government spending still amounts to more than a third of the size of its economy. Latin America's government spending, in general between a quarter and a third of GDP and in some cases higher due to particularly burdensome debt servicing, is much greater than the size of spending in today's prosperous nations when they were at a similar stage of development. Additionally, the size of government is measured not only by the size of public spending but also by a host of other factors weighing on the productive capacity of citizens.

Tax policy was theoretically designed to reduce the burden of taxation and simplify, as well as harmonize, the system. But vast inequality in the treatment of big corporations and small businesses, of employees and self-employed people, of various industries and agriculture, and, more generally, of savings, production, and consumption has made sure that the allocation of resources is profoundly influenced by political power and that certain groups obtain rents at the expense of others. Mexican tax exemptions for assembly plants, maquiladoras, and tax-free enclaves, *zonas francas*, are obvious examples of government use of tax policy to direct resources toward particular trades, as was Argentina's selective VAT policy freeing the cable, health insurance, and advertising industries from that duty altogether and permitting certain trades to pay half of the general 21 percent rate. Meanwhile, all sorts of taxes crept back into Peru just as the burden of taxation was supposedly coming down. An "extraordinary solidarity tax" in the midst of recession, for instance, hurt the few taxpaying businesses. Belying the transitory nature expressed in its pompous title, the tax continues to exist. A "selective consumption tax" heavily increases the price of fuel transfers to car drivers and owners of industrial plants. Although consumption was targeted in all countries, the bulk of taxation in Latin America, from income to VAT to other types of tax, has continued to penalize capital and therefore create incentives for immediate consumption.

While trade barriers were lowered and commerce became the object of deregulation, tariffs and other types of obstacles have varied considerably from capital goods to manufactures to agricultural and livestock products, in a labyrinthine web of wealth redistribution. Latin Americans miss the basic premise that the real objective of exchange is consumption and that exports are the means to obtain the resources for imports. In an ideal world, a country would get all of its imports without needing to sell anything in order to obtain the foreign exchange to buy them with. Because we live in a less than ideal world, countries must export in order to import, or to attract enough capital to pay for their imports if their exports are not high enough to cover the costs. There is something bizarre about governments negotiating trade deals, and a dizzying number of deals were negotiated in recent years that created bureaucratic bodies and separate arrangements according to who the partner was. After all, it is not governments but citizens who trade, and what is traded is not speeches and clauses—the stuff of trade negotiations—but, simply, goods and services. The variety of trade deals and negotiations in the western hemisphere indicates that no government sees trade as a spontaneous activity by people who want to benefit themselves and each other. They see it as a military exercise that aims to take as much territory as possible and concede as little as possible. One wonders what effect this approach to trade would have on Richard Cobden, who believed that politics and commerce should not be mixed and brought prosperity to Britain after forcing the repeal of the corn laws in the mid-nineteenth century.

The absurdity of the situation was such that many countries found themselves back in negotiations after reaching bilateral deals. Such was the case with the United States and Chile, who, after signing their own agreement, were also involved in Free Trade Area of the Americas talks, and of Peru, which, after becoming an associate member of MERCOSUR, engaged in negotiations with its own partners again, this time as a member of the Andean Community of Nations, which was seeking a deal with them. All of these countries were at the same time discussing FTAA and, of course, participating in the Doha Round of world trade talks. All of this in the name of citizens wanting to trade with one another spontaneously and freely.

Reform did not bring about real "free trade." Guatemala's tariffs aimed at Tyson's poultry products and Mexican duties on concrete imports benefited powerful local lobbies. So did Mexico's barriers against Chinese footwear and Starking apples, and Peru's protection of dairy and flour products. In Argentina, high tariff protection in the automobile industry diverted large amounts of local capital toward car manufacturing, with the number of producers more than doubling by the new millennium. That same country actually ended up raising tariffs on seventy-one of a total of ninety-seven groups of items to comply with the rules of the South American Common Market. In Chile, agriculture is more heavily protected from competition than are other activities, and export-related forest plantations have received subsidies. In Colombia, coffee growers have actually been formally represented in the executive branch. Despite all the bias in favor of the export economy, only Mexico, Central America, and Argentina have improved their market shares abroad. The region's participation in world trade is still a modest 6.1 percent. The selective use of tariffs hurt consumers and benefited a few producers; the use of subsidies for certain exports missed the real point of commerce, which is to sell in order to obtain foreign currency with which to buy imports, not to sell for the sake of selling. This amounted to a distortion of the very nature of an activity that was created, in the beginnings of civilization, with the purpose of expanding consumption among individuals who discovered that by selling certain goods in whose production they specialized they could obtain goods that others produced and they desired. What is even more perplexing is that a country like the United States has chosen to help reinforce rather than undermine protectionist privilege. The 2003 negotiations for a free trade agreement between Central America and the United States conditioned the accord on Central America's defining its own common market first, with more liberal countries having to adapt to their less free neighbors within that region. Washington also required Central American compliance with a battery of U.S. regulations and excluded certain items from the accord.

Financial deregulation came with government guarantees aimed at promoting private credit so that the beneficiaries of privatization could expand. In Mexico, the cost eventually shifted to the taxpayers, who paid $68 billion to rescue the banks. In Peru, the cost was borne by those who had savings, as well as by producers and creditors when a long liquidity crisis interrupted the chain of payments (just under $1 billion of taxpayers' money was also employed in Peru, rescuing banks from irresponsible lending policies caused by government guarantees). Under implicit or explicit insurance, banks have inadequate incentives to remain sufficiently liquid. The opposite happened in Venezuela, where, after a rise in oil revenue due to monetary devaluation, in order to help the banks that were inundated by an excess of liquidity in local currency, the government sold them special bonds. The fact that Latin American governments extended deposit and credit guarantees did not stop them from mandating various levels of bank reserves.

Labor legislation, the area where reform was least profound, also managed rewards and penalties. Labor laws dating to Perón's days held back productivity in Argentina and made reform synonymous with double-digit unemployment in the eyes of the country. As has happened in other areas of the economy with the government's interventionist bias, the system that raises the cost of employing people has had specific beneficiaries—in this case a labor oligarchy, which receives direct income from taxpayers and which, as in many other countries, is dangerously empowered by industry rather than company-based collective bargaining (which itself limits the freedom of workers and managers to contract). This makes, for instance, all metallurgical workers, whether they are involved in building submarines or manufacturing nails, subject to common collective-bargaining rules. Members of the government's labor department supervise salaries and employment conditions established by negotiations between business and labor corporations rather than individuals. It is common across the region to find all sorts of government-inspired councils purporting to bring together employers, workers, and bureaucrats in the interest of the people. They entrench rather than disperse obstacles facing the unemployed. In Brazil, high, inflexible labor costs ingrained in its 1988 constitution have remained largely untouched because of vested interests both at the federal and state levels. The same can be said of most other countries' labor legislation. In Mexico, it is estimated that labor laws have nearly doubled the hourly cost of labor.

These institutional pockets of privilege go a long way toward explaining why unemployment has risen in half of the Latin American nations since the early 1990s despite private enterprise. Ironically, illegal immigrants from poorer neighboring nations find it easier than local people to obtain jobs in richer Latin American countries. The underground economy makes it harder for the rich and powerful to control the entire labor market with restrictive regulations.

Other areas where reform was much less prevalent simply watched the system's unfairness perpetuate itself. The liberal professions, for instance, continued to be highly restrictive, denying membership of legally and exclusively licensed associations to those who could not comply with norms designed to place obstacles to entry, unless they used cronyism or blatant corruption to penetrate the sacred chamber. Under such uncompetitive rules, clients have had less protection from malpractice and fraud than they might have had if privilege did not dominate the game.

The Rules of the Game

The exploitative, unfair nature of reform in all areas is perpetuated by the legal system. Nowhere in Latin America was the legal system the object of meaningful change. The region's legal systems, based on a tradition whose remote origins lie in Justinian's codified version of Roman law and Napoleon's positive law, give the authorities discretion over everything from constitutional to economic to family matters. Such interference makes the law an instrument of politicians, who use it, under the guise of public policy, to allocate favors and costs. Under such arrangements, there is no independent judiciary. At every level, decisions are corruptly bought, and citizens are treated unfairly unless they wield political influence. In the absence of high standards, the law is a mercantilist mechanism of juridical transfers from those who are at a disadvantage to cronies honored by the system. It is the prime source of discrimination and exploitation against the powerless.

Reformers not only failed to follow the principle of individual property rights, they also did not regard the law as a higher source of morality than government decision making. As a result, the individual was left naked in the face of political power. Instead of repealing bad laws, governments assumed that free societies are built from above by passing all sorts of new laws, just as economic nationalism had been. Inevitably, reform consolidated positive, legislative law as a perverse instrument of fragmentary, temporary rights. No wonder the ghost of illegitimacy began to visit Latin American republics once again at the beginning of the twenty-first century, with the streets of many countries bursting with fiery demonstrators who called themselves "civil society" toppling governments in Ecuador, Argentina, and Peru, engaging in anguished struggle with Venezuela's authoritarian regime, and threatening to replace presidents in other parts. In a region that is still unable to rescue 211 million citizens, more than half the population, from poverty's grip, many feel they have nothing to lose. In contrast, East Asia, despite severe setbacks, reduced the proportion of the population living on less than $1 a day from 26 to 15 percent (in Chile, an exceptional case, one million people have come out of poverty since the return of democracy).

There are important lessons to be gleaned from Latin America's story of crooked reform. The most important is that symptoms should not be mistaken for causes. Governments thought that private investment, not the rule of law, brought forth development. Conversely, private investment and growth are symptoms of the capitalist society that only the rule of law enables. By reforming investment laws, maintaining nominal exchange rates, granting access to assets, and promoting expanded credit through private banks, governments attracted much foreign, and even some domestic, investment. But investment and aggregate growth were generated by economic nationalism and, before that, by experiments in private property. Even some African nations, such as South Africa, Nigeria, Angola, Ghana, and Mozambique—an area of the world Latin America looks upon with a sense of superiority—have attracted much foreign capital in the last decade. But governments failed to remove themselves as the source of the law so that clear, abstract, predictable rules applied equally to all would permit the contract society to flourish—a longer-term, but ultimately much more just, sustained, and successful way of generating investment and growth. It would be dangerous to underestimate the far-reaching effects of these policies simply because some of them also take place today in the United States, western Europe, and Japan. What brought prosperity to these nations was the absence of such policies in the past, and even under disproportionately big governments, most of their citizens continue to enjoy a measure of individual rights and institutional protections greater than those in Latin America.

It should come as no surprise that in the given circumstances Latin America's average investment rate has not amounted to more than 21 percent of GDP, as opposed to twice that rate in East Asia (since 2000, Latin America's investment rate has been much lower, in many cases no more than 15 percent). Corporatism, state mercantilism, privilege, wealth transfer, and political law conspired to prevent high accumulation of capital. Consequently, the rate of growth of capital accumulation during the 1990s (except in Chile and Costa Rica) was lower than during economic nationalism's strongest years between 1950 and 1980—Brazil, Mexico, Argentina, and Peru did not even reach a 3 percent annual rate. Under such conditions and with low productivity, despite all the foreign investment and a few impressive years, Latin America's GDP grew at an annual average rate of 3.4 percent during the entire decade, very modest considering the rise in population. By the year 2000, growth had ceased and the economies of the region continued to stagnate. The capitalist miracle had fast become a mirage.

Latin American governments did what they had done many times before—they used the law as a credible commitment to specific parties, guaranteeing their own property rights. Indeed, many of the regimes that provided these guarantees seemed strong enough to sustain them for some time (a few were dictatorial, such as Mexico's PRI and Peru's Fujimori, and in Argentina and Brazil, democracy did not prevent presidents from changing the constitution so they could ensure reelection). But the type of arrangement whereby governments and private investors trade property rights for fiscal revenue and credit is by definition unstable. Commitments can always be undone by future governments when it is the government and not the law that secures rights. That is why crony capitalism feeds on corporatism, state mercantilism, privilege, wealth transfer, and political law. In the absence of the long-term commitment of the rule of law, private interests need to maximize immediate profits the same way that government needs to maximize capital flows and ultimately the revenues that come from its cronies' high rates of return.

Under such circumstances, private interests have a stake in making the rules, and politicians have a stake in the profits. This form of integration between the public and the private spheres serves as the commitment to and guarantee of support of parties, government, and private enterprise who trade with one another. Corruption, therefore, either in the blatant form, as has been the case in almost every country in the reform years, or under the guise of wealth transfers, is just as naturally part and parcel of crony capitalism as is predation.

If the rule of law is the environment in which risk is reduced to the bare minimum because the government, the greatest potential threat, is itself removed as a source of that risk, crony capitalism is the compromise by which governments ill prepared to limit their power secure their subsistence, and private parties that would not otherwise invest because of high risk agree to do so. Historically, limited government has existed in few places. All other societies are variations on the limited rights environment. Sometimes those variations involved high degrees of autonomy from government interference in matters such as civil law and trade. But in all societies where the rule of law is limited, the government and private parties collude to exchange rights and liberties for support.

The kind of society that results from that exchange is not based on liberal capitalism. Latin America's reforms constitute a variation, however much things are or look better than under economic nationalism, on the long history of crony capitalism. No country has successfully achieved development by playing by the rules of crony capitalism. Such systems develop specific parties for a limited period of time, not entire nations. Even taking international factors into consideration, it is no surprise that by the year 2000 even those privileged parties had ceased to grow in a region that saw itself once more in the grips of financial chaos and economic depression. It is even less surprising that no country saw a boom in small- and middle-sized businesses, which create many jobs in capitalist countries. In fact, lack of business opportunity largely accounts for the fact that many who lost their jobs because of privatization had to subsist in the underground economy (privatization had a negative impact on formal employment of 40 percent in Argentina, 55 percent in Peru, 36 percent in Mexico, 23 percent in Colombia, and 10 percent in Brazil). The fragmentary nature of property rights makes them too risky a prospect for banks that prefer to lend money to their own related businesses and business partners. Agriculture, which in many Latin American countries still employs around 30 percent of the population, is in a particularly sorry state, in part because its small entities lack access to any form of credit, in part because, like most of the economy, it cannot generate its own savings due to statism.

The knowledge, including technology, that modern globalization allows underdeveloped countries to absorb in little time is far superior, even in relative terms, to that offered by international exchange when today's capitalist nations were starting the rise to prosperity in the eighteenth and nineteenth centuries. But the flow of knowledge and opportunity from exchange with foreign nations is only a factor in development if the rules of the game and the attitudes and customs that go with them over a long period of time guarantee very limited government, horizontal property rights, and a network of institutions that reflect and flow from the contract society, respected—and protected—by the political arrangements. This concept goes beyond partisan politics. In fact, both the left and the right have contributed to Latin America's underdevelopment.

The New Millennium

As one might expect, the failure of sophistic reform in Latin America during the 1990s caused a dearth of reform in the new millennium. Brazil's Luiz Inacio "Lula" da Silva and Argentina's Néstor Kirchner have emerged as symbols of the decade. They stand in direct response to left-wing "populism" and right-wing "neoliberalism." Their vision purports to go beyond the policies of fiscal and monetary profligacy that caused hyperinflation in the 1980s, and beyond the policies of crony privatization and protoliberalization that caused unemployment and high debt in the 1990s. They believe that the government should promote growth through public spending without causing inflation and incurring new debt, and protect the economy from globalization by using regional-bloc negotiating power rather than high tariffs. President Kirchner has invoked Roosevelt's New Deal as a paradigm for Latin America and launched a momentous program of public works. Both Brazil and Argentina have decided to revitalize MERCOSUR, the South American bloc of trading partners, with a view to constructivist, European Union–style integration (steps have been taken to incorporate the Andean countries via negotiations for a trade agreement between MERCOSUR and the Community of Andean Nations).

In trying to steer a middle course between the inflationary 1980s and the privatizing 1990s, they fail to see that both experiences were variants of the same evil. In the 1980s, the state, a producer of goods and services, used a suffocating tangle of compulsion mechanisms, including currency manipulation, to coerce citizens into sustaining what Octavio Paz once called the Philanthropic Ogre; in the 1990s, the state, having transferred production to private enterprise, used a suffocating tangle of compulsion mechanisms, excluding inflation, to coerce citizens into sustaining a coterie of monopolies that, in exchange for exclusive rights, supported the Philanthropic Ogre through credit and some taxes. The result at the end of the 1980s was hyperinflation and stagnation. The result at the end of the 1990s was default and stagnation.

It is clear that Latin Americans are still missing the point about underdevelopment, by addressing symptoms and not causes. President Lula thought that capping and taxing monthly pensions, increasing the retirement age so that the fiscal situation would not get out of hand, and using state agencies to fight poverty would turn his country around. In Argentina, the surplus created by stopping debt servicing in 2002 and the growth generated by exports due to currency devaluation (and consumption of capital) gave President Kirchner the confidence to announce a public works program worth $1 billion in its first phase and possibly $3 billion in the long run. And through MERCOSUR, both countries aim to replicate at the regional level the kind of state prevailing at the national level. Everywhere else, from Mexico to Peru, new authorities were content to maintain the status quo, fooling themselves into believing that moderate growth after a long period of recession marks real progress. Corporatism, state mercantilism, privilege, wealth transfer, and political law are alive and kicking in Latin America.

How Reform Succeeded Better Elsewhere

There have been many occasions in the recent past when poor countries rose to prosperity. Such cases, including much of Europe and Japan after World War II, differ from Latin America in that the fundamentals of liberal capitalism were already in place even if the economy and society were in ruins. Judicial institutions, even financial systems, were quickly restored as part of the environment in which reconstruction took place. The result was a more homogeneous distribution of income than in Latin America, where reform, despite some impressive growth years, actually widened the gap between the elites and the rest, not allowing for upward mobility and the emergence of a strong middle class. Latin America has a Gini coefficient—a typical measure of income inequality—approximately fifteen points above the average of those of the rest of the world. During the reform years, the wealthiest 20 percent of the population received on average 60 percent of the national income in each country, sixteen times more than the poorest 20 percent—a ratio of richest to poorest double the size of Asia's. In France, Germany, the United Kingdom, the United States, and Canada just after the devastation of World War II, the richest 10 percent of the population received on average 30 percent of national income, whereas the richest 10 percent absorb almost half of Brazil's income today.

In 1948, when Israel was created, there was no development as such in that country. But there was a capitalist culture that quickly translated into a society where most people could participate in the creation of wealth. That is what made Israel relatively prosperous even in the face of socialist policies and U.S. transfers. In that sense, Israel was born with a middle class. In Latin America, meanwhile, institutional arrangements inimical to liberal capitalism, under a system of justice profoundly subservient to the government and to ever-changing, obscure legislative and political law that attempted to dictate the conduct of individuals in everything from commerce to family life, kept millions of people away from free-market capitalism.

There are contemporary cases of successful reform where the effort was made to abolish privilege. In New Zealand, the emergence of a Labor government in 1984 unexpectedly opened the gates of reform. In the 1930s, that country was considered one of the pioneers of cradle-to-grave welfare, and the asphyxiating weight of the state was such that between 1950 and the 1980s the rate of economic growth was half that of the member countries of the Organization of Economic Cooperation and Development (OECD). Socialism was so strong that even after capitalist reform, a New Zealand journalist was able to state that his country was "reformed by Hayekians, run by pragmatists and populated by socialists." A number of principles presided over the changes. They were done very quickly (according to Roger Douglas, one of the leaders of reform, opponents find it more difficult to fire at "a rapidly moving target"), they aimed simultaneously at various parts of the political economy, and, instead of trying to design a capitalist society with constructivist policies, they removed obstacles that hindered private contract and competition and reduced pockets of privilege. By the time the Labor government left power, the ethos of reform was so powerful that the succeeding National government decided to expand it.

But what did the abolition of privilege translate into in terms of actual policy? Tax reform translated into low, mostly flat taxes, and disposable income rose between 6 and 8 percent; all tariffs fell to a 5 percent level; banks were no longer required to hold their deposits in the central bank, and controls on all financial prices were lifted; monopoly rights of trade unions to workforce representation were removed, and the law of contract displaced collective bargaining as the axis of relations between managers and workers; industrial reform recognized the freedom of entry of "potential" competitors rather than actually conferring the right to enter a market on specific parties or regulating competition; investment reform removed discrimination against investors, which placed foreign capital on an equal footing with domestic capital; farm policy eliminated subsidies and, unlike what happened in Latin America, high public spending did not creep back in, because both manufacturers and farmers called for sound government finances to reduce pressure on real interest and exchange rates (government spending was actually reduced from 41 percent of GDP in the early 1990s to 35 percent in 1996). New Zealand's reform is still far from complete, but it has been much more coherent and consistent than Latin America's, underpinned by institutions, both legal and political, that removed themselves to a large extent as the source of success and failure of specific individuals and groups. The results are clearly seen in the greater access to capital enjoyed by millions of people in that country.

It is fair to say that New Zealand enjoys an advantage over Latin America: its culture is far less burdened by centuries of statism. But Latin America's reforms did not fail because of cultural resistance to change. They failed because they did not dismantle many factors contributing to that very culture.

There are other countries that have successfully translated partial reform into real gains for the population. Ireland, one of the poorest nations of western Europe, whose principal export until recently was human capital from emigration, was able to double the size of its economy in the 1990s to spectacular gains for millions of ordinary citizens. By the new millennium, the country, a hub of technological investment in Europe, had ceased to export people. With a population one-fourth the size of Chile's, it was able to put out goods and services worth almost 40 percent more than the output of that South American country even with moderate, selective reform. Low taxes and few regulations lured foreign companies into an environment that, unlike Latin America's, offered strong judicial guarantees. Irish reform was less ambitious than Latin American reform—the lesson being that it is not the quantity of reform but its nature that counts. Limited reform under political guarantees for horizontal property rights goes a long way in comparison with extensive reform under precarious juridical institutions and fragmentary property rights. For instance, Estonia's improvement after the bold elimination of tariffs, which were brought down to zero in the 1990s, and the emergence of solid legal frameworks for investors indicate that removing the government as an instrument of privilege creates overall progress (lack of equally audacious reforms in some other areas notwithstanding).

By contrast, in eastern Europe, despite major advances in relation to pre-1989 socialism, reform had results only slightly better than Latin America's in the 1990s. Fiscal realism, liberalization, and privatization were treated as objectives in themselves, not as policies responding to a new and radically different vision regarding the role of the state in society. Polish researcher Grzegorz W. Kolodko blames the loss of one-quarter of the combined GDPs of former COMECOM countries between 1990 and 1998 on the fact that "a lack of institutional development turned out to be the missing element in transition policies based on the Washington Consensus."

The exclusion of most Latin American citizens from rights conferred on a chosen oligarchy explains why most private investment was financed by volatile foreign capital and not by domestic savings, which remained low. Capital could not spread and accumulate in a sustained way over a long period of time. Economies that do not grow significantly do not generate large savings or sustained investment. A large percentage of bank credit went to consumption rather than investment. Only Chile has been able to achieve consistent domestic savings rates of 25 percent or more of GDP. The general pattern has been dependency on foreign investment. The consequences of vulnerability to fluctuations in foreign investor confidence became painfully obvious with Chile's 1982 financial crisis, Mexico's peso devaluation in 1994–95, Argentina's default at the turn of 2002, the 40 percent loss of value of Brazil's real in early 2003, and the hemispherewide stagnation that started toward the end of the 1990s and has continued almost to the middle of this decade (Chile's high savings insulated that country from financial turbulence in later years). Subsequent stabilization in those nations does not detract from their financial vulnerability in the absence of strong domestic savings.

Whether these events were caused by lack of domestic transparency and stability, international contagion, or world slowdowns, they brought the fragility and inconsistency of reform into the open. The 1990s reproduced in Argentina, Brazil, Mexico, and Peru a pattern seen in some countries of the region in the 1970s: massive capital inflows and a corresponding overvalued exchange rate delivering abundant cheap imports, followed by loss of confidence, massive capital outflows, and eventually recession. And, at the end of the day, with exceptions like Mexico and Brazil, Latin America's economy was still mainly exporting primary products (even Chile is highly dependent on them). The fact that so much foreign capital is a short-term investment owes a great deal to the absence of universal property rights. It should come as no surprise that Mexico received such large amounts of short-term capital when, even under reform, article 25 of the constitution continued to establish that the state "plans, leads, directs and manages" the economy. The same goes for the introduction of private property in the countryside under Carlos Salinas, constrained by a 6,200-acre limit on companies as well as by article 27 of the constitution, declaring the government to be the owner of the land. Diffuse rights as opposed to individual rights do not generate capitalism. Constructivist, to use Friedrich Hayek's famous term, as opposed to individual-minded reform is the best way of making good the dictum expressed by one of the characters in Lampedusa's novel *The Leopard*: "If we want everything to stay just as it is, everything must change."

Underdevelopment, then, is not a fatal condition; it is the result of international conspiracies or the consequence of insufficient capital. It is first and foremost a vested interest that creates a nasty mind-set in those who live under it for too long.

9

Corruption and the Ethical Abyss

Latin American reform was corrupt, meaning that many reformers stole other people's money and property. An army of public servants found opportunities for personal profit in the transition from economic nationalism to private enterprise while an army of local and foreign businessmen knew that the road to success lay not in seducing consumers but in seducing those who called the shots. Consequently, almost every country—Chile and Brazil much less so than Mexico, Peru, and Argentina, to mention a few—found itself under an ethical shadow that, by the time reform failed to deliver what it had promised, fueled reaction against capitalism. Three presidential impeachments on corruption charges in Latin America during the last decade of the twentieth century indicate not how much corruption there was but rather how few Latin American leaders paid the proper price for what they partook in and encouraged. Democracies were really kleptocracies.

Recently, Latin American nations have been increasingly occupying dishonorable positions in the rankings offered by organizations, like Transparency International, that compare relative levels of corruption around the world. Andres Oppenheimer describes Latin American corruption as investment opportunities drew business from multinational corporations willing to play by the local rules of the game and as domestic interests sought to secure their positions in partnership with politicians, bureaucrats, and military officials wanting a stake in the feast. Under ambiguous wording, some European countries, among them Germany, even allowed kickbacks paid by their businessmen abroad to be deducted from taxes. The atmosphere of the 1990s, when leading capitalist nations were themselves embroiled in a culture of corporate deceit that became public only when giants like Enron collapsed, did not exactly restrain investors from engaging in corrupt practices abroad as much as local interests did in the countries where they invested.

The unusually high volume of corruption during the reform years is directly connected to the increased opportunities from expanded investment and from the fact that immense asset divestitures passed through the discretion of politicians and bureaucrats. But it is a mistake to view corruption as a cause of reform failure or, more widely, of underdevelopment. Corruption was a feature of Latin American life before the reforms took place and continues today, when reform has ceased. It is not the volume but the permanent nature of corruption that needs to be addressed by looking at it as a symptom of the illegitimacy of the law rather than as a human evil conspiring against Latin America.

Corruption is not just a means to obtain profits in countries where profit is a function of power and not of initiative and enterprise; it is a consequence of the loss of legitimacy of the law and of the state, and of those moral values that make possible civilized coexistence in any society. There is no separation between the government and the state, between the political and the administrative: public service is a vehicle of patronage by which politicians reward supporters on a massive scale, who in turn view their appointments as business and profit opportunities that are missing in the private economy. Those who occupy administrative positions exploit the rest—until a change of government brings in new beneficiaries of the same type of practice. *Clientelismo*, the word that describes that phenomenon, means more than a corrupt practice: it sums up Latin America's view of what a government is and the function it serves. Few people have any respect for the services provided by the state; at the same time, people look desperately at public office as the only available source of social mobility and profit, ideally through the direct exercise of an administrative position or, alternatively, through alliances with those who hold it, even at the low end of the bureaucratic edifice. It is hard to overstate the corrosive ethical effect of this distortion arising from the displacement of opportunities from the private to the public sphere. James M. Buchanan and Gordon Tullock's insights into the state as a space in which or through which individuals seek to maximize profits just as they do in the marketplace find in Latin America particularly raw confirmation. The institutional framework being what it is, such self-serving behavior does not produce the positive general results that public choice theory ascribes to self-interest in political matters under the right set of incentives. Self-interest on the part of the public official and his cronies in a parasitic state reinforces the mechanism of the state as an instrument of predation against productive individuals. Corruption joins other forms of redistribution as an additional factor of exploitation. It exploits those on whom taxes are levied and from whom money is borrowed, of course, but also the very poor, the people in whose name the government took wealth from productive individuals in the first place.

New regulations amounting to cumbersome barriers to entry into the market replaced previous ones as the privatization of the state engendered opportunities for the bureaucracy. Recent research in both developed and underdeveloped countries has confirmed that strict regulation does not secure higher-quality products, greater profitability for firms, better environmental or health results, as it purports to do. What it does encourage is much higher levels of corruption. This has certainly been the case in Latin America, where the high cost of doing business, a field virtually untouched by reform, has turned potential producers into candidates for lucrative government posts or government-protected markets. In Mexico, it takes 112 business days and 15 different procedures at a cost of almost 60 percent of per capita GDP just to be able to operate a start-up company. In Brazil, it takes 67 business days and 15 procedures at a cost of almost 70 percent of per capita GDP. In Peru, it takes 171 business days and 14 procedures at a cost of 21 percent of per capita GDP. Corruption is the natural creature of such environments. Although corruption allows some of those excluded from the system to buy their way in, it consolidates the exclusion of those who are unable to follow suit, it raises the cost of doing business, and it empowers the bureaucrat.

The illegitimacy of the law and of government triggered revolution at the turn of the twentieth century. At the turn of the twenty-first century, the new illegitimacy has caused devalued human relations. From this divorce comes disrespect for human life, as we see in the explosion of crime and violence from Mexico City to São Paulo, and from Lima to Buenos Aires; distrust of the entities and the people that make up the state, as we see in the attitude of ordinary citizens toward police officers, judges, or even minor symbols of the legal order such as streetlights; and aggression against other people's property, as takes place even among informal economy entrepreneurs who have so struggled against the government in order to procure some property for themselves. A culture of cynical disbelief in anything that is not illicitly obtained has emerged as a consequence of the illegitimacy of the law and the state. It pervades all levels of society, rich and poor, public and private.

Failure to address this fracture in society is by far the greatest flaw of Latin American reform, one that is not immediately obvious or quantifiable. Corruption is the symptom of that fracture. As we will see, the fact that reform expanded the scope of opportunities for public officials is not the only factor that explains it. There are two other factors: reform hindered the evolution of civil society, and the prevailing justice system was left untouched.

Civil Society and the Poor

In recent years, as migrants transformed the cities into sprawling urban centers—not attracted by the opportunities of industrialization, as happened in nineteenth-century Europe, but by utter despair because of conditions in the countryside—a new type of society began to emerge. In Peru and Mexico, with a strong Indian presence, this new society had an important mestizo cultural dimension, visible in everything from the music to the types of Sunday fairs, folklore activities, and associations arising out of that bustling new world. Throughout Latin America, this urban phenomenon spawned a multitude of voluntary arrangements, a mutuality of cooperating families through which all types of neighborhood, trade, and civic associations started to provide the sorts of services the state was unable to provide. Poor people found ways to divide property on newly occupied land, set up security arrangements, distribute water or electricity from nearby sources, pave roads, adjudicate disputes, negotiate transport routes, construct markets, clean up the environment, share sports facilities, practice religion, distribute food among the destitute—in essence, to sustain life through peaceful community. Thousands of organizations, committees, associations, and congregations sprang from the struggle for survival.

Prosperity did not result in the end because the conditions necessary for liberal capitalism were not present, but private effort was able to generate the minimal social safety nets and law enforcement services that the politicians have been good at offering and bad at delivering despite big government. If it had not been for grassroots organizations, government aid in the form of food, milk, or public works budgets would not have been brought to the shantytowns. "Mothers' clubs" and "glass-of-milk committees" are just two examples of how poor Peruvian women set up extensive grassroots networks. Shantytowns in many Latin American countries are in fact nascent civil societies. The moral dimension of these webs of voluntary associations and civic organizations is important because they are deeply connected to the concept of rights. Poor people's associative and spontaneous exercise of rights provides a firm ground for development should official institutions cease to concentrate officially sanctioned rights on those satellites of privilege orbiting the government. Compassion and solidarity in Latin America are not government benefits: they are a private, even primeval, effort to sustain life.

The phenomenon is not unlike what took place in Great Britain and the United States in the nineteenth century, when civic associations, fraternal orders, friendly societies, and urban development organizations provided social services like health care, unemployment insurance, education, and even security, or delivered so-called public goods such as roads and highways. Welfare was not a government program but a trait of civil society. Even today, migration from cities to suburbs created by private developers in the United States serves as a powerful example of the human instinct of community. According to the Community Associations Institute, there are some 205,000 Common Interest Developments in the United States, housing more than 40 million people, in which contracts and agreements serve to set up many types of services for the benefit of those who reside in the communities.

The very notion of civil society in developed nations belies the caricature depicting free-market capitalism as an exploitative, profit-obsessed machine that drains the spirit of compassion for others. Western philosophy gives form to the idea of civil society in the eighteenth century, but the roots of the idea can be traced to the Greeks and the Romans. The idea of people helping one another in a space called community is present in John Locke's writings, in the concept of social mutuality in David Hume's work, and in the moral sentiments that are a part of Adam Smith's teachings. Those philosophers would have been fascinated by the contemporary Latin American resonance of what they described and valued in their own countries centuries ago.

The Latin American elites failed to see the importance of what was happening not only as a potential for prosperity but also as a foundation of the type of civic virtue, of moral character, that breeds civilization. Instead of seeing a nascent civil society, they saw hordes of dark-skinned violators of the law who did not pay taxes, who resented the rich and held predatory instincts against the property of the better-off—uneducated migrants invading the cities with their hybrid, unrefined mestizo culture (but they also saw lots of votes and opportunities for political patronage). It is a tragic irony that, by excluding it from the closely knit world of legal protection, full property rights, and official recognition with all the benefits that such status entails, the Latin American elites have worked hard at turning this promising civil society into the projection of their very fears and prejudices. So the entrepreneurial instinct and the community ethos in large parts of the population coexisted more and more in the last few years with an attitude of deep social corruption born of frustration and of racial and social resentment. This degradation is particularly dangerous in societies that are not fully integrated and where there is no solid middle class. Elitist, exclusive reform, the type that reshuffles privilege rather than removes impediments to participation and social mobility, has accelerated the descent into a moral abyss.

By stifling civil society in early republican life, corporatist, state-mercantilist, privilege-driven, wealth-transferring Latin American political law brought about a crisis of legitimacy of the state and of the legal order at the end of the nineteenth century, which resulted in the Mexican Revolution. Civil society was stifled again throughout the twentieth century by a system based on the same principles of oppression. This time, rather than revolution, a migrant society that turned its back on the law and created its own rules was born. But there was a limit to how long these parallel societies could coexist without real integration (the fact that there is no real integration does not mean there is no contact; both worlds cross paths daily). By failing to reconcile both worlds, to accommodate the political institutions to a reality that surpasses the cozy arrangements of the elite, the state failed to understand where the solution to the crisis of legitimacy lay. The response this time was corruption on a wider, more pervasive scale than ever before. In Peru, where this phenomenon is particularly acute, social resentment is rife, human relations are deteriorating even further, and the spoken and written word are losing all value. Andreski's words, written many decades ago, ring even truer today: "Once a society is pervaded by parasitic exploitation, the choice is only to skin or be skinned." This is the profound significance of corruption.

Countries where a stronger civil society has existed traditionally, like Costa Rica, Chile, and Uruguay, have experienced the least corruption. Chile's nineteenth century saw the emergence of a civil society even under a powerful state. The presence of migration from places like Catalonia and the Basque country, where civil society was strong, helped encourage a type of civic, rule-of-law culture that survived even when, much later, political instability and dictatorships arose.

Latin American reform failed to strengthen civil society by working against the grassroots, bottom-to-top system of rights as the population carved out for itself a peaceful existence on the margins of the law. Many of the myriad private arrangements and contracts, often family-based, with which poor people sustain life or defend themselves from adversity enter into conflict with one another, sometimes through violent competition for land on which to settle but also through gang warfare arising from rivalries among neighborhoods or through the formation of armies of thugs at the service of political machines. By failing to provide a homogeneous institutional framework for spontaneous arrangements, the governments of Latin America have contributed to the corruption of the social fabric and to a state of cynicism that runs contrary to the kind of moral character necessary to sustain civilized life.

Organizations that function as channels for government subsidies for the poor have not been allowed or encouraged to become corporations, raise money elsewhere, and turn their decentralized, grassroots networks of social workers into more productive entities able to strengthen the community and improve the quality of life around them. Parents' associations, which raise small amounts of money to buy books and pencils for their children, and sometimes even bricks for the buildings in which they attend school, have been given very little say in the administration of education in most countries. The myriad Protestant religious organizations that have sprung up in poor neighborhoods in the last few decades have not been placed on an equal footing with Catholic institutions, a discrimination that works against the civilizing implications of these groups' activities. The discouragement of private patronage because of overburdening taxation and the bureaucratic obstacles placed in their way has hindered efforts to enhance cultural associations, especially of artisans, that play a key role among the poor. The same can be said of sports-based activities. The practical effect of this neglect is much worse than just unrealized potential. It is the proliferation of civil cynicism, social resentment, and distrust of the law.

It is no longer a rebellion against the government in the name of doing informal business or a struggle for the preservation of an individual space against the intrusion of political force. It is, more fundamentally, a reaction against the very idea of a legal and moral order in its basic, life-valuing form and an affirmation of illegality for illegality's sake.

Justice, the Cinderella of Reform

It is often said that the judicial system is the Cinderella of Latin America's public sector because of the minute budgets it is assigned. Most countries devote between 1 and 2 percent of their national budgets to the judicial system, and almost all of that money is spent on salaries. But the amount of money politicians give to the courts and judges bears little relation to the importance they assign to them, which is why all governments and their cronies devote vast amounts of time and resources to controlling and corrupting them. Perhaps politicians fear that increasing funds would also increase the power of the justice system and therefore its independence.

In no Latin American nation has there been profound judicial reform. The countries in which the justice system is less corrupt and more immune from the meddling of politicians are also ones where strong civilian institutions were long in place (Costa Rica being a case in point) and where ethical standards and the separation of powers were traditionally greater. The rest continue to have weak judicial systems and have engaged either in no reform at all, despite international funding and bureaucratic reviews, or very limited reform of some type or other with the result that the origin of the problem has actually been reinforced.

This does not mean that those in positions of power did not entertain lively discussions—sometimes even acting on them—about everything from changing the way judges are appointed to increasing budgets, updating technology, reshuffling the court structure, elevating the level of training, and decentralizing the judicial network. But in the new millennium, Latin America is left with opinion polls that consistently put the judicial system at the top of the list of the most corrupt, inefficient, and untrustworthy institutions. The economic implications of inadequate judicial institutions are considerable. Conservative estimates by multilateral bodies point to a 15 percent incidence of such a factor in economic growth due to lack of investor trust.

The problem does not lie in the way judges are appointed, because no matter what mechanism is used, the power of government is such that judges are subservient to those who run it (or to the prosecutors acting in its name). It is of no real consequence, either, by how much the budget is increased, how many new courts there are and how they divide the load, how many computers are made available, how sophisticated the level of training is, or how many judges work from the provinces as opposed to the capital city. The real problem lies in the dearth of independence from both the government and political law, high costs of access for ordinary citizens, and inefficiency. By not attacking these factors, or doing so partially, all attempts at judicial reform have failed. Brazil's new 1988 constitution embraced what looked like ambitious judicial reform, carried out with much enthusiasm in the ensuing years. The result of greater access to the courts was that pending cases increased ten times in the following decade. In Ecuador, there are more than half a million backlogged cases, lasting a little less than two years on average.

Decisions continue to be made on the basis not of justice but of the legislation controlled by politicians and of how much relative power the parties involved wield even at the low end of the scale. Ultimately, the Latin American justice system, like the rest of the public sector but to much worse effect, depends on the incentives judges have to be fair or unfair, and it is usually the case that those incentives work against what is right because the courts are an extension of the general condition of power as an instrument of discrimination. Since the benefits of judicial reform are not immediate, the incentive for decision makers to reverse the situation is nil. It does not matter that ordinary citizens at large reject the system that victimizes them, because the weakness of civil society, itself closely related to the inadequacy of the judiciary, means that the issue of real reform is subject to the incentives or disincentives of the elites. The elites brought about the transition from economic nationalism to private enterprise because the cost of the former system had become unbearable. There is no equivalent pressure—at least not yet—to overhaul the justice system. In fact, the continuous subservience of judges to the powerful is one of the very reasons why the elites managed to turn reform in the 1980s and 1990s into a reshuffling of power rather than a reversal of the status quo.

The absence of real judicial reform in a context of economic reform has made the problem more acute. Though limited, shallow, and even deceitful, economic reform has expanded the scope of market transactions, creating far greater demand for dispute-resolution mechanisms (the emerging society born out of migration to the cities had also exposed the need for an adequate judicial system). The more complex the interactions between individuals and groups, the more necessary it becomes to solve disputes and enforce contracts. Informal or private arrangements (and justices of the peace, who operate like arbitrators in countries like Peru) have helped limit the devastating effect of corrupt, inefficient, and untrustworthy courts, but the price has been the widening divide between the country in which the majority of people live and do business, and the country in which a minority monopolizes the law.

Only when elites have had an interest in promoting legal and judicial updating so as to adapt the institutions to their expanded economic activities have they adjusted the legal and the judicial systems somewhat in order to keep up with international standards. This was the case in Argentina, for instance, where the laws and the courts tried to adopt American and European rules regarding the relationship between managers and shareholders, and other issues related to the functioning of firms. These changes and adaptations, however, tend to reflect activities of the powerful business groups connected to the government, not to permit the incorporation of citizens with equal rights into the process of law and justice.

That is why the constant amendment of commercial codes by Latin American countries since the nineteenth century, with Argentina and Brazil registering the greatest number of changes since 1850, has not necessarily benefited the population at large. Since legal codes made by politicians and not court decisions based on merit determine law and justice in Latin America, the modernization of the system means only the modernization of the legal codes. But those legal codes and the courts that enforce them are themselves part and parcel of the wider reality of countries where power and influence determine what is right. At any given time, there are typically hundreds of thousands and even millions of cases pending beyond reasonable periods of time in Latin American courts, and almost all of them involve people who command little influence and small businesses that do not have government contracts and do not employ powerful lobbies. Just as economic reform was conditioned by corporatism, state mercantilism, privilege, wealth transfer, and political law—the very system that produced the evils it was supposed to cure—the tiny judicial reform has tended to mirror the system that created the problems it was meant to solve.

The fact that judicial institutions serve the rich and powerful much better than the rest of the population does not mean that formal businesses enjoy all the guarantees they would like. A survey of U.S.

firms in the chemical and pharmaceutical industries conducted in the mid-1990s found that half of U.S. firms considered Argentina's intellectual property protection too weak to warrant the transfer of the latest technology to that country; 55 percent of them had the same opinion about Colombia, 51 percent about Venezuela, 45 percent about Mexico, and 42 percent even about Chile. Piracy becomes, in this case, an ironic form of revenge by those who lack any legal protection against those benefiting from greater protection of their property but who are nonetheless exposed to the pervasive precariousness and corruption of the law in society at large.

Three factors stemming from the failed reforms of the last decade, then, have strengthened corruption: the expansion of opportunity for public officials, the further weakening of civil society and the absence of a judicial system worthy of that name.

PART IV

Turning the Tide

10

Liberty for Latin America

Development cannot be decreed or legislated. Yet all underdeveloped countries are governed, whether by socialists, conservatives, or utilitarian liberals, as if it could be. It can therefore be said that turning the tide involves, first and foremost, the political class coming to terms with the impotence of those who hold the monopoly of coercion to force prosperity on the real world. No law or decree designed to encourage production or distribute wealth is able to turn a poor country into a prosperous one. Napoleon is said to have remarked that it was vanity that made the French Revolution, everything else being a pretext. The concept could be extended to the role of government in contemporary—or historic—Latin America. Accepting the impotence of coercion in the field of human betterment will therefore be an act of extreme political humility. The institutions of civilization have resulted from a long evolutionary process, not deliberate design.

If the function of government is approached from this standpoint, does it mean those in charge should simply stand aside and watch? No. Since any incoming administration inherits a heavy legacy of coercive laws and norms that constitute the accumulated vanities of previous administrations and legislatures, it cannot sit idle. That legacy in Latin America actually translates into hundreds of thousands of rules that govern not just the economy but also the lives of people in each country, together with the bureaucracy that enforces them and a dependency on government support on the part of those who live in extreme poverty. Those rules are the lifeline of the corporatist, state-mercantilist, privilege-driven, wealth-transferring, political law–based state. But that is not all that any new administration inherits from its predecessors. It also inherits an underdeveloped society that functions under those rules, however it chooses to respond to them, including disobedience and the use of parallel, spontaneous rules.

If government cannot legislate progress but presides, by legacy, over a sea of coercive norms and a society that lives or survives under those norms, what can it do? It can do many things, bearing in mind that reform ultimately involves undoing more than doing. Had the statist system never come into being, any factional demand on the government not met by the authorities would entail only a frustrated expectation. But the given situation is more sensitive, in that reform will remove ongoing commitments made long ago by the authorities, thus affecting, in the short run, existing beneficiaries, not just expectations.

The acts of reform fall into one of four categories. The first two, cleansing the law and sanctifying the choices of the poor, are two sides of the same coin. The third, empowering the justice system, is a natural consequence of the previous two. The last, providing a gentle and secure transition for those who currently depend on the government for their subsistence or for services such as health and education, is the only humane response to the given situation.

Cleansing the Law, Sanctifying the Choices of the Poor

The first mission requires subjecting the whole body of laws and norms to a painstaking scrutiny that judges each one by the same standard. The standard is set by five questions: Does it relate to individuals in general or to corporations? Does it make success or failure dependent on state interference? Does it favor particular groups of people, and does it therefore discriminate against the rest? Does it transfer wealth from one group of citizens to another? Does its coercive power, either to make something happen or to forbid, derive from political law—that is, from the authority of the politicians or bureaucrats who passed the norms—or, rather, from a higher principle of which those politicians were careful guardians?

The second mission (which is really the other side of the same coin) amounts to an act of learning. The government engages in an equally diligent scrutiny of the way people have responded to those norms and laws in the conduct of their everyday business. The gap between the law and real life, and therefore between the objectives the government originally set out to realize and the way society deviated from them, is a source of great inspiration. This holds true both in cases in which the people ignored the laws and norms, and in cases in which coercion was able to impose itself, because even when government is able to force compliance with its commands, it cannot prevent the ultimate outcome of a regulation from deviating from the original intention. What is the purpose of this highly complex procedure by which the government observes the myriad ways people conduct business and lead their lives? Quite simply to learn from it and, except where criminal behavior is involved, make sure that no law or norm contradicts what people do in real life, with the purpose of sanctifying the uses, customs, and choices of ordinary citizens.

The two procedures, cleansing the law and sanctifying choice, are intimately connected. If you purge government coercion of corporatism, state mercantilism, privilege, wealth transfer, and political law, you end up liberating society in such a way that most of the choices of ordinary people, which government does not seek to anticipate or determine, automatically become legitimate. Conversely, if you set out only to study how people violate the law in order to start a business, sell or buy a product or a service, exercise the ownership of a home, adjudicate a dispute, organize in order to share the costs of common objectives and develop a community, and you then sanction those actions, you end up with a set of norms that largely amount to expurgating the existing law of statism.

The double procedure, however, is necessary because human imperfection and the accumulation of inadequate coercion mean that those who set out to cleanse the existing law can still end up with a set of institutions that hinder or contradict the conduct of real people. Grounding the process of political hygiene, the legal cleansing, in the choices and interactions of people in real life acts as a safeguard.

This process will set the individual free. In every area—from monetary to fiscal, tax, trade, financial, investment, labor, or any other policy—the result will be liberating the Latin American citizen from authoritarianism.

Citizens will not be exploited by a monetary policy that debases money through the artificial expansion of credit or devaluation, or by unduly high interest and exchange rates that raise costs and make products more expensive abroad. Nor will citizens be forced to trust one, and only one, particular banknote issuer.

Citizens will not face competition from any entity owned, subsidized, or protected by government in any sort of productive or commercial activity.

Citizens will not be taxed simultaneously as producers, savers, investors, and consumers, or punished for creating more wealth than others. (Sales taxes are currently the only significant sources of fiscal revenue; it would make sense to concentrate taxation at that end of things during the transition to the free society, abolishing income, corporate, and capital gains taxation. A low sales tax grounds taxation in a measure of personal choice, a healthier way of going about the process of expropriation that is signified by taxation.)

Citizens will not be forced to pay more than is necessary for the goods and services they buy because of direct or indirect tariffs, nor will anything be taken away from them to encourage their neighbors' exports or to pay a penalty for wanting to export something themselves.

They will not be robbed in order to reward irresponsible bankers for the losses incurred by a financial institution through credit given to government cronies, nor will they be constrained by any law as seekers of credit or as investors who want to move money into or out of the country. They will not face restrictions as providers of financial services, such as having to place reserves in the central bank or suffering the consequences of open market operations aimed at influencing rates, being constrained from setting interest rates according to choice or having to comply with forced, ever-changing levels of fractional reserves.

They will not suffer expropriation in order to subsidize the investments of others, nor will they face barriers to entry, subtle or unsubtle, in any legal activity whatsoever, or impediments to obtaining and freely disposing of profits. Those who already participate in agriculture, industry, commerce, and any service activity, including the utilities, education, and all other sensitive areas, will not be able to stop them, by any direct or indirect legal mandate originating in the political system, from entering or exiting the field if they wish in order to compete with existing producers in the pursuit of consumer interest or to bow out. Likewise, professional associations will not usurp the role of the courts by preventing people, with the use of political norms and laws, from engaging in any profession.

Money will not be stolen from people in order to support organized labor against their wishes, and the people will be able to determine wages and other employment benefits through direct private contract with employers should they wish to.

These are a few examples of how purging current law of its exploitative soul, and heeding the instincts of ordinary citizens as they have shaped response to coercion in daily life, will empower the individual. It will not do away with compassion and enthrone egotism, or destroy community and open the doors to a Darwinist struggle for survival. It will eliminate the perverse effect of authority on the free association and exchange among ordinary people of a mostly peaceful, sensible, and hardworking disposition. They will exercise compassion and enhance their community because it is apparently part of human nature to do so and because the type of environment that results from such social inclinations is the best guarantee of individual and family-based success. History has repeatedly proved that the more free people are, the more responsibly they act. Nothing builds moral character better than liberty. Human flaws will still exist in a free society, but the transformation of the law will make sure the better instincts of people find reward and put up a much better fight than they do today against the darker ones.

The legal system affects conduct through incentives and disincentives that come from coercion and reward, but also through its influence on individuals' perceptions and evaluations of themselves. In that way, sustained institutional frameworks guaranteeing freedom can engender a cultural evolution toward those values that today seem to distance Latin Americans from free-market capitalism.

The repeal of thousands of laws and norms, as well as the transformation of the very nature of the law, will lower what economists call transaction costs and offer a sense of security beyond anything Latin American citizens have witnessed. I am skeptical of figures that anticipate the infinite choices of free individuals, but there is no question that liberty will beget prosperity. There are those who say, for instance, that a flat income tax of 10 percent (something I am not advocating) would increase tax revenue by 4 percent of GDP and, taking into account the fact that much of the underground economy would turn legal, perhaps by even 7 percent. There are those who maintain that, with the end of the system that forces millions of people to do business illegally, Peru could see the size of its economy grow by more than 50 percent. These figures sound perfectly reasonable, as would any others that prognosticate a huge increase in the amount of wealth created after the liberation of Latin America. The effect of taking corporatism, state mercantilism, privilege, wealth transfer, and political law out of the legal system would be the immediate end of second-class citizenship, the condition shared by millions of Latin Americans. And, clearly, if the cost of doing business legally was reduced so that incorporating a business involved two procedures, two working days, and negligible costs, as is the case in Canada, as opposed to forty procedures, eighty-two working days, and more than two and a half times the per capita rate of GDP, as is the case in Bolivia, friendly transaction costs and increased security would expand wealth beyond the imagination even of enthusiastic economists who like to anticipate figures. The liberation of the British from the restrictive corn laws in the mid-nineteenth century turned that country into an economic powerhouse. There is no telling what wonders the liberation of Latin Americans from a million corn laws would do.

Empowering the Justice System

The suggested reforms have no meaning without a healthy justice system. In Latin America, there is no justice system. There is an authoritarian political system and the courts are its instruments. In the cases in which no corruption or politically motivated persecution is involved and people are actually able to access the courts, what passes for a justice system is an institution that simply applies the body of laws, norms, and regulations—several hundred thousand in each country—produced by the political system. The courts function as the agencies of the government and of those who have power.

In order for reform of the political system to take place, a justice system needs to come into being. Since the essence of the reform means, to a large extent, displacing the law from the political sphere in order to restore rights and liberties, the courts of justice need to become the new hosts of the legal process. Their function will not be, of course, to produce laws the way politicians have done before. That would simply turn the courts of justice into the old government. The justice system will adjudicate disputes based on those principles of law that, divorced from the political system, have become inalienable guarantees of the liberty of the people. Those principles will have to be clearly spelled out in some form of constitution, at least until such time when the natural course of society makes it irrelevant, if it ever does. Even though common law is a much better tradition than legal codes, it is still possible to envision a situation in which simple and clear codes give written guidelines to judges, as long as they do not in any way deviate from the constitutional principles of liberty.

An essential reason why "capitalist" reform failed is that it attacked the size of the state—the symptom—without attacking the role of the government as the source of the rules governing the economy and life in general, with the result that the size actually increased. Better results would have taken place and liberal capitalism would have made greater gains, even had no assets been privatized, if the government's attitude to rule making had been fundamentally transformed. With real reforms, norms will be much more legitimate and their authority greater. Under a system in which no government limits the freedom of the people but in which, through the courts of justice, it protects every single citizen's life, property, and right to conduct business as he or she pleases, the crisis of legitimacy suffered by the Latin American state in the nineteenth and twentieth centuries is unthinkable. Liberal reform is about removing from the sphere of the state the very causes of its illegitimacy. What could be less compassionate than a government that invades a person's liberty and uses the courts to apply the very laws those courts should be forestalling in order to uphold individual rights—which, after all, is their proper mission?

The courts will not automatically produce impeccable results. The current judges are not trained well enough to understand every possible issue and conflict arising out of the modern economy. By placing severe restrictions on power and therefore also on the discretion of the judges, who are ultimately bound by the principles of individual rights, the ground is laid for better-functioning courts. Everything else, including adjustment to technological advances and modern complexities, will flow from the very flexibility and openness of a system that will no longer be subjected to political law and will be closer to the people.

During the transition and for years to come, there is no doubt that those who used the political system to obtain favors and exclude others from activities they sought to control will attempt to make courts the vehicles of their interests. But, since the courts will no longer be subject to political law and will therefore be empowered to perform their proper function, the incentives to comply with special interests will be far smaller. At the same time, a much more vibrant, active, and vigilant civil society, emboldened by its new freedom, will have more weapons at its disposal in order to denounce those attempts. It will for the first time have the law on its side. Special interests will not disappear, but the power of the justice system will generally have the means to resist them.

As in the cleansing of the law, the transformation of the courts will need to pay close attention to the way ordinary people have been conducting their business. Since justice will not be imposed on litigants but will emerge from their cases according to principles instead of political laws and norms, it makes sense to sanctify the myriad ways the poor, excluded from the judicial network, have organized in order to set up alternate methods of dispute resolution. Justices of the peace, arbitrators, and other adjudicators of disputes at the grassroots level, such as those existing in the Indian communities of the Andes, should be encouraged and protected by the new arrangements.

A Gentle Landing for Those Aboard

It is a fact that, through the type of arrangements that have prevailed in Latin America, many people have come to rely on the government for the satisfaction of basic needs. Millions depend on various forms of welfare assistance simply to survive and, more extensively, a major segment of the population has come to depend on the government for access to health care and education. This state of affairs is in great part created, decade after decade, by the absence of liberty and the transfer of individual responsibility to the heart of government. The challenge for liberal reform is to reconcile the objective of making the state retreat with the survival of that part of the population that already depends on the government for basic needs such as food and shelter, as well as for health and education, two services regarded as vital if not necessarily involving immediate life-and-death situations for the majority.

Strictly speaking, the purging of every form of corporatism, state mercantilism, privilege, wealth transfer, and political law from the entire body of official norms will do away with these government provisions, since everything that does not involve national defense, law enforcement, and the administration of justice easily falls under the rubric of predation. What is Latin America to do?

In the long run, liberty will give people the means to survive and access to health care and education, which, rid of government intervention and subject to the power of consumers, will be provided at low cost (as happens in many developed countries, private corporations will, for instance, find it natural to attract employees and retain the loyalty of those already employed by offering health insurance benefits to which they will be asked to provide modest contributions). Charity will move from the heart of government to the heart of individuals, and mainstream society will care for the destitute through private institutions, more lovingly than any government ever has. But, while the transition expands opportunity and devolves a sense of responsibility to each individual (there will be a time when not devoting a chunk of personal income to the education of one's children and to medical bills will be inconceivable), what kind of landing are we to offer those passengers who happen to be on the failing plane?

Three principles must be upheld. The government cannot provide any of the services involved, only the means to access them. The government must focus the subsidies, either through tax credits, vouchers, cash, or loans, strictly on those who are not in any way able to pay. Last, a careful timetable for a gradual phasing out of these subsidies will be established, even if extended over a long period of time—the timetable will be adjusted to reflect the conditions of the beneficiaries but will in no case function under the principle of permanent entitlement. The gradual reduction of the subsidies will permit even further lowering of sales taxes that will provide the government revenue during the transition.

The transition from dependency to independence can quickly start to empower those citizens relying on the government for satisfaction of their essential needs. Citizen vesting in the ownership of assets currently controlled by the state—first and foremost a matter of justice—will spread property and capital, and create incentives for productive management (regulatory agencies, of course, will be abolished). Since the assets need to be handed back to civil society, there is no choice but to transfer them to someone. Because the workers and managers have already mixed their labor with the resources that are to be privatized, and because privatization—a government action—might, in the short run, affect those who depend on a government job, it is only fair to transfer fractional shares to them. The new owners will be able to dispose of those shares as they see fit. This process will include the transfer of ownership of public schools and health centers to teachers and doctors, and of public television networks to cultural workers currently employed in that area. Since citizens not directly employed by the state are by virtue of the statist system dependent on the government for sheer survival, it would also make sense to extend ownership of some of the privatized assets to those in extreme poverty (who would join the current workers and managers as new shareholders). The principle here would be that of compensatory justice for a situation that is clearly a legacy of statism. Unlike all other people affected by statism, the very poor depend not partially but totally on government handouts. That wholesale dependence creates a philosophical opportunity for including them among the beneficiaries of the transfers. Extending ownership beyond that, to society at large, might result in so many shares and types of shares as to make the system impossible. There is, undoubtedly, a philosophical case to be made for that too, but my proposal would draw the line at workers, managers, and the very poor who currently depend on the government for sustenance.

Worker participation in the ownership of companies in which they work has enhanced overall performance in the United States, where one-fifth of employees own shares in the firms that employ them. A recent study indicates that productivity rises in the first year that a company opens share ownership to its workers and that the company continues to boast higher productivity than other firms in later years. Employee participation in the ownership of American companies dates back to Thomas Jefferson's administration. Albert Gallatin, Jefferson's secretary of the treasury, said, "The democratic principle upon which this nation was founded should not be restricted to the political processes but should be applied to the industrial operation." In Latin America, the privatization of state companies that are still under government control through wide employee share-ownership schemes would not only encourage participation in the economic process and benefit productivity. In the immediate run, it would help the transition by turning the uncertainties regarding job stability once the companies become private into opportunities and incentives. Nothing builds the kind of moral character necessary for a free, responsible society better than seeing its positive workings early on. But there is another reason why the transit to a free society will be aided by the spread of ownership. The process will strengthen the citizens' capacity to resist future encroachments on liberty by political representatives. Since authorities are always a danger to people's freedoms, property can give citizens a weapon to protect their space. Isabel Paterson alluded to this idea in *The God of the Machine*: "If the representative takes office simply on a formal expression of opinion, or signal, it is thought he must be amenable to subsequent opinion in like form. On the contrary, since the representative is permitted to release *real physical energy*, no further signal will be obeyed *unless the voters retain in their private control a corresponding but preponderant power of resistance to any misapplication of the power delegated to their representatives*."

The granting of legal status—a direct consequence of ending the costly and discriminatory legal system—to the multitude of shantytown community associations, many of which are family based, will gradually allow them to access credit or charity donations at home and abroad, lessening dependency and enhancing responsibility. But there is a way the government can help accelerate the process of becoming less indispensable to the poor: by allowing the organizations that now function exclusively as channels of state subsidies to turn into corporations. Since the few remaining subsidies will now come in the form not of products or services but of money, these organizations, intermediate bodies between the individual and the mighty state, will acquire total autonomy from government bureaucrats, gradually being able to raise funds from private sources and engage in productive activities. Many of them have strong decentralized networks of social workers at the grassroots level, through which food and other basic supplies are currently distributed. In each local area, groups of families, mostly headed by women, are in charge. The gradual transition from dependency to responsibility—from an unethical to an ethical society—will be eased by the transition of passive subsidy-distributing networks into productive corporations.

The spread of ownership and the transformation of the legal nature of subsidy-distributing channels will, then, be two ways that the government, in the very process of divesting itself of its previous role, will facilitate civil society's expansion.

What about health care and education? Is there any way the government can ease the transition from the dependency culture to the culture of responsibility? Tax-supported compulsory schooling was not standard in the northern states of the United States until the last decade before the Civil War. The system was not imported in the South until after that conflict. In Latin America, not until the end of the nineteenth century did public education embrace large sections of the population. Instead of becoming a tool of development, it has sustained underdevelopment despite enjoying more public funding in relative terms than in other parts of the world (in early times it did help reduce illiteracy). The gap between Latin America and other developing regions has increased over the last three decades to the extent that its citizens on average have two fewer years of schooling than what would be expected given the region's per capita income, a standard well below that of Asia and similar to that of sub-Saharan Africa. Only a small proportion of the population completes secondary or higher education, and universities are divorced from the productive life of business and do not contribute to technological research of any kind. Between 30 and 40 percent of public funding is concentrated at the university level, a form of bottom-to-top wealth distribution since those who pursue higher education are the elite class. The relatively few skilled workers earn much more than the rest, making the educational system a vehicle for the inequality it is supposed to correct. Problems in elementary education are compounded, of course, by health and nutrition problems. These in turn are part of the wider problem of inadequate public health, which, like education, absorbs between 3 and 4 percent of GDP in each country, by no means a smaller proportion than in the better-performing developing nations.

The transition to a free society requires that the government cease to provide education and instead, following Milton Friedman's formula, provide funding to parents so that their children have access to the institutions currently reserved for a small minority. Provided the government does not stifle competition, costs and fees will not be high in the private sector. Provided the government does not limit initiative by exercising a dictatorship over the curriculum, schools will offer a better education. Provided the government does not establish barriers between learning and business, education will be firmly grounded in the productive life of society, and the institutions of learning will become engines of scientific and technological advancement (as is, for instance, Mexico's Instituto Technológico de Monterrey, a notable exception in the region).

Various countries have slowly moved toward subsidizing the people directly rather than providing health care and education. The result is increased choices available. Peter Bauer has correctly stated, "I regard the extension of the range of choice, that is, an increase in the range of effective alternatives open to the people, as the principal objective and criterion of economic development." New Zealand separated the purchasing from the provision of health care services by setting up four regional authorities that use state funds to buy health care services from private providers that are free to bid for contracts. In education, fees were introduced at the university level, and government-guaranteed loans to be repaid through the tax system were made available to cover tuition costs and living expenses. In Chile, a kind of voucher system has been in place for some years, resulting in around 45 percent of students attending private school (the figure includes the almost 10 percent who pay fees out of their own pockets), while 55 percent attend public schools run by local governments. Gradually, schools have asked beneficiaries of the voucher program for additional fees. Because reform has not gone far enough (the national government, among other things, still controls the curriculum), mathematics and science surveys for thirteen-year-olds show that Chile is still behind poorer countries such as Tunisia and Indonesia, although it is doing better than other Latin American nations, where very little, if any, reform has taken place (there has been limited reform in Nicaragua, and a pilot voucher program was introduced in one Colombian province). Chile's government has also gradually moved from providing health services to allowing individuals to opt out of the public program and use their earnings to buy private insurance. More than one-third of workers have moved to the private system.

These reforms do not constitute a comprehensive transition to a system in which the government only provides funds directly to the beneficiaries so that they can access the much-better-run private institutions, in an environment in which the absence of political bias allows many more organizations to offer them education and health services at truly competitive prices, substantially raising their quality of life.

The transition itself, as we saw in the case of extreme poverty, will generate mediating institutions that strengthen the social fiber and open the doors to fruitful, healthy cooperation by individuals.

Parents' associations already exist in many countries to raise money to buy anything from pencils to concrete or bricks. With access to legal incorporation, they will be able to involve themselves in their children's education through mechanisms that make teachers more accountable and even participate in efforts to provide private education.

Since legal discrimination will cease and Protestant churches, lay associations, and other faith-based organizations will be placed on an equal footing with Catholicism, all sorts of religious groups closely linked to grassroots communities will be able to play a part in the education and even the preventive health care of the people.

Since taxation will be transformed and capital will be liberated from many constraints, private patronage will surface, as it has done in all societies in which the government did not discourage it. Education will be a direct beneficiary. Other, indirect ways will also contribute to the cultivation of individuals. Once able to join the legal system, artisan associations and other neighborhood-based cultural groups will be able to compete for private funds.

Since discrimination against all types of education will disappear, home-based schooling will be another option for learning, involving the family more closely and, through the getting together of various families, even neighborhoods.

New universities, institutes of technology, and technical colleges will no longer be at a disadvantage because of official protection of long-established centers. As a result, better institutions of higher education will be available and competition will reduce costs.

All sorts of sports associations will enjoy access to legal status and be on an equal footing with sports institutions previously considered "official," and with other kinds of organizations. Access to private funds will be increased as hindrances such as double or triple taxation are removed from private capital and money becomes more available.

Liberty for Latin America

The British statesman Edmund Burke defined the American Revolution as "a revolution not made, but prevented." The modern idea of revolution—born in the eighteenth century—involves the violent overturning of the established order and the emergence of an all-powerful central authority. The old idea, in a more literal sense, evoked the image of the wheel gyrating toward its original position, of things being restored to their proper place. By restoring liberty, the rightful condition of the individual, the American heroes undertook the latter form of revolution—and thus, in Burke's insightful description, prevented the former.

The history of Latin America is replete with violence against the individual, a recurrent revolution of the wrong kind. The many symptoms of individual sovereignty sparkling in the thick night of oppression indicate that such is not the natural, voluntary fate of Latin Americans. The recurrence, generation after generation, of the five principles of oppression, however, has ingrained in the minds of many people certain presuppositions that conspire against their own liberation. There is such a thing as an inertia of oppression. The idea that certain things cannot be different, that blame for the harm brought about by certain institutions is attributable to particular individuals in charge of them and not to the very nature of those institutions, needs to be dispelled.

It is about time, then, for the wheel to turn to that original position that never actually existed in the recorded history of the region but that from time immemorial has seemed to be the common longing—a sort of nostalgia—of those who do their best, so far with painful results, to survive and defeat the adversities that power throws in their way. It is, in fact, not a purely Latin American longing. Every nation that has liberated itself from servitude seems to have responded to its newly found freedom with the familiar resolve of individuals who, though not accustomed to it in practice because of ancient traditions of oppression, have never ceased, in their gut instincts, to strive for a condition they know to be right. To be sure, equally powerful instincts of violence against liberty inhabit human society, and therefore, once conquered, freedom is a permanent revolution of the restoring kind, never a foregone conclusion.

My hope is that one of these days, by making the right kind of revolution, Latin America will prevent the umpteenth revolution of the wrong kind. And then, challenged by the enemies of liberty, who will never cease to be active, it will begin what promises to be an enthralling history of permanent revolution, turning the wheel of the individual to its rightful place.

Appendix

AVERAGE ANNUAL REAL PER CAPITA GDP GROWTH IN LATIN AMERICA

Country	*2000–2003*	*2004 (est.)*
Argentina	−3.9	2.8
Bolivia	0.1	2.1
Brazil	0.8	1.8
Chile	1.9	3.2
Colombia	0.3	1.7
Costa Rica	0.2	0.7
Dominican Republic	0.9	−1.0
Ecuador	1.7	3.2
Guatemala	0.0	0.9
Honduras	0.5	0.0
Mexico	0.7	1.9
Nicaragua	0.0	1.0
Panama	0.2	1.3
Peru	1.5	2.4
Uruguay	−4.8	3.9
Venezuela	−6.9	5.6

Source: International Monetary Fund.

ECONOMIC GROWTH IN LATIN AMERICA

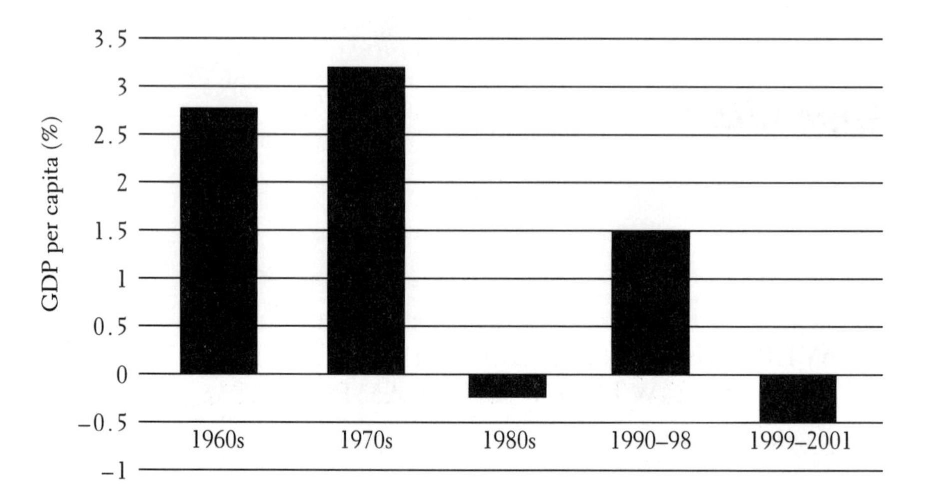

Sources: World Bank; Economic Commission for Latin America and the Caribbean (ECLAC).

SIZE OF GOVERNMENT 2000–2001

Country	*1*	2	3	4	5	6	7	8
Argentina	7,933	17%	5.9%	15.9%	15.3%	18.7%	17%	22.2%
Bolivia	952	15.8%	33.8%	18.2%	10.7%	9.9%	8%	42.6%
Brazil	4,624	24.9%	17.1%	20.5%	19.2%	—	—	23%
Chile	5,354	16.5%	28.2%	23.4%	24.5%	22.9%	18.4%	62.6%
Colombia	2,290	27.1%	40.2%	12.2%	13.7%	—	—	42.3%
Costa Rica	3,912	22.9%	23.2%	17.1%	19.3%	14.5%	13%	94.3%
Dominican Republic	2,062	10.9%	24.8%	23.7%	14.2%	—	—	69.1%
Ecuador	1,425	13.3%	18.1%	16.8%	28.4%	—	—	73.2%
El Salvador	1,752	10.4%	23.4%	17%	1.8%	24.2%	20.1%	70.3%
Guatemala	1,558	8.4%	16.4%	16.8%	8.9%	—	—	47.9%
Honduras	711	16.1%	—	35%	21%	—	—	98.7%
Mexico	3,819	14.2%	10.5%	23.3%	21.5%	—	—	64.6%
Nicaragua	466	17.1%	48.3%	34.4%	–6.6%	14.1%	12.8%	121.3%
Panama	3,279	22.1%	17.1%	30.2%	24.4%	—	—	72.1%
Paraguay	1,700	9.2%	35.7%	22.1%	7%	—	—	55.6%
Peru	2,368	13.4%	20.8%	20.1%	18.2%	24.7%	20.1%	33.8%
Uruguay	6,115	15.3%	23%	13.9%	12.5%	16.9%	15%	40%
Venezuela	3,300	10%	42.4%	17.5%	29.9%	42.9%	27.8%	46.4%

1. GDP per capita (constant 1995 US$)
2. General government consumption as share of total consumption
3. Government enterprises and investment as a share of gross investment
4. Gross capital formation (% of GDP)
5. Gross domestic savings (% of GDP)
6. Taxes on income, profits, and capital gains (% of total taxes)
7. Taxes on income, profits, and capital gains (% of current revenue)
8. Trade (% of GDP)

Sources: World Bank; Fraser Institute, *Economic Freedom of the World: 2003 Annual Report.*

TRADE

MEAN TARIFF RATE, 2001

Country	*Rate(%)*
Argentina	12.6
Bolivia	9.5
Brazil	14.4
Chile	8.0
Colombia	12.8
Costa Rica	5.4
Dominican Republic	9.0
Ecuador	12.8
El Salvador	7.4
Guatemala	7.2
Honduras	7.9
Mexico	16.2
Nicaragua	3.2
Panama	9.5
Paraguay	10.9
Peru	13.0
Uruguay	11.1
Venezuela	7.5

Source: Fraser Institute, *Economic Freedom of the World: 2003 Annual Report.*

REGULATIONS
2001

Country	*Hiring and firing practices*	*Starting a new business*	*Time with government bureaucracy*
Argentina	2.4	2.7	5.0
Bolivia	3.8	2.8	4.3
Brazil	5.5	4.6	6.3
Chile	3.2	4.9	6.3
Colombia	2.9	3.4	6.0
Costa Rica	5.5	4.0	5.3
Dominican Republic	4.6	4.8	5.8
Ecuador	2.9	2.9	5.5
El Salvador	6.4	5.2	7.0
Guatemala	4.6	3.8	4.8
Honduras	3.3	2.0	5.5
Mexico	3.1	3.0	4.3
Nicaragua	5.9	4.0	7.0
Panama	2.5	4.9	6.0
Paraguay	2.2	4.2	6.0
Peru	4.9	2.9	5.8
Uruguay	2.7	3.5	5.8
Venezuela	3.2	3.0	5.3

Source: Fraser Institute, *Economic Freedom of the World: 2003 Annual Report*. The figures rate the regulatory environments on a scale of 1 (least free) to 10 (most free).

LEGAL SYSTEMS
2001

Country	*Judiciary independence*	*Impartial courts*
Argentina	1.0	1.4
Bolivia	1.4	2.1
Brazil	5.3	4.6
Chile	5.4	5.4
Colombia	3.9	4.0
Costa Rica	5.9	5.5
Dominican Republic	3.8	3.3
Ecuador	1.0	1.3
El Salvador	3.3	3.9
Guatemala	1.7	1.9
Honduras	1.7	2.0
Mexico	3.0	3.4
Nicaragua	1.5	2.2
Panama	2.5	3.2
Paraguay	1.7	1.9
Peru	2.2	3.0
Uruguay	7.1	5.2
Venezuela	0.5	0.9

Source: Fraser Institute, *Economic Freedom of the World: 2003 Annual Report*. The figures rate the legal systems on a scale of 1 (least independent and impartial) to 10 (most independent and impartial).

ECONOMIC GROWTH
1990s

Country	*GDP per capita growth (annual average compound)*	*Capital formation growth (annual average compound)*
Argentina	4.6%	2.5%
Bolivia	1.8%	3.3%
Brazil	0.1%	2.6%
Chile	6.1%	6.8%
Colombia	1.9%	3.8%
Costa Rica	1.4%	4.6%
Mexico	1.2%	2.4%
Peru	2.8%	2.9%

Source: André A. Hofman / Economic Commission for Latin America and the Caribbean (ECLAC).

PRODUCTIVITY
1990s

Country	*Capital productivity growth (annual average compound)*	*Labor productivity growth (annual average compound)*
Argentina	2.7%	4.3%
Bolivia	1%	0.8%
Brazil	–0.7%	0.4%
Chile	0.9%	4.8%
Colombia	–0.2%	1.6%
Costa Rica	–0.6%	0.9%
Mexico	0.7%	0%
Peru	1.7%	1.6%

Source: André A. Hofman / Economic Commission for Latin America and the Caribbean (ECLAC).

REGULATION OF ENTRY

Country	*Number of procedures for start-up companies to be allowed to operate legally*	*Time in business days for start-ups to be allowed to operate legally*	*Cost for start-ups to be allowed to operate legally as % of GDP per capita (1997 data)*
Argentina	24	71	23%
Bolivia	40	82	260%
Brazil	30	67	67%
Chile	24	78	11%
Colombia	34	55	12%
Ecuador	24	141	15%
Mexico	30	112	57%
Panama	14	14	31%
Peru	28	171	21%
Uruguay	18	105	5.5%
Venezuela	30	124	11%

Source: Simon Djankov, Rafael La Porta, Florencio López de Silanes, and Andrei Schleifer, Harvard Institute of Economic Research.

SIZE OF THE INFORMAL ECONOMY 2000

Country	*Informal economy as % of GDP*	*Informal economy (current US$ in billions)*	*Informal economy GDP per capita*
Argentina	25.4	704.7	1894.8
Bolivia	67.1	54.1	664.3
Brazil	39.8	2267.7	1424.8
Chile	19.8	134.9	908.8
Colombia	39.1	308.3	789.8
Costa Rica	26.2	38.3	998.2
Dominican Republic	32.1	59.8	683.7
Ecuador	34.4	42.6	416.2
Guatemala	51.5	96.5	865.2
Honduras	49.6	28.7	426.6
Mexico	30.1	1684.9	1526.1
Nicaragua	45.2	9.5	180.8
Panama	64.1	60.1	2089.7
Peru	59.9	311	1245.9
Uruguay	51.1	99	3066
Venezuela	33.6	400	1448.2
Average	41.81	396.57	1166.19

Source: Friedrich Schneider, "Size and Measurement of the Informal Economy in 110 Countries Around the World."

Notes

Introduction

3 *A few years ago, Latin America was thought to be:* The term "Latin America" was coined by French sociologists in the nineteenth century. It is widely used, although in Spain "Iberoamerica" is more common.

3 *The sweeping reforms taking place from the Río Grande:* The expression "Washington Consensus" was coined in 1990 by economist John Williamson of the Institute for International Economics.

3 *Thus far, however, the shift to capitalism:* "*Se vogliamo che tutto rimanga com'è, bisogna che tutto cambi.*" Giuseppe Tomasi di Lampedusa, *Il Gattopardo* (Milan: Feltrinelli, 1960), p. 42. The English translation of the quote is mine. The English edition of the book gives a slightly different translation: "If we want things to stay as they are, things will have to change." *The Leopard* (New York: Pantheon Books, 1960).

4 *The year 2003 brought more stability to countries like Argentina:* The report by the Economic Commission for Latin America and the Caribbean (ECLAC) that refers to the "lost half-decade" is quoted in "Wanted: A New Regional Agenda for Economic Growth," *The Economist*, April 26, 2003, pp. 27–29.

6 *For them, development, if reforms:* The "culturalist" side, constituting a wide range of different viewpoints and even conflicting ideologies, includes Max Weber, Albert Nock, Edward Banfield, Lucian Pye, Lawrence E. Harrison, Francis Fukuyama, and Mariano Grondona, to name but a few. See Max Weber, *The Protestant Ethic and the Spirit of Capitalism* (New York: Scribner, 1958); Albert J. Nock, *Our Enemy, the State* (New York: William Morrow, 1935); Edward C. Banfield, *The Moral Basis of a Backward Society* (Chicago: Free Press, 1958); Lucian W. Pye, *Asian Power and Politics: The Cultural Dimensions of Authority* (Cambridge, MA: Harvard University Press, 1985); Lawrence E. Harrison, *Underdevelopment Is a State of Mind: The Latin American Case* (Lanham, MD: Madison Books, 2000); Francis Fukuyama, *Trust: Social Virtues and the Creation of Prosperity* (New York: Free Press, 1995); Mariano Grondona, *Las condiciones culturales del desarrollo económico: Hacia una teoría del desarrollo* (Buenos Aires: Ariel-Planeta, 1999).

6 *The institutions limiting freedom:* Like the "culturalists," the "institutionalists" comprise a very broad range of views and even conflicting ideologies. Peter Bauer, Robert Dahl, and Douglass North are some of them. See Peter T. Bauer and Basil

S. Yamey, *The Economics of Underdeveloped Countries* (Chicago: University of Chicago Press, 1957); Robert A. Dahl, *Polyarchy: Participation and Opposition* (New Haven, CT: Yale University Press, 1971); Douglass C. North, *Institutions, Institutional Change and Economic Development* (New York: Cambridge University Press, 1990).

6 *Institutionalists think, as John Waterbury has written:* Quoted in William Ratliff, "Development and Civil Society in Latin America and Asia," *Annals of the American Academy*, September 1999, p. 98. The quote is taken from John Waterbury, *Exposed to Innumerable Delusions: Public Enterprise and State Power in Egypt, India, Mexico and Turkey* (New York: Cambridge University Press, 1993).

6 *Likewise, culturalists think:* Daniel Etounga-Manguelle, "Does Africa Need a Cultural Adjustment Program," in *Culture Matters: How Values Shape Human Progress*, ed. Lawrence E. Harrison and Samuel P. Huntington (New York: Basic Books, 2000), p. 75.

6 *even for Tocqueville, "too much importance is attributed":* Alexis de Tocqueville, *Democracy in America* (New York: Alfred A. Knopf, 1994), p. 322.

7 *Looking at the world from the other side:* Throughout this book, I use the word "liberal," unless the context indicates otherwise, in its classical sense, referring to ideas of free trade and limited government.

Chapter 1: The Five Principles of Oppression

13 *If no other evidence were available:* Although Herbert Spencer analyzed the role of war in the formation of the state, Ludwig Gumplowicz and Franz Oppenheimer are credited with being the first to develop a theory of conquest and confiscation. See Herbert Spencer, *The Principles of Sociology* (New York: Appleton, 1896–97; Ludwig Gumplowicz, *La lutte des races sociales: Recherches sociologiques* (Paris: Guillaumin, 1893), translated from the German, *Der Rassenkampf: Sociologische Untersuchungen* (Innsbruck: Wagner'sche Univ. Buchhandlung, 1883); Franz Oppenheimer, *The State: Its History and Development Viewed Sociologically* (New York: Vanguard Press, 1926).

13 *They became in effect states capable:* See Robert L. Carneiro, "A Theory of the Origin of the State," in *The Politicization of Society*, ed. Kenneth S. Templeton, Jr. (Indianapolis: Liberty Press, 1979), pp. 37–51.

13 *Peaceful subsistence communities continued to exist:* Archaeologists have recently determined that the city of Caral, built as early as 2627 B.C. and located in the Supe River Valley of Peru, is the most ancient site in the Americas. It appears that it thrived on exchange and not on war, as the absence of weapons, mutilated remains, and battlements indicates. The inhabitants traded their cotton and fruit crops with fishing communities of the coast in return for food. See Ruth Shady Solís, Jonathan Haas, and Winifred Creamer, "Dating Caral: A Preceramic Site in the Supe Valley on the Central Coast of Peru," *Science* 292 (April 27, 2001): 723–26.

14 *Between the third and ninth centuries* A.D., *the Maya city-states:* The term "Incas" is derived from the word "Inca," which refers to the ruler of the Quechua peoples in the Valley of Cuzco area, but it has come to refer by extension to the entire civilization. The term "Aztecs" was coined after the conquest of Mexico. Before the con-

quest, the term "Nahua" would have been more appropriate, designating various groups, of which the Mexicas became the dominant one, in the Valley of Mexico. The Triple Alliance of the Mexica with the Aculhua and the Tepaneca made possible a formidable expansion that went beyond the valley on a large scale. Numerous alliances as well as subordinated tribes constituted what is known as the Aztec Empire, a less pervasive, less centrally controlled, and less "imperial" type of organization than that of the Incas.

16 *The* kuraka, *or local chief, was charged with enforcing the obligations:* John Murra, "Social, Structural and Economic Themes" and "On Inca Political Structure," in *Systems of Political Control and Bureaucracy in Human Societies*, ed. Vern F. Ray (Seattle: American Ethnological Society, 1958), p. 34.

16 *The Inca decided what public works were needed:* Luis E. Valcárcel, *Historia del Perú Antiguo*, 3 vols. (Lima: Editorial Juan Mejía Baca, 1964), 1: 44, 131, 555.

17 *Among the Aztecs, the nobles received rights:* Michael D. Coe and Rex Koontz, *Mexico: From the Olmecs to the Aztecs*, 5th ed. (New York: Thames & Hudson, 2002), p. 195.

17 *The law was an extension of the king:* Incidentally, under both the Aztecs and the Incas, the royal courts had a reputation for fairness, and homicide, theft, adultery, and drunkenness were severely punished.

17 *All five principles made the ancient Latin American state an instrument:* Franz Oppenheimer, *The State: Its History and Development Viewed Sociologically* (New York: Vanguard Press, 1926), pp. 12–13.

18 *In that world, rights and liberties were corporate:* Howard J. Wiarda, *The Soul of Latin America* (New Haven, CT: Yale University Press, 2001), pp. 61–64.

18 *Under the title of* fueros, *local kingdoms:* Clarence H. Haring highlights the contrasts between Castile and Aragon, the two kingdoms unified under Isabella and Ferdinand. Aragon had a more limited government and a greater tradition of individual rights. In Castile, the towns had enjoyed a measure of autonomy, subsequently ruined by wars between them and between them and the aristocracy, itself in permanent struggle with the Crown. Absolutism rose over that chaos to impose state order. See Clarence H. Haring, *The Spanish Empire in America* (New York: Harcourt, 1963), p. 2.

18 *At the close of the fifteenth century, the unified monarchy:* Since 1248, the Saracens had been confined to Granada. They were expelled from Spain altogether in 1492.

18 *The state began to appropriate:* Douglass North and Robert Paul Thomas, *The Rise of the Western World* (Cambridge: Cambridge University Press, 1973), p. 86.

19 *Society was geared toward the maintenance:* Clarence H. Haring, *The Spanish Empire in America* (New York: Oxford University Press, 1947), p. 6.

19 *Those rights limited private property and the possibility:* North and Thomas, *Rise of the Western World*, pp. 85–88.

20 *Such was the principle of state mercantilism in Iberia:* The voracity of the state, of course, only increased with the colonies of the New World. Despite huge remittances from European colonies such as the Low Countries and New World colonies such as Mexico and Peru, the Spanish monarchy was chronically underfunded. Clarence Haring argues that, because Spain had not developed the "economic type," it was unable to benefit from the wealth of the colonial empire, which

came to be a "liability." See Haring, *The Spanish Empire in America* (Oxford edition), pp. 28–29.

20 *The encomiendas, large grants of serf labor:* Robert G. Keith, "*Encomienda, Hacienda* and *Corregimiento* in Spanish America: A Structural Analysis," *Hispanic American Historical Review* 51, no. 3 (August 1971).

20 *As a result, price ceilings were set on wheat:* North and Thomas, *Rise of the Western World*, p. 130.

21 *The absolutist monarchy of unified Spain:* Kenneth L. Karst and Keith S. Rosenn, *Law and Development in Latin America: A Case Book* (Berkeley: University of California Press, 1975), p. 30.

21 *He had married the idea:* Adam Seligman, *The Idea of Civil Society* (Princeton, NJ: Princeton University Press, 1992), p. 19.

21 *Although many scholars defended the space:* The idea of natural law present in Aquinas's philosophy (influenced by Aristotelian thought) limited, however, the power of divine right. This doctrine was used by many Spanish theologians and jurists to question Spain's conquest of Mexico and Peru, and to demand a humane treatment of Indians. See Carl Watner, " 'All Mankind is One': The Libertarian Tradition in Sixteenth Century Spain," *Journal of Libertarian Studies* 8, no. 2 (Summer 1987).

21 *It is inaccurate to say that this awesome power:* Lewis Hanke states that the idea of natural law had been very much alive before the advent of absolutism and that, even when the divine nature of the king's rule was established, the philosophers and jurists of Spain held that the state was bound by certain laws of nature. See *Las teorías políticas de Bartolomé de Las Casas* (Buenos Aires: Talleres S.A. Casa J. Peuser, 1935), pp. 30–40.

21 *But the divine aura of the Crown:* Guillermo Lohmann Villena, *Ideas jurídico-políticas en la rebelión de Gonzalo Pizarro: La tramoya doctrinal del levantamiento contra las leyes nuevas en el Perú* (Valladolid. Seminario Americanista, Secretariado de Publicaciones de la Universidad, 1977), p. 29 (my translation).

21 *In theory, as in the sixteenth-century:* Bernice Hamilton defines natural law as understood by these writers to mean, broadly, that which is reasonable and at the same time generally accepted, as well as doing "unto others as you would they should do unto you." See *Political Thought in Sixteenth-Century Spain: A Study of the Political Ideas of Vitoria, De Soto, Suárez and Molina* (Oxford: Oxford University Press, 1963), pp. 11–15. It was not exactly the same as individual-based natural rights because there was still an emphasis on the idea of community, but it was close, since many of the implications of natural law as understood by these thinkers, including property, were based on the individual. Eventually, John Locke developed the philosophy of natural law, translating it into natural rights. See Murray N. Rothbard, *The Ethics of Liberty* (New York: New York University Press, 1998), pp. 21–24.

21–22 *In practice, since the king was the divine:* Juan de Mariana, a Jesuit, advocated the greatest limits on the authority of the ruler. For him, the king's power was superior to that of Parliament only in matters of war, foreign policy, and possibly justice. In contrast, Francisco Suárez thought that the ruler needed no consent from the community unless specified. See Hamilton, *Political Thought in Sixteenth-Century Spain*, pp. 41–42.

22 *The imposition of the Iberian mold on the pre-Columbian:* Disease was by far the most devastating effect of the Europeans' encounter with the American natives. Smallpox, measles, chicken pox, typhus, and other pandemics killed millions of Indians. See Alfred W. Crosby, "*Conquistador y Pestilencia:* The First New World Pandemic and the Fall of the Great Indian Empires," in *Readings in Latin American History, Vol. 1: The Formative Centuries*, ed. Peter J. Bakewell, John J. Johnson, and Meredith D. Dodge (Durham, NC: Duke University Press, 1985), pp. 35–49.

22 *In Mexico, for instance, land ejidos:* The Jesuits ran closed, totalitarian Indian preserves in Paraguay. Under a policy of *reducciones*, Peru's viceroy, Francisco de Toledo, uprooted thousands of villages and concentrated them in certain valleys, disrupting established ethnic, ecological, and political patterns. See John Murra, "Current Research and Prospects in Andean Ethnohistory," *Latin American Research Review* 5, no. 1 (Spring 1970): 9. For a comprehensive report of the viceroy's decrees, see *Francisco de Toledo: Disposiciones gubernativas para el virreinato del Perú* (Seville: Escuela de Estudios Hispano-Americanos, Consejo Superior de Investigación Científica, Monte de Piedad y Caja de Ahorros de Sevilla, 1986).

22 *In order to colonize certain areas:* Clark S. Knowlton, "Land-Grant Problems Among the State's Spanish-Americans," *New Mexico Business* (June 1967): p. 2.

22 *On the other side of the social spectrum:* Charles Gibson, *The Aztecs Under Spanish Rule: A History of the Indians of the Valley of Mexico, 1519–1810* (Stanford, CA: Stanford University Press, 1964), pp. 58–81.

23 *It received income from land rents:* John Lynch, *The Spanish American Revolutions, 1808–1826* (New York: Norton, 1973), p. 10.

23 *As the foremost corporation in the corporatist:* Wiarda, *The Soul of Latin America*, p. 133.

23 *Their presence was particularly:* Gibson, *The Aztecs Under Spanish Rule*, pp. 127–32.

23 *This is the reason why the state held:* In the eighteenth century, when the Bourbons replaced the Hapsburgs, the Jesuits were even expelled from the colonies.

23 *Spain's and Portugal's aim:* The patrimonial state really worked on the premise that the king was the "proprietor" of the colonies, which made him the personal dispenser of privileges in America.

24 *In the early period, Brazil:* William P. Glade, *The Latin American Economies: A Study of their Institutional Evolution* (New York: American Book, 1969), pp. 159–60.

24 *The political and economic organization:* Ibid., p. 156.

24 *Sugar was introduced, trade remained:* Werner Baer, *The Brazilian Economy: Growth and Development* (Westport, CT: Praeger, 1995), pp. 12–14.

24 *Local government, tied to large estates:* The period in which Portugal came under Spain's control, between 1580 and 1640, did see a greater measure of centralized administration.

24 *By then, trading monopolies were set up:* Small traders and the Jesuits reacted strongly, and an authoritarian crackdown ensued. Politics and the economy became more controlled than ever before in the colony. See A.J.R. Russell-Wood, "Preconditions and Precipitants of the Independence Movement in Portuguese America," in *From Colony to Nation: Essays on the Independence of Brazil*, ed. A.J.R. Russell-Wood (Baltimore: Johns Hopkins University Press, 1975), pp. 13–29;

Caio Prado Júnior, *História econômica do Brasil* (São Paulo: Editôra Brasiliense, 1967), p. 54.

24 *As a result of the dearth of free trade:* According to L. A. Clayton, in the first years of the eighteenth century, no more than 14.5 percent of the ships that departed from Callao, Peru, were destined for Panama, the viaduct for legitimate trade with Spain. See "Trade and Navigation in the Seventeenth-Century Viceroyalty of Peru," in Bakewell et al., *Readings in Latin American History*, p. 190.

25 *The only real market:* In the seventeenth century, when the Crown was in fiscal trouble, in order to obtain their salaries the colonial officers signed deals with merchant capitalists in exchange for supplying cash and equipment to the Indians so they would produce an export crop for the merchants to trade in. See Brian R. Hamnett, *Politics and Trade in Southern Mexico, 1750–1821* (Cambridge: Cambridge University Press, 1971), pp. 5–7.

25 *Local government and colonial bureaucratic:* The Crown even authorized such sales in Peru in 1633. Kenneth J. Andrien, "The Sale of Fiscal Offices and the Decline of Royal Authority in the Viceroyalty of Peru, 1633–1700," *Hispanic American Historical Review* 62, no. 1 (February 1982): 49–71.

25 *In the eighteenth century, when the French Bourbons:* Under the Bourbons, the laws barring foreigners from the colonies were relaxed, and some of the scientific advances of Europe were exported to the American territories.

25 *But the central command structure:* In the case of Brazil, more directives and regulations than ever flowed from Lisbon, under absolutist and centralizing policies. See Russell-Wood, "Preconditions and Precipitants of the Independence Movement," pp. 15–26.

25 *Intendencias, which replaced local government:* The representatives of royal authority in the colonies were, in ranking order, the viceroy, the *oidores* or judges who were part of the Audiencia, and the corregidores, who were local-level magistrates and district officers. There were also the cabildos, or local municipalities, the only ones in which Creoles were represented. Those removed from the main cities often included Indian chiefs or caciques. The intendencias, based on the French model, came into being in the eighteenth century and replaced the local-level *corregimientos* and *alcaldías mayores*.

25 *From a spiritual and an ideological point:* Wiarda, *The Soul of Latin America*, p. 108. John Lynch calls the eighteenth-century reforms "essentially an application of control" seeking to strengthen ties between the colonies and the metropolis at the expense of Creoles. Even the decision to allow Indians to refuse to work in the haciendas or to pay back debts not freely contracted was a move to weaken the power of Creoles and an assertion of imperial control. So was the expulsion of the Jesuits, the extension of a state tobacco monopoly, and the direct administration of the sales tax called *alcabala*. See *The Spanish American Revolutions*, pp. 2, 7–12.

25 *In exchange for political support:* For an account of the colonial economy, see Carlos Rodríguez Braun, *La cuestión colonial y la economía clásica* (Madrid: Alianza Editorial, 1989).

26 *For instance, large land grants:* Knowlton, "Land-Grant Problems," pp. 2–3.

26 *The state tolerated:* Charles Gibson argues that the native *títulos* (property titles) for community land possession were a response to Spanish encroachment, usurpation, and legalism. See *The Aztecs Under Spanish Rule*, p. 271.

26 *In general, the colonial elite:* The Indians, though liable to demands for tribute and labor, were, strictly speaking, not slaves. The encomenderos were eventually weakened by the Crown, which saw them as an obstacle to centralized power. Much later, the landowning hacendados established a less conspicuous domination over Indian tribute and labor, and were thus able to avoid the direct assault of the Crown. See ibid., p. 59.

26 *Originally, Martim Afonso distributed:* E. Bradford Burns and Julie A. Charlip, *Latin America: A Concise Interpretive History* (Upper Saddle River, NJ: Prentice Hall, 2002), pp. 36, 37.

27 *Unlike in the English colonies:* Celso Furtado, *Formação econômica do Brasil* (Rio de Janeiro: Editôra Fundo de Cultura, 1961), pp. 41–42, 56, 63.

27 *This system of rigid wealth transfer:* David A. Brading states that by 1810, with 4,945 listed haciendas and estancias, there were little more than 4,000 families who belonged to the landlord class in Mexico. See "Government and Elite in Late Colonial Mexico," in Bakewell et al., *Readings in Latin American History*, p. 243.

27 *Before that time:* Indian depopulation due to various epidemics made it easier for colonists to capture land in the sixteenth and seventeenth centuries. When the Indian population began to grow again, the only way of attaching themselves to the land was through laboring in the haciendas.

27 *They went on to develop:* In his study of the founding of new societies, Albert Galloway Keller contrasts "farm colonies" with "exploitative colonies." Settlers in the former type were generally fleeing from political or social discontent, had moderate ambitions, did not exploit a particular crop or commodity, developed small freeholds, and did not produce a wide class divide. In the latter type of colony, settlers were looking for easy wealth, exploited a particular crop or commodity, used servile, organized labor on a massive scale, concentrated property through large estates with absentee owners, and produced a class-based society. The North American colonies belong in the former group, as do, to a certain extent, Argentina and Chile. Mexico, Peru, and the English colonies in the West Indies belong in the second group. This would explain why Argentina and Chile were spared some of the characteristics that hold back development in other Latin American countries. See Albert Galloway Keller, *Colonization: A Study of the Founding of New Societies* (Boston: Ginn & Company, 1908).

27 *Back in Spain:* The *Recopilación de leyes de los reynos de las Indias* (Madrid: Ediciones Cultura Hispánica, 1973), promulgated in 1680, gives a good idea of the prolific nature of Iberian legalism in the colonies. It contains, however, only a small percentage of all the laws relating to the Indies up to that moment.

27 *Almost one million laws:* Alfonso García-Gallo speaks of "hundreds of thousands" of norms and laws, of "such an enormously intense legislative activity that few things went without regulation" and of "mandates mostly driven by casuistry aimed at solving specific matters in a particular place." See *Los orígenes españoles de las instituciones americanas: Estudios de derecho indiano* (Madrid: Real Academia de Prudencia y Legislación, 1987), pp. xiii, 124, 132 (my translation).

27–28 *A chasm opened between:* Ricardo Levene states that they developed an attitude of "contempt" for the law. See *Introducción a la historia del derecho indiano* (Buenos Aires: Valerio Abeledo, 1924), pp. 30–33.

28 *It created a gulf:* According to Kenneth Karst and Keith Rosenn, "the diversity of

means for transmitting the royal will to the colonies was nearly matched by the diversity of means for colonial administrators to frustrate that will." They go on to say that "the result was bureaucratic confusion, administrative delay, mistrust of government officials, and disrespect of law." See Karst and Rosenn, *Law and Development in Latin America*, p. 37.

28 *The colonial officials themselves reserved:* A well-known saying dating from colonial times attributed to many officials who chose to disregard the law while paying lip service to the Crown. Following old legal doctrine, Spain's laws had actually contemplated disobedience in certain instances since the fourteenth century. See Alfonso García-Gallo, *Estudios de historia del derecho indiano* (Madrid: Instituto Nacional de Estudios Jurídicos, 1972), p. 100.

28 *This was true not only of Spanish:* In Brazil, the proliferation of laws and decrees was comparable to that of the rest of Spanish America. Karst and Rosenn sum it up in this way: "Scanning the confused and contradictory mass of statutes, orders, opinions, regulations, letters patent, decrees, edicts, and instructions appropriately called *legislação extravagante* (literally, extravagant legislation) through which the Sovereign's will was transmitted to the Brazilian colonies, one is amazed that the administrative machine functioned at all." See *Law and Development in Latin America*, p. 40.

28 *Order was maintained through fear:* Wiarda, *The Soul of Latin America*, pp. 107–26.

28 *The problem was that the change:* John Lynch goes as far as to say that in Colombia, "independence ended the Spanish colonial monopoly, but foreign trade continued to be subject to restrictions, and there was nothing approaching free trade." See Lynch, *The Spanish American Revolutions*, p. 258.

28 *By the time the blood dried:* John Lynch refers to Peruvian liberals as "prisoners of their society" and states that "they demanded no more than political reform and equality for Creoles within the colonial framework." The aristocracy, for its part, "clung fanatically to their power and privilege." Referring to Mexico, he says, "Mexican society retained its immutable form, for independence had certain built-in safeguards against change." See ibid., pp. 158, 159, 329.

28 *Until the late nineteenth century:* Kenneth L. Sokoloff, "The Evolution of Suffrage Institutions in the New World," in *Crony Capitalism and Economic Growth in Latin America*, ed. Stephen Haber (Stanford, CA: Hoover Institution Press, 2002), pp. 95–98.

29 *Through various means:* In Venezuela, according to John Lynch, "independence reaffirmed the power of the land-owning class. The colonial aristocracy did not survive in its entirety, but its ranks were replenished by new, plebeian entrants. Estates confiscated by royalists were restored to their owners or descendents, while the republican government confiscated the property of its enemies." See ibid., p. 222.

29 *By the end of the nineteenth century:* Paulo Drinot, "Peru, 1884–1930: A Beggar Sitting on a Bench of Gold," in *An Economic History of Twentieth-Century Latin America*, ed. Enrique Cárdenas, José Antonio Ocampo, and Rosemary Thorp, 3 vols. (New York: Palgrave, 2000), 1: 161.

29 *By then, 95 percent:* Burns and Charlip, *Latin America*, p. 201.

30 *A good illustration is provided:* In correspondence with Thomas Jefferson, Dom João,

the prince regent who was driven from Portugal by the invasion of Napoleon's army and settled in Brazil, alluded to the "well-founded liberal principles, religious as well as political, that we possess." Although, under the influence of José da Silva Lisboa, an admirer of Adam Smith, he opened trade with other nations, his cronies monopolized public office, and numerous restrictions protecting Portuguese interests continued to exist. See Clarence H. Haring, *Empire in Brazil: A New World Experiment with Monarchy* (Cambridge, MA: Harvard University Press, 1958), pp. 5–9.

30 *Immigration was subsidized:* Glade, *The Latin American Economies*, pp. 298–304.

30 *Coffee producers were closer:* Furtado, *Formação econômica do Brasil*, pp. 133–36; Thomas H. Holloway, *The Brazilian Coffee Valorization of 1906: Regional Politics and Economic Dependence* (Madison: State Historical Society of Wisconsin, 1975), pp. 56–75.

31 *The stage was set:* Jesús Eduardo Rodríguez, Teresa Sosa de Bocaranda, and Vilma Clavier, "Marketing Ideas in Venezuela," in *Fighting the War of Ideas in Latin America*, ed. John Goodman and Ramona Morotz-Baden (Dallas: National Center for Policy Analysis, 1990), p. 51.

32 *Finally, lack of penetration:* Karst and Rosenn, *Law and Development in Latin America*, pp. 65–66.

32 *Anything governments and parliaments:* This phrase, quoted in another context, is attributed to the French jurist Marcel Planiol by Alberto Benegas Lynch, *Las oligarquias reinantes* (Buenos Aires: Atlantida, 1999), p. 45.

32–33 *Whether that caudillo was José Gaspar:* José Ortega y Gasset, *Mirabeau o el político* (Madrid: El Arquero, 1927), p. 17.

Chapter 2: The Twentieth Century: The Hour of the Snail

36 *The revolution failed to make:* John P. Powelson and Richard Stock, *The Peasant Betrayed: Agriculture and Land Reform in the Third World* (Washington, DC: Cato Institute, 1990), pp. 35–37.

37 *The constitution explicitly directed:* Burns and Charlip, *Latin America*, p. 206.

37 *In the 1930s, Lázaro Cárdenas:* Rosario Varo Berra, "La reforma agraria en México desde 1853: Sus tres ciclos legales" (Los Angeles: UCLA Program on Mexico, 2002), pp. 130–40.

38 *Through what has aptly been called:* Stephen Haber, Noel Maurer, and Armando Razo, "Sustaining Economic Performance Under Political Instability," in Haber, *Crony Capitalism*, p. 35.

40 *As a result, by the 1970s:* Maura de Val, *La privatización en América Latina* (Madrid: Editorial Popular, 2001), p. 108.

40 *As we have seen, the Mexican Revolution:* Powelson and Stock, *The Peasant Betrayed*, pp. 35–37.

40 *The methods varied:* Ibid., pp. 141–42.

40 *The transition that took place:* Some countries, such as Brazil, did not engage in full-scale land reform, so concentration of property was perpetuated according to the old legacy. The response was the massive "landless" peasant movement, which in the 1980s engaged in violence against, and was the object of violence by, the big owners.

40–41 *This new form of concentration:* Oscar Muñoz Gomá, *Estrategias de desarrollo en economías emergentes: Lecciones de la experiencia latinoamericana* (Santiago de Chile: Facultad Latinoamericana de Ciencias Sociales, 2001), p. 53.

41 *By the 1950s:* Burns and Charlip, *Latin America*, p. 239.

41 *The result was much less efficiency:* Ernest Feder, *The Rape of the Peasantry: Latin America's Landholding Problem* (Garden City, NY: Anchor Books, 1971), Chapters 5–9.

41 *The old legacy of elitism:* Matt Moffett, "In Brazil, the Poor Stake Their Claim on Huge Farms," *Wall Street Journal*, July 11, 2003.

42 *"At times," wrote the Colombian writer:* Germán Arciniegas, *The State of Latin America* (New York: Alfred A. Knopf, 1952), p. 356. (The Spanish original is titled *Entre la libertad y el miedo* [Mexico City: Ediciones Cuadernos Americanos, 1952], p. 315.)

42 *The oligarchic state had become:* That is how Victor Bulmer-Thomas refers to the Latin American state of the twentieth century vis-à-vis the state of the nineteenth century. See "Economic Performance and the State in Latin America," in *Liberalization and Its Consequences: A Comparative Perspective on Latin America and Eastern Europe*, ed. Werner Baer and Joseph L. Love (Northampton, MA: Edward Elgar, 2000), p. 18.

44 *Since rich countries "monopolize" capital:* For a good dissection of Raúl Prebisch's argument, see Peter T. Bauer, *Dissent on Development* (Cambridge, MA: Harvard University Press, 1976), pp. 234–71.

44 *According to the ECLAC model:* Ibid.

45 *It needed to make sure:* Gunnar Myrdal, "Development and Underdevelopment: A Note on the Mechanism of National and International Economic Inequality" (Cairo: National Bank of Egypt, Fiftieth Anniversary Commemoration Lectures, 1956), p. 64.

45 *This nationalist view of political economy:* See J. A. Hobson, *Imperialism: A Study* (Ann Arbor: University of Michigan Press, 1965), and Vladimir Il'ich (Lenin), *Imperialism, the Highest Stage of Capitalism: A Popular Outline* (New York: International Publishers, 1969).

45 *A later development of structuralism:* Fernando Henrique Cardoso and Enzo Faletto, *Dependency and Development in Latin America* (Berkeley: University of California Press, 1979).

45 *Raúl Prebisch himself had:* Bauer, *Dissent on Development*, p. 236.

46 *By 1932, the region:* Burns and Charlip, *Latin America*, p. 228.

46 *The export model under British influence:* de Val, *La privatización de América Latina*, p. 25.

47 *Mexico, geographically much closer:* Alan Taylor attributes later differences in the depth of economic distortions between the Southern Cone and Central America to the differing extents of these early capital controls. See "Latin America and Foreign Capital in the Twentieth Century: Economics, Politics, and Institutional Change," in *Political Institutions and Economic Growth in Latin America*, ed. Stephen Haber (Stanford, CA: Hoover Institution Press, 2000), pp. 133–34.

48–49 *By the end of the 1960s:* Burns and Charlip, *Latin America*, p. 238.

49 *Mexico's economy could boast:* John Goodman and Ramona Marotz-Baden, "The War of Ideas in Mexico," in Goodman and Morotz-Baden, eds., *Fighting the War of Ideas in Latin America*, p. 63; Muñoz Gomá, *Estrategias de desarrollo*, p. 186.

51 *If one sticks to the statistics:* André A. Hofman, "Economic Growth and Performance in Latin America" (Santiago de Chile: United Nations Economic Commission for Latin America and the Caribbean [ECLAC], 2000), p. 15. This document is part of the project "Growth, Employment and Equity: Latin America in the 1990s," financed by the government of the Netherlands. Muñoz Gomá, *Estrategias de desarrollo.*

51 *But if one looks at the statistics:* Bauer, *Dissent on Development*, pp. 34, 32.

51 *Some countries, such as Brazil:* Lawrence E. Harrison, *The Pan-American Dream* (New York: Basic Books, 1997), pp. 80, 125.

51 *The differences in economic growth:* Hofman "Economic Growth and Performance in Latin America," p. 16.

52 *By the 1980s, Latin America's GDP:* Taylor, "Latin America and Foreign Capital in the Twentieth Century," pp. 124–25.

54 *Despite vast amounts:* Ibid., p. 139.

55 *In Brazil, for instance:* The import/GDP ratio was 16 percent in 1947–49. It later decreased, but by 1974 it was back at 14 percent. Baer, *The Brazilian Economy*, p. 79.

56 *Oil revenues were four times:* Rodríguez, Sosa de Bocaranda, and Clavier, "Marketing Ideas in Venezuela," p. 48.

56 *In Mexico, the growth:* John Goodman and Ramona Morotz-Baden, "Winning the War of Ideas in Latin America," in Goodman and Morotz-Baden, eds., *Fighting the War of Ideas in Latin America*, p. 8.

56 *Capital flight in that same:* John A. Gavin, "Mexico, Land of Opportunity," *Policy Review* 39 (1987): 32–35; Paul Craig and Karen LaFollette Araujo, *The Capitalist Revolution in Latin America* (Oxford: Oxford University Press, 1997), pp. 170–71.

56 *By 1980, one of every two:* The rise of interest rates in the United States in 1979–80 caused a spike in the cost of borrowing and debt servicing, making matters worse for Latin America. Joseph L. Love and Werner Baer, "Introduction," in Baer and Love, eds. *Liberalization and Its Consequences*, p. 3.

56 *By the mid-1980s, public:* Rodríguez et al., "Marketing Ideas in Venezuela," p. 50; Goodman and Morotz-Baden, "The War of Ideas in Mexico," in Goodman and Morotz-Baden, eds., *Fighting the War of Ideas in Latin America*, p. 66.

57 *Such policies propped up:* Manuel F. Ayau, "The Role of Higher Education in Guatemala," ibid., pp. 138–41.

58 *In any case, the financial episodes:* Michael Gavin, Ricardo Hausmann, and Ernesto Talvi, "Saving Behavior in Latin America: Overview and Policy Issues" (Washington, DC: Inter-American Development Bank, Office of the Chief Economist, Working Paper 346, 1997), p. 15; de Val, *La privatización en América Latina*, p. 37.

58 *It is no surprise that Mexico's:* Mario Baeza and Sidney Weintraub, "Economic and Political Constants/Changes in Latin America," in *The United States and the Americas: A Twenty-First-Century View*, ed. Albert Fishlow and James Jones (New York: Norton, 1997), p. 39.

60 *Mentioning that the "lost decade":* Hofman, "Economic Growth and Performance in Latin America," p. 13.

Chapter 3: Friendly Fire from the United States

62 *Latin Americans admired their northern:* Alexander von Humboldt, referring to the growing anti-Spanish sentiment that started to become explicit in the latter part of the eighteenth century, observed, "The Creoles prefer to be called Americans. Since the Peace of Versailles, and in particular since 1789, they are frequently heard to declare with pride, 'I am not a Spaniard, I am an American,' words which reveal the symptoms of a long resentment." Quoted in Lynch, *The Spanish American Revolutions*, p. 1. By 1900, only Argentina, Chile, Cuba, and Mexico had achieved even 10 percent of the United States' GDP per capita. It is very likely that Uruguay was in that same group, but there are no figures for that country at the turn of the century. See Bulmer-Thomas, "Economic Performance and the State in Latin America," p. 13.

62 *Equally perplexing is the fact:* From the first stirrings of Latin America's independence movements, the founding fathers of the United States saw opportunities for commerce and for weakening the presence of hostile European powers in the region. In a private letter to William Claiborne written in 1808, Thomas Jefferson stated, "We consider their interests and ours as the same, and that the object of both must be to exclude all European influence from this hemisphere." See *The Writings of Thomas Jefferson*, 10 vols., ed. Paul L. Ford (New York: Putnam, 1892–99), 9: 213. However, Brazil's favoritism toward British trade soon dampened U.S. hopes of much increase in trade in the early nineteenth century. See Stanley E. Hilton, "The United States and Brazilian Independence," in Russell-Wood, ed., *From Colony to Nation*, p. 114.

63 *This lack of awareness:* One must, however, embarrassingly acknowledge the foresight of the founding fathers and other American leaders of the nineteenth century, who did not believe that free societies would emerge after independence. "Their people are immersed in the darkest ignorance and brutalized by bigotry and superstition," wrote Jefferson to the Marquis de Lafayette in 1813. For his part, John Quincy Adams wished "well" the Latin American "cause," but admitted that he had seen "no prospect that they would establish free or liberal institutions of Government." See *The Writings of Thomas Jefferson*, 9: 435; *Memoirs of John Quincy Adams, Comprising Portions of His Diaries from 1795 to 1848*, ed. Charles F. Adams, 12 vols. (Philadelphia: Lippincott, 1874–77), 5: 324–25.

63–64 *In the wake of the Spanish-American*: Although it is by no means as well-known as the Marxist tradition, there is an important classical liberal anti-imperialist tradition. Adam Smith inaugurated it in his *An Enquiry into the Nature and Causes of the Wealth of Nations* (1776) by demolishing the policies of mercantilism that had served to legitimize colonial empires. The Manchester School went much further with the writings of Richard Cobden in the nineteenth century. The Anti-Imperialist League (founded in 1898) took up the same cause in the United States. Individualist writers like Garet Garret denounced the close link they saw between the New Deal and imperialism in the 1930s. Frank Chodorov, a disciple of Albert J. Nock, castigated foreign entanglement as a threat to individual liberty. In the decades after World War II, Murray Rothbard and Leonard Liggio, among others, attacked the interventionist foreign policy derived from the cold war, while Joseph Stromberg, as had Garret before, identified a natural connection between statism at home and empire abroad. For a review of this tradition, see Alan Fairgate, "Non-Marxist Theories of Imperialism," *Reason*, February 1976, pp. 46–52. For discussion of Cobden's views on English foreign policy, see William Dawson, *Richard Cobden and Foreign Policy* (London: Allen and Unwin, 1926). For a history of the early anti-imperialist movement in the United States, see E. Berkeley Tompkins, *Anti-Imperialism in the United States: The Great Debate, 1890–1920* (Philadelphia: University of Pennsylvania Press, 1970). Also see Garet Garret, *The People's Pottage* (Caldwell, ID: Caxton Printers, 1953); Charles H. Hamilton, ed., *Fugitive Essays: Selected Writings of Frank Chodorov* (Indianapolis: Liberty Press, 1980); Murray N. Rothbard, *Left and Right: The Prospects for Liberty* (San Francisco: Cato Institute, 1979); Leonard Liggio, "Why the Futile Crusade," *Left and Right* (Spring 1965): 4–22; Leonard Liggio, "Palefaces or Redskins: A Profile of Americans," *Left and Right* (Autumn 1966): 48–60; Murray N. Rothbard, "Transformation of the American Right," *Continuum* 2 (1964): 220–31; Joseph Stromberg, "The Political Economy of Liberal Corporatism," *Individualist* (May 1972): 2–11. Also see Sheldon Richman, "New Deal Nemesis: The 'Old Right' Jeffersonians," *Independent Review* 4, no. 2 (Fall 1996): 201–48.

64 *By then, 16 percent:* Albert Fishlow, "The Western Hemisphere Relation: Quo Vadis?" in Fishlow and Jones, eds., *The United States and the Americas*, p. 21.

65 *As in the case of trade:* Ibid.

65 *The very term "Latin America":* Andres Oppenheimer, *Bordering on Chaos: Guerrillas, Stockbrokers, Politicians and Mexico's Road to Prosperity* (Boston: Little, Brown, 1996).

65–66 *Interventionism against left-wing:* The School of the Americas, which trained some sixty thousand Latin American officers in half a century, produced at least six hundred identified human rights violators and a dozen dictators. It operated in Panama between the 1940s and the 1980s, and was then moved to Fort Benning, Georgia. It was closed in 2001 and replaced with another military academy for hemispheric officers.

66–67 *The Alliance for Progress stated:* Fishlow, "The Western Hemisphere Relation," p. 20.

67 *Franklin D. Roosevelt protected agriculture:* In regard to U.S. protectionism in general, it must be stated that Latin America has obtained some preferential access through the Generalized System of Preferences (GSP), the Caribbean Basin Initiative (CBI), the Andean Trade Promotion and Drug Enforcement Act (ATPADEA), and other mechanisms.

68 *Manufacturing, as Peter Bauer:* Bauer, *Dissent on Development*, pp. 142–45.

70 *At the end of the century, narcotics:* Eva Bertram, Morris Blachman, Kenneth Sharpe, and Peter Andreas, *Drug War Politics: The Price of Denial* (Berkeley: University of California Press, 1996), pp. 26, 81, 105–109.

70 *Funding for drug eradication:* Bruce M. Bagley, "The New Hundred Years War?: U.S. National Security and the War on Drugs in Latin America," in *The Latin American Narcotics Trade and U.S. National Security*, ed. Donald J. Mabry (New York: Greenwood, 1989), p. 46.

70 *Equally, failure of "source" countries:* The Drug Abuse Acts of 1986 and 1988 condition foreign aid and trade preferences for drug-producing and drug-transiting

countries on their active participation in the war on drugs. See Ted Galen Carpenter, *Bad Neighbor Policy: Washington's Futile War on Drugs in Latin America* (New York: Palgrave, 2003), pp. 124, 146.

71 *Between 50 and 60 percent*: Eduardo Buscaglia and William Ratliff, *War and Lack of Governance in Colombia* (Stanford, CA: Hoover Institution Press, 2001), p. 5.

71 *Terrorist groups grossing hundreds:* For the effects of the war on drugs on corruption in Mexico, see Carpenter, *Bad Neighbor Policy*, pp. 175–85.

71–72 *Drug-financed terrorist groups:* Buscaglia and Ratliff, *War and Lack of Governance*, p. 9.

73 *Out of a total of 400,000 acres:* Alvaro Vargas Llosa, "Back from the Dead—With U.S. Help," *San Francisco Chronicle*, August 18, 2002.

73 *In fact, coca cultivation:* Tina Hodges and Kathryn Lebedur, "Bolivians Pay Dearly for U.S. War on Drugs," *Miami Herald*, November 14, 2002.

73 *It is therefore no surprise:* According to *The Economist*, a gram of cocaine sold for $150 in 2001. The price was $490 in 1981 and $110 in 1996, a record low year. See "Stopping It: How Governments Try—and Fail—to Stem the Flow of Drugs," *The Economist*, July 28, 2001, p. 11. In 2003, the price was around $100.

73 *Within Colombia's borders:* "The Balloon Goes Up," *The Economist*, March 8, 2003, p. 37. Also see Sarah Peterson, "People and Ecosystems in Columbia: Casualties of the Drug War," *Independent Review* 6, no. 3 (Winter 2002): 427–40.

73 *As Steven Wisotsky has said:* Steven Wisotsky, *Beyond the War on Drugs: Overcoming a Failed Public Policy* (Buffalo, NY: Prometheus Books, 1990). Also see Bruce L. Benson and David W. Rasmussen, "Predatory Public Finance and the Origins of the War on Drugs, 1984–1989," *Independent Review* 1, no. 2 (Fall 1966): 163–89, and Jeffrey Miron, *Drug War Crimes: Consequences of Prohibition* (Oakland, CA: Independent Institute, 2004).

74 *The Bolivian military uprooted*: Vargas Llosa, "Back from the Dead."

75 *By then, amid official U.S.*: According to Rensselaer W. Lee III, farmers make between four and ten times more money on coca leaves than raising legal crops such as cacao, oranges, or avocados. See *The White Labyrinth: Cocaine and Political Power* (New Brunswick, NJ: Transaction Publishers, 1989), pp. 26–27.

76 *Just as interventionism and condescension:* Alan Riding, *Distant Neighbors: A Portrait of the Mexicans* (New York: Vintage Books, 1989).

77 *Additional obstacles hindering:* Nancy Birdsall, Nora Lustig, and Lesley O'Connell, "The United States and the Social Challenge in Latin America: The New Agenda Needs New Instruments," in Fishlow and Jones, eds., *The United States and the Americas*, pp. 100–101.

77 *In a sense, the United States:* W. B. Allen, *George Washington: A Collection* (Indianapolis: Liberty Classics, 1988), p. 525.

78 *Objections against trade would:* It is estimated that protectionism in the United States is equivalent to a national sales tax of 6 percent on average. See "Protectionism in America: Watch Your Wallet," a report prepared for Consumers for World Trade (Washington, DC: Trade Partnership, November 1, 2003).

78 *Thomas Paine might have:* Thomas Paine, *Common Sense* (New York: Penguin, 1986), p. 86.

Chapter 4: What Could Have Been

81 *What turned out to be decisive:* Of course, those who negotiated rights in essence negotiated privileges, because they did not negotiate in the name of individual rights per se but for their own. We saw something similar in Spain with the *fueros*, except that the process of extending liberty to more and more groups was eventually interrupted. For the idea of *fuero* as privilege and other ways freedoms were granted as privileges in medieval Europe, see José Ortega y Gasset, *El tema de nuestro tiempo* (Madrid: Espasa Calpe, 1988), pp. 165–66.

83 *Douglass North and Robert Paul Thomas:* North and Thomas, *Rise of the Western World*, pp. 29–35.

83 *The system that prevailed:* Nathan Rosenberg and L. E. Birdzell Jr., *How the West Grew Rich: The Economic Transformation of the Western World* (New York: Basic Books, 1986), pp. 37–60.

84 *The space that opened up:* North and Thomas, *The Rise of the Western World*, p. 84. Margaret Thatcher argues that, by inserting the word "freemen" in the Magna Carta, the barons who forced King John to accept limits to his authority inaugurated a tradition that made it possible to extend their privileges over time to all the population (unlike demands made of their kings by nobles in other countries). Their wisdom, she believes, is all the more admirable considering that the barons were uncultured, warlike men. See Margaret Thatcher, *Statecraft: Strategies for a Changing World* (New York: HarperCollins, 2002), p. 470.

85 *Similarly trade, greatly animated:* It was the continuous American production of silver that permitted Europe to export bullion to Asia without experiencing any market shortage of specie. For an account of colonial mining, see David A. Brading and Harry E. Cross, "Colonial Silver Mining: Mexico and Peru," in Bakewell et al., eds., *Readings in Latin American History*, pp. 129–56.

85 *The remote origins of the concept:* Friedrich A. Hayek, *The Constitution of Liberty* (Chicago: University of Chicago Press, 1978), pp. 164–67.

85 *The codes themselves did not:* David Hume, *The History of England: From the Invasion of Julius Caesar to the Revolution in 1688* (Indianapolis: Liberty Classics, 1983), 2: 520. This edition is based on the edition of 1778 that includes the author's last improvements.

85–86 *In more general terms:* Nock, *Our Enemy, the State*, p. 73.

86 *Had such heresies been:* See John W. Danford, *Roots of Freedom: A Primer on Modern Liberty* (Wilmington, DE: ISI Books, 2000), pp. 37–40.

86 *Institutions, politics, and culture all:* Vilfredo Pareto attributes the Reformation to a wave of religious sentiment in northern Europe as opposed to more worldly values in southern Europe. See *The Rise and Fall of Elites: An Application of Theoretical Sociology* (New Brunswick, NJ: Transaction Publishers, 1991), p. 40.

86 *This happened as the English Parliament:* North and Thomas, *The Rise of the Western World*, pp. 155–57.

87 *John Locke's ideas about:* The cultural roots of liberty, as the evolution of institutions, can be traced back to a time long before Locke and other writers, of course. The Judeo-Christian tradition traces it as far back as four thousand years ago, in the person of Abraham. The Greek philosophers discussed freedom (the Stoics in particular came up with the idea of "natural law"), and Friedrich A. Hayek places the

origin of the concept of the rule of law in the word *isonomia*, by which ancient Greece referred to the equality of laws for all men (Hayek, *The Constitution of Liberty*, p. 164). Those with knowledge of ancient Chinese culture indicate that between the seventh and third centuries B.C. the idea of a government of laws rather than of men also emerged. The Roman jurists further developed the Greek tradition. Later, the Gregorian reformers also brandished some ideas of freedom in their struggle with the state, a conflict that stimulated the development of canon law.

87 *And he went on to say*: Quoted in Albert J. Nock, *Mr. Jefferson* (Tampa, FL: Hallberg Publishing, 1983), p. 51.

87 *After a diplomatic mission*: Quoted ibid., p. 63.

88 *Latin America today is in many ways*: The Bank of England was created in the seventeenth century by businessmen who traded favors from the authorities for credit via the acquisition of government bonds. Like seventeenth-century England, Latin American financial institutions buy government bonds in exchange for favors heaped on them and the industries linked to their owners.

89 *Bruno Leoni has written*: Bruno Leoni, *Freedom and the Law* (Indianapolis: Liberty Fund, 1991), pp. 50–52.

89 *In Roman times*: "*Natura omnes homines liberi sunt et aequales*" (All men are free and equal by nature) was a rule of Roman law. See Donald R. Kelley, "The Private Life of Liberty," in *Liberty/Liberté: The American and French Experiences*, ed. Joseph Klaits and Michael H. Haltzel (Washington, DC: Woodrow Wilson Center Press, 1991), pp. 13–17.

89 *Justinian's Corpus Juris Civilis*: Karst and Rosenn maintain that Roman law had gone from being grounded in real-life experience to being idealistic and rigid in the latter part of the Roman Empire. Consequently, Justinian's codification (the first comprehensive codification of Roman law; previous codifications, before the fall of Rome, had been mere compilations of customary law and some legislation) was already somewhat removed from real-life experience. See Karst and Rosenn, *Law and Development in Latin America*, p. 30.

89 *As the English historian Lytton Strachey wrote*: Lytton Strachey, *Queen Victoria* (New York: Penguin Books, 1971), p. 177.

90 *Latin America did not import from continental Europe*: Hayek, *The Constitution of Liberty*, pp. 196–200.

90 *Government was so far removed*: David Friedman, "Private Creation and Enforcement of Law: A Historical Case," *Journal of Legal Studies* 8 (March 1979): 406.

90 *The law merchant was born*: Bruce Benson, "Justice Without Government," in *The Voluntary City: Choice, Community and Civil Society*, ed. David T. Beito, Peter Gordon, and Alexander Tabarrock (Ann Arbor: University of Michigan Press, for Independent Institute, 2002), pp. 127–33.

90 *During the seventeenth and eighteenth centuries*: Ibid., p. 142.

91 *Gerald W. Scully has shown*: Gerald W. Scully, "Statism Versus Individualism and Economic Progress in Latin America," in Goodman and Morotz-Baden, eds., *Fighting the War of Ideas in Latin America*, pp. 211–12.

91 *Indeed, some have argued*: Edgardo Buscaglia and William Ratliff, *Law and Economics in Developing Countries* (Stanford, CA: Hoover Institution Press, 2000), p. 10.

92 *The settlers did not arrive:* Since the native hunters were not an organized labor force, the Virginia Company, the Massachusetts Company, the Dutch West India Company, and others brought labor from Europe under bond; they also imported slaves from Africa. See Charles Austin Beard and Mary R. Beard, *The Rise of American Civilization* (New York: Macmillan, 1934), pp. 11, 35–37, 44–45, 55.

93 *But the culture of local self-government:* In contrast, English plantation colonies in the West Indies tended to mirror the type of government and society developed in Spanish America. See Lowell J. Ragatz, *The Fall of the Planter Class in the British Caribbean, 1763–1833: A Study in Social and Economic History* (New York: Century Co., 1928), pp. 3–36.

93 *As a recent book:* Hernando de Soto, *The Mystery of Capital: Why Capitalism Triumphs in the West and Fails Everywhere Else* (New York: Basic Books, 2000), pp. 116–20, 145–147, 188.

94 *Terry Anderson and Peter Hill:* Terry L. Anderson and Peter J. Hill, "The Evolution of Property Rights," in *Property Rights: Cooperation, Conflict, and Law*, ed. Terry Anderson and Fred S. McChesney (Princeton, NJ: Princeton University Press, 2003) pp. 120–38.

94 *One must not overlook:* Clark Knowlton illustrates how the land tax, open violence, homestead laws, the economic cycle, the establishment of national forests, irrigation and flood control projects, fencing, and public welfare had the effect, at various stages from the middle of the nineteenth century to the early twentieth century, of expropriating vast amounts of land from the original owners. See "Land-Grant Problems," pp. 5–11.

94 *Under such arrangements:* Richard Cobden, *The Political Writings of Richard Cobden* (New York: T. F. Unwin and Kraus, 1969), p. 36.

95 *It would be wrong to conclude:* In 1935, Albert J. Nock wrote, "Heretofore in this country sudden crises of misfortune have been met by a mobilization of social power. In fact (except for certain institutional enterprises like the home-asylum, city-hospital and country-poorhouse) destitution, unemployment, 'depression' and similar ills have been no concern of the State, but have been relieved by the application of social power." See Nock, *Our Enemy the State*, p. 5.

95 *In fact, research has rediscovered:* David T. Beito, " 'This Enormous Army': The Mutual-Aid Tradition of American Fraternal Societies," and David G. Green, "Medical Care Through Mutual Aid: The Friendly Societies of Great Britain," in Beito et al., eds., *The Voluntary City*, pp. 182–96, 204–19. Also see David G. Green, *Reinventing Civil Society: The Rediscovery of Welfare Without Politics* (London: Institute of Economic Affairs, Health and Welfare Unit, 1993).

95 *Other "public goods":* Daniel Klein, "The Voluntary Provision of Public Goods? The Turnpike Companies of Early America," in Beito et al., eds., *The Voluntary City*, pp. 76–91.

95 *It is hardly surprising:* See George W. Liebmann, *Solving Problems Without Large Government: Devolution, Fairness and Equality* (Westport, CT: Praeger, 2000), pp. x, 1, 6–8, 11–15.

95 *Latin America's political and economic:* Lawrence Harrison has written extensively about the influence of cultural values in Latin America's underdevelopment. See, for instance, *The Pan-American Dream.*

96 *Jeffrey Rogers Hummel has:* Jeffrey Rogers Hummel, *Emancipating Free Slaves, Enslaving Free Men: A History of the American Civil War* (Chicago: Open Court, 1996), pp. 223–25.

96 *The government printed fiat money:* Murray N. Rothbard, *What Has Government Done to Our Money?* (Auburn, AL: Ludwig von Mises Institute, Auburn University, 1990), p. 83.

96 *The next phase of interventionism:* Robert Higgs, *Crisis and Leviathan: Critical Episodes in the Growth of American Government* (New York: Oxford University Press, 1987), p. 21. Also see Robert Higgs, *Against Leviathan: Government Power and a Free Society* (Oakland, CA: Independent Institute, 2004).

Chapter 5: The Liberal Tradition

100 *Tenochtitlán was jealous:* N. James, *Aztecs and Maya: The Ancient Peoples of Middle America* (Charleston, SC: Tempus, 2001).

100 *Through commercial activity:* John A. Garraty and Peter Gay, eds., *The Columbia History of the World* (New York: Harper, 1972), p. 649. Also see Gibson, *The Aztecs Under Spanish Rule*, pp. 15–22.

100 *The* pochtecas *specialized:* James, *Aztecs and Maya*, p. 121.

100 *Although the empire was essentially:* Eric R. Wolf, *Envisioning Power: Ideologies of Dominance and Crisis* (Berkeley: University of California Press, 1999), p. 184.

100 *Under the heavy weight:* Robert B. Revere maintains that the marketplace originated in the "ports of trade" situated on the periphery of ancient empires, on the coasts, or near certain rivers, where exchanges among strangers took place without much interference from the states, which acted as "neutral" entities and had little interest in those areas (before that time, trade in the cradles of civilization was mostly a state activity, so there was trade without markets). The states began to interfere with the "ports of trade" after the first quarter of the first millennium B.C. See "Ports of Trade in the Eastern Mediterranean," in *Trade and Market in the Early Empires: Economies in History and Theory*, ed. Karl Polanyi, Conrad M. Arensberg, and Harry W. Pearson (Glencoe, IL: Free Press, 1957), pp. 38–61.

100 *The state intervened more directly:* The quote is by Anne C. Chapman, who argues that long-distance trade bound together the two great culture areas of Mesoamerica—Tenochtitlán (Aztecs) and Yucatán (Maya descendants)—and distinguishes between state-regulated long-distance trade and the home marketplace. See "Port and Trade Enclaves in Aztec and Maya Civilizations," ibid., pp. 114–16.

101 *Significantly, merchants even had:* Wolf, *Envisioning Power*, p. 185.

101 *Long before the Classic period:* James, *Aztecs and Maya*, p. 69.

102 *Notarial records show* kurakas: Karen Spalding conducted extensive research on the records of the city of Huánuco, in Peru. See "*Kurakas* and Commerce: A Chapter in the Evolution of Andean Society," *Hispanic American Historical Review* 53, no. 4 (November 1973): 586–88.

102 *An entire class of merchants:* Archivo Nacional del Perú, Sección Histórica, Derecho Indígena, Cuaderno 491.

102 *The greatest Indian rebel:* Lillian Estelle Fisher, *The Last Inca Revolt: 1780–1783* (Norman: University of Oklahoma Press, 1966), p. 30.

102 *Each ayllu consisted of an agrarian:* Fray Domingo de Santo Tomás defines "ayllu" as lineage, generation, or family. *Lexicón, o vocabulario de la lengua general del Perú* (Lima: Instituto de Historia, 1951), p. 232.

102 *The families owned the land: Relación de las costumbres antiguas de los naturales del Pirú,* a text written in colonial times, published anonymously in 1879, and later attributed to the mestizo Jesuit Blas Valera, states that, once the division of the land took place among ancient Peruvians, the understanding was that not even the king and his nobles could tread on the private plots. See *Antigüedades del Perú,* ed. Henrique Urbano and Ana Sánchez (Madrid: Historia 16, 1992), p. 101.

102–3 *Inevitably under such a system:* Alvaro Vargas Llosa, *The Madness of Things Peruvian* (New Brunswick, NJ: Transaction Publishers, 1994), pp. 89–90.

103 *The* kuraka *supervised and represented:* Spalding, "*Kurakas* and Commerce," pp. 584–85.

103 *Evidence of many disputes between:* Thomas C. Patterson refers to "kin-civil" conflicts arising when rulers were no longer able to dominate their kin. He also indicates that exploitation by the ruling elite often was masked under traditional relations based on the cooperation of close kin, eventually triggering rebellion. See *The Inca Empire: The Formation and Disintegration of a Pre-Capitalist State* (New York: Berg Publishers, 1991), pp. 50–51, 161.

103 *Anyone who visits a market fair:* Carlos Antonio Mendoza Alvarado, who has conducted extensive research on Indian markets in Guatemala, states that "indigenous markets are institutions stemming from the Guatemalan Maya culture, based on free and voluntary exchange by their members, and on the value of their word (oral contracts), constituting meeting places where information is also exchanged and intercultural relations take place." See *Aproximación al funcionamiento de los mercados indígenas de Guatemala: Consideraciones económicas sobre el mercado de Tecpán* (Guatemala City: Universidad Francisco Marroquín, 1999), p. 5 (my translation).

104 *In the mid-1540s: Las leyes nuevas, 1542–1543; reproducción de los ejemplares existentes en la Sección de Patronato del Archivo General de Indias* (transcription and notes by Antonio Muro Orejón) (Seville, 1945).

105 *In documents such as Representación de Huamanga:* Guillermo Lohmann Villena, *Ideas jurídico-políticas en la rebelión de Gonzalo Pizarro: La tramoya doctrinal del levantamiento contra las leyes nuevas en el Perú* (Valladolid: Seminario Americanista, Secretariado de Publicaciones de la Universidad, 1977), p. 41.

105 *A much more systematic:* Carl Watner writes about them as constituting a "libertarian tradition." See " 'All Mankind Is One,' " p. 293.

106 *They based their beliefs on natural law:* Jesús Huerta de Soto, "Principios básicos de liberalismo," *Revista Hispano Cubana* 4 (May–September 1999): 105, 107.

106 *The first scholars "to grasp":* Michael Novak, *This Hemisphere of Liberty: A Philosophy of the Americas* (Washington, DC: American Enterprise Institute, 1990), p. 45.

106 *"Only God" knows what:* This quote by the Spanish Jesuit Juan de Lugo is taken from Huerta de Soto, "Principios básicos del liberalismo," p. 107.

106 *Alejandro Chafuén has aptly:* Alejandro Chafuén, *Christians for Freedom* (San Francisco: Ignatius Press, 1986).

107 *History paid more attention:* Richard M. Morse, "The Heritage of Latin America,"

in *The Founding of New Societies: Studies in the History of the United States, Latin America, South Africa, Canada and Australia*, ed. Louis Hartz (New York: Harcourt, 1964), pp. 153–59.

109 *Francisco de Miranda: The Diary of Francisco de Miranda, Tour of the United States, 1783–1784*, ed. William Spencer Robertson (New York: Hispanic Society of America, 1928), p. 121.

110 *Juan Bautista Alberdi:* Juan Bautista Alberdi, *Bases y puntos de partida para la organización de la República Argentina* (Buenos Aires: Plus Ultra, 1996).

110 *Commercial banks, for instance:* Alberto Benegas Lynch, *Fundamentos de análisis económico* (Buenos Aires: Abeledo-Perrot, 1986), pp. 311–12.

110 *In 1910, the volume:* Alberto Benegas Lynch, "Rediscovering Freedom in Argentina," in Goodman and Morotz-Baden, eds., *Fighting the War of Ideas in Latin America*, p. 122.

110 *By the 1920s, its economy:* Grondona, *Las condiciones culturales del desarrollo económico*, p. 445.

110 *Later events, coupled with:* Mariano Grondona addressed the fact that his country is the only one in the world to have "undeveloped" itself, that is, to have attained a situation of development and then to have descended into underdevelopment. See ibid., pp. 445–68.

112 *Another important factor was:* Karst and Rosenn, *Law and Development in Latin America*, p. 654.

112 *But perhaps Chile's contemporary:* By 1900, Argentina and Uruguay were Latin America's most successful countries in terms of both economic performance and social advances. Chile was next, together with Cuba. Mexico shared some of the economic results of the second group but was less advanced in matters such as literacy.

112 *It is estimated that the informal economy:* Austrian professor Friedrich Schneider at Johannes Kepler University of Linz conducted a study of the size of the informal economy in 110 countries around the world. The figure comes from adding the value (in U.S. dollars) of the informal economy in all 110 countries. "Size and Measurement of the Informal Economy in 110 Countries Around the World" (Washington, DC: World Bank, July 2002), pp. 6, 8, 11, 13, 16, 18.

113 *Housing, transport, manufacturing, retail:* Enrique Ghersi, "The Informal Economy in Latin America," *Cato Journal* 17 (Spring–Summer 1997). See http://www.cato.org/pubs/journal/cato_journal.html.

113 *Informal employment accounts for:* Rudá Ricci, "A Economia Politica da Argentina," Minas Gerais, 2002; Francesco Neves, "Making Do," *Brazzil*, June 1999. See http://www.brazzil.com.

113 *Brazil's Amazon region involves:* Gary D. Libecap, "Contracting for Property Rights," in Anderson and McChesney, eds., *Property Rights, Cooperation, Conflict, and Law*, p. 151.

113 *These are just a few examples:* According to Friedrich Schneider, the informal economy represents an average of 41 percent of the total size of the economy in Latin America. "Size and Measurement of the Informal Economy," p. 11.

114 *Isaiah Berlin had an eye:* Isaiah Berlin, *Vico and Herder: Two Studies in the History of Ideas* (London: Hogarth, 1976), p. 68.

114 *American anthropologist William Mangin:* William Mangin, "Latin America Squatter Settlements: A Problem and a Solution," *Latin American Research Review* 2, no. 3 (Summer 1967): 65–98.

114 *As early as 1971, anthropologist:* Keith Hart, "Informal Income Opportunities and Urban Employment in Ghana," *Journal of Modern African Studies* 11, no. 1 (March 1973): 67.

115 *Even before that time, studies had been conducted:* One case study was conducted in some barrios of Caracas, Venezuela. Kenneth L. Karst, Murray L. Schwartz, and Audrey J. Schwartz, *The Evolution of the Law in the Barrios of Caracas* (Los Angeles: Latin American Center, University of California, 1973), pp. 17–30, 42–44, 45–47, 48–54.

115 *In her famous book:* Rose Wilder Lane, *The Discovery of Freedom* (New York: Arno Press, 1972), pp. 167, 165–70.

115 *Much of the trade conducted:* When the monarchy fled to Brazil after the invasion of Portugal by Napoleon's army, one of the most important measures of economic liberalism was to authorize the open sale of any commodity in the streets and door to door. See Emília Viotti da Costa, "The Political Emancipation of Brazil," in Russell-Wood, ed., *From Colony to Nation*, p. 51.

115 *In the 1970s, many:* Philip Mattera, *Off the Books: The Rise of the Underground Economy* (New York: St. Martin's Press, 1985), pp. 35–39.

116 *A recent study demonstrates:* Alan B. Krueger, "A Study Looks at Squatters and Land Titles in Peru," *New York Times*, January 9, 2003. The study was conducted by Erica Field, a Ph.D. student in economics at Princeton University.

116–17 *It is estimated that the worldwide:* de Soto, *The Mystery of Capital*, p. 5.

117 *In Peru, for instance:* Alberto Mansueti in collaboration with José Luis Tapia and Instituto de Libre Empresa, *La Salida*, e-book (Lima: Instituto de Libre Empresa, 2003). See http://www.ileperu.org.

Chapter 6: When Things Looked Right, They Were Wrong

122 *Even before exercising power:* Brazil was a case in point. Dom Pedro I, the first Brazilian emperor, had a supposedly "liberal" penchant but ruled like an autocrat and held control of the judiciary, some concessions to liberals notwithstanding. For his part, Dom Pedro II brought many liberals into government at the beginning of his long reign, but power was centralized and exclusive, as well as corrupt. Later, despite his constitutional role as a "moderating power" and his tolerant disposition, he tended to meddle in politics and hold back calls for major reform, including the abolition of slavery. See Haring, *Empire in Brazil*, pp. 18–43, 53–62, 93–96, 165.

123 *Liberals were Rousseau-type liberals:* Wiarda, *The Soul of Latin America*, p. 6.

124 *In the spirit of enhancing:* James, *Aztecs and Maya*, p. 148.

126 *The town, as Stanislav Andreski wrote:* Stanislav Andreski, *Parasitism and Subversion: The Case of Latin America* (New York: Schocken Books, 1969), p. 2.

127 *The planters constituted:* Burns and Charlip, *Latin America*, p. 23.

127 *By 1830, the conservative landowning:* His dictum was: "The stick and the cake, justly and opportunately administered, are the specifics with which any nation can be cured, however inveterate its bad habits may be." Simon Collier, *Ideas and Pol-*

itics of Chilean Independence, 1808–1833 (Cambridge: Cambridge University Press, 1967), p. 359.

130 *In Uruguay, José Batlle y Ordoñez:* Positivism, under the watchwords "Order and Progress," was influential in the republican movement that, helped by a military coup d'état, toppled the Brazilian monarchy in 1889. Benjamin Constant, who taught at the Military Academy in Rio de Janeiro, was a major force behind the spread of positivism. See Haring, *Empire in Brazil*, pp. 139–41.

130 *One of positivism's leading intellectual:* Laureano Vallenilla Sanz, *Cesarismo democrático: Estudios sobre las bases sociológicas de la constitución efectiva de Venezuela* (Caracas: Tip. Universal, 1929).

130 *Foreign investment tripled:* Alan Knight, "Export-Led Growth in Mexico, c. 1900–1930," in Cárdenas et al., eds., *Economic History of Twentieth-Century Latin America*, 1: 127–30.

131 *Díaz allowed bankers to write:* Stephen Haber, Noel Maurer, and Armando Razo, "Sustaining Economic Performance Under Political Instability," in Haber, ed., *Crony Capitalism*, pp. 39–40.

132 *A few decades later, oil fueled Mexico:* Venezuela's oil boom started in the 1930s, in an atmosphere of monetary stability, when the currency was still pegged to one gram of gold and was issued by commercial banks. The country experienced its oil-led "golden age" in the 1950s.

135 *Public investment was used directly:* Bulmer-Thomas, "Economic Performance and the State in Latin America," p. 32.

135 *The trend continued in the 1980s:* Baer, *The Brazilian Economy*, p. 3.

136 *It also became evident:* Between the 1950s and the 1980s, Latin American dictatorships raised public spending by 13 percent every year, more than twice the rate of democracies. The figures can be found in the *Monthly Financial Statistics 1954–85* (International Monetary Fund, Washington, DC).

136 *Multiple government actions:* The term "rent-seeking," describing the competition among private interests for "rents" stemming from government actions that produce profits for some at the expense of others, was originally coined by Anne Krueger in "The Political Economy of Rent-Seeking," *American Economic Review* 64 (1974): 291–300.

136 *By the early 1990s:* Baer, *The Brazilian Economy*, pp. 3–4.

Chapter 7: The Fever of Change

137 *Reform takes place when:* This term was used by Stanislav Andreski in *Parasitism and Subversion* to describe the predatory nature of Latin America's political and economic system. The author derived the concept of parasitism in part from the work of the French sociologist Charles Comte. See *Traité de législation, ou exposition des lois générales suivant lesquelles les peuples prospèrent, dépérissent, ou restent stationnaires* (Paris: Chamerot, 1835).

138 *Those who depended on government:* Carlos Rangel, *Third World Ideology and Western Reality: Manufacturing Political Myth* (New Brunswick, NJ: Transaction Books, 1986).

142 *By 1996, thanks to monetary:* "Latin American Finance," *Financial Times*, London, March 14, 1997.

143 *Mexico and Argentina reduced:* James Gwartney and Robert Lawson, *Economic Freedom of the World: 2003 Annual Report* (Vancouver: Fraser Institute, 2003), pp. 41, 53, 62, 111. Some countries, such as Brazil, made slight variations on their top marginal tax rates after they slashed them. The figures refer to 2001, a year after reform had largely stopped throughout the continent. In the previous years, therefore, in the midst of reform, some countries had even lower top marginal tax rates (Brazil's was 25 before it went up to 27.5 percent).

143 *Argentina's maximum tariff level:* Hernán Büchi and Juan A. Fontaine, "Agenda para América Latina: Afinando la estrategia" (Santiago de Chile: Instituto Libertad y Desarrollo, November 1996), p. 50. The figures are based on statistics from the World Bank and the Economic Commission for Latin America and the Caribbean. In Chile, the average was 8 percent in 2003, with most items taxed at 6 percent. There have been slight variations in other countries. In the Andean countries, for instance, the top tariff is now 20 percent.

143 *Although the average tariff for the region:* Fishlow, "The Western Hemisphere Relation," p. 31.

144 *By 1997, nearly 20 percent:* Abraham F. Lowenthal, "United States–Latin American Relations at the Century's Turn: Managing the 'Intermestic' Agenda," in Fishlow and Jones, eds., *The United States and the Americas*, p. 115.

145 *In fact, by the late 1990s:* Gary C. Hufbauer, Jeffrey J. Scott, and Barbara R. Kotschwar, "U.S. Interests in Free Trade in the Americas," in Fishlow and Jones, eds., *The United States and the Americas*, p. 70.

145 *By 2003, it was close to $600 billion:* Interactive Tariff & Trade Data Web, U.S. International Trade Commission, Washington, DC, 2002. See http://dataweb.usitc.gov.

147 *In part thanks to NAFTA:* Hufbauer, Scott, and Kotschwar, "U.S. Interests in Free Trade," p. 71.

147 *The response of foreign investors:* Another source of foreign capital for Latin Americans is the remittances from relatives living in the United States and other countries. Total remittances in 2002 amounted to $32 billion and in previous years the total amount has exceeded $20 billion. See Enrique Iglesias, "Don't Shortchange Latin America's Largest Aid Program," *San Francisco Chronicle*, May 1, 2003.

147 *By the mid-1990s, annual capital:* Gavin, Hausmann, and Talvi, "Saving Behavior in Latin America," p. 15; "The Americas in 1997: Making Cooperation Work," a report of the Sol M. Linowitz Forum (Washington, DC: Inter-American Dialogue, May 1997), p. 13; "Inversiones extranjeras directas en América Latina y el Caribe," Secretaría Permanente del Sistema Económico Latinoamericano (SELA), Caracas, October 8–10, 2001. See http://sela2.sela.org/WM2/WM10.aspx?menu=1&url=http://www.lanic.utexas.edu/~sela/AA0/ES/menu/finanin1.htm.

147 *More than half of U.S. involvement:* Hufbauer, Scott, and Kotschwar, "U.S. Interests in Free Trade," p. 62.

148 *But drawing parallels between Chile:* When oil prices are high, oil-producing countries such as Venezuela and Ecuador also have relatively high domestic savings due to the oil "rent" enjoyed by the state. In the case of Panama, which has savings rates above the regional average, the country's attraction as an international financial center accounts for the results.

148 *Annual economic growth measured:* Igor Paunovic, "Growth and Reforms in Latin America and the Caribbean in the 1990s" (Santiago de Chile: Economic Commis-

sion for Latin America and the Caribbean [ECLAC], 2000), p. 13. This document is part of the project Growth, Employment and Equity: Latin America in the 1990s, financed by the government of the Netherlands.

149 *However, it is still the case:* Hofman, "Economic Growth and Performance in Latin America," pp. 20–26.

151 *The recession of the early 1980s:* Arturo T. Fontaine, Harold Beyer, and Eduardo Novoa, "Democracy and Dictatorship in Chile," in Goodman and Morotz-Baden, eds., *Fighting the War of Ideas in Latin America*, p. 107.

152 *By 1991, halfway into Salinas's:* de Val, *La privatización en América Latina*, pp. 242–43.

152 *The rest of the region followed:* Laurence Whitehead offers a comparative analysis of privatization in various Latin American countries. See "Privatization and the Public Interest: Partial Theories, Lopsided Outcomes," in Baer and Love, eds., *Liberalization and Its Consequences*, pp. 262–92.

152–53 *Carlos Menem managed to sell:* During the 1990s, 154 privatization contracts were signed by the federal government (the figure excludes the many transfers made in the form of concessions, as well as provincial and local government privatizations). The revenue from privatizations undertaken by the federal government amounted to more than $19 billion. See Sebastián Galiani, Paul Gertler, and Ernesto Schargrodsky, "Water for Life: The Impact of the Privatization of Water Services on Child Mortality," Working Paper 154 (Stanford, CA: Stanford University, CRED PR, November 7, 2002), p. 7. See http://www.nber.org/~confer/2002/urcw02/gertler.pdf.

153 *In 1994, twenty-nine companies were transferred:* de Val, *La privatización en América Latina*, pp. 265–67.

154 *By 2001, the Brazilian government:* Francisco Anuatti-Neto, Milton Barossi-Filho, A. Gledson de Carvalho, and Roberto Macedo, "Benefits and Costs of Privatization: Evidence from Brazil," January 15, 2002, p. 1. The paper was developed with financial backing from the Inter-American Development Bank and the Foundation Institute of Economic Research.

154 *The long-distance carrier, Embratel:* Jack Epstein, "Unbundling Telebrás," *Time International*, August 10, 1998, p. 37.

155 *By 2001, the electricity sector:* Anuatti-Neto, Barossi-Filho, Gledson de Carvalho, and Macedo, "Benefits and Costs of Privatization," p. 2.

155 *Between 1995 and 1996:* Paunovic, "Growth and Reforms in Latin America and the Caribbean," p. 27.

157 *By the end of the decade:* de Val, *La privatización en América Latina*, p. 45.

157 *The combined European investments:* "La inversión directa europea en América Latina: Los réditos de la apertura y privatización" (Caracas: Sistema Económico Latinoamericano [SELA], June 2000).

158 *Profitability in the privatized firms:* "The Privatization Paradox," *Latin American Economic Policies* 18 (second quarter): 1 (Washington, DC: Research Department, Inter-American Development Bank, 2002), based on research conducted by Alberto Chong, Virgilio Galdo, and Eduardo Lora. See http://www.iadb.org/res/publications/pubfiles/pubN-18-2002.pdf.

158 *The improvement in the quality of service:* Ibid., p. 6.

158 *Research has found that after 1995:* Galiani, Gertler, and Schargrodsky, "Water for Life," p. 25.

159–60 *The reform, which was extended:* José Piñera, "Liberating Workers: The World Pension Revolution" (Washington, DC: Cato Institute, 2001), p. 2.

160 *Staggering numbers of people:* Ibid., pp. 5–7. These figures have grown since 2001. In Peru, for instance, the number of participating workers is now close to 3 million.

160–61 *Private pension funds have accumulated:* These figures have grown since 2001 except for Argentina, owing to the collapse of that country's finances.

Chapter 8: The Capitalist Mirage

162 *We have seen that it is possible:* Pascal Salin, *Libéralisme* (Paris: Odile Jacob, 2000), p. 10 (my translation). Also see William C. Mitchell and Randy T. Simmons, *Beyond Politics: Markets, Welfare and the Failure of Bureaucracy* (Boulder, CO.: Westview Press, for the Independent Institute, 1994).

163 *First, the essence of structural reform:* Roger Douglas, "Turning Pain into Gain: Lessons from the New Zealand Experience," speech given to the Atlantic Institute for Market Studies, Halifax, Canada, January 1995. See http://www.aims.ca/commentary/pain.htm. For a comprehensive analysis of the challenges of reform, see Douglas's *Unfinished Business* (Auckland: Random House, 1993), esp. Chapter 10, "The Politics of Reform: The Art of the Possible."

163 *George Reisman has made a similar point:* George Reisman, *Capitalism: A Treatise on Economics* (Ottawa, IL: Jameson Books, 1996), p. 975.

163 *Douglas's second observation on transition:* Douglas, "Turning Pain into Gain."

165 *Had governments been aware of this:* In "A One Day Plan for the Soviet Union," an essay on post-Communist reform, Yuri N. Maltsev recommended applying the homesteading principle and, where it was not feasible, the distribution of shares throughout society using a scheme proposed by the Czech reformer Vaclav Klaus. In order to avoid the chaos resulting from too many shares, each citizen would be given a certificate that could be exchanged for a certain number or variety of shares. Quoted in Murray N. Rothbard, "How and How Not to Desocialize," *Review of Austrian Economics* 6, no. 1 (1992): 72–74.

167 *There took place:* Andreski, *Parasitism and Subversion*, p. 77. Also see Alvaro Vargas Llosa, "Latin American Liberalism: A Mirage?" *Independent Review* 6, no. 3 (Winter 2004): 427–38.

167 *Murray Rothbard was thinking:* Murray N. Rothbard, "Justice and Property Rights," in *Egalitarianism as a Revolt Against Nature and Other Essays* (Auburn, AL: Ludwig von Mises Institute, 2000), p. 92.

168 *In Venezuela, the government:* Natan Zaidman, "Venezuela," in *Telecommunications in Latin America*, ed. Eli M. Noam (New York: Oxford University Press, 1998), p. 122.

168 *Electricity monopolies were ceded:* Andrew Powell, "On Restructuring, Regulation and Competition in Utility Industries: The Experience in the United Kingdom and Implications for Latin America" (Washington, DC: Inter-American Development Bank, April 1995), p. 30.

171 *It is a common flaw:* Andrew Powell, "On Restructuring, Regulation and Competition," pp. 9–11.

171 *Had there been no government-induced monopolies:* By "competitive process" I refer to competition as entrepreneurship, that is, as an ongoing process of discovery that benefits all participants, not as a scramble in which those able to wield the most power drive other producers off the market and dictate conditions. See Israel Kirzner, *Competition and Entrepreneurship* (Chicago: University of Chicago Press, 1973), pp. 88–134.

172 *As Arthur Seldon has observed:* Arthur Seldon, *Capitalism* (Cambridge, MA: Basil Blackwell, 1990), p. 164.

172 *That is a reason why in countries like the United States:* "Business Regulations in America: Gaming the Rules," *The Economist*, July 26, 2003, p. 12.

173 *Responding to pressure:* Laurence Whitehead has written about the difficulties of introducing competition and obtaining optimum market results through regulation in the context of government-granted monopolies and privileges. See "Privatization and the Public Interest," pp. 264–71. The issue is also addressed with specific reference to the telecommunications monopolies in Noam, *Telecommunications in Latin America*.

173 *This does not imply, of course:* Users are charged for their water in Chile, but a direct subsidy is given to poor people so they can meet the cost.

174 *At the turn of the new millennium:* "Mexico's Economy: The Sucking Sound from the East," *The Economist*, July 26, 2003, pp. 35–36.

176 *By 2003, despite the withdrawal of the requirement:* "Safety First: Mexican Pension Funds," *The Economist*, April 26, 2003, p. 66.

176 *In parts of Brazil's 750,000-square-mile:* Anthony Hall has written about the Brazilian government's policy of encouraging large groups, via subsidies, to settle in the Amazon region since the 1960s, which has resulted in encroachment on small farmers as well as Native Americans, with grave social consequences. Since 1971, the government has retained the legal power to give land to settlers virtually anywhere. At first, small claimants were favored, but gradually much larger interests, including cattle ranchers, became the dominant beneficiaries. One group particularly affected has been "rubber tappers" (*seringueiros*), who earn their living by extracting and subsistence farming in the northwest. The intact rubber stands, vast reserves of land and timber, have been taken over by these large concerns favored by government intervention. The reaction of the small farmers (and landless peasants) has been violent, and conflict has extended to other zones. Grassroots movements have forced some concessions from the government, but the very nature of the conflict has strengthened rather than weakened the role of the political authorities in the Amazon region. See "Privatizing the Commons: Liberalization, Land and Livelihoods," in Baer and Love, eds., *Liberalization and Its Consequences*, pp. 235–38, 241–43.

177 *Even under a currency board policy:* Steve Hanke, "Argentina: Caveat Lector," Cato Institute, Twentieth Annual Monetary Conference, New York, October, 17, 2002, p. 2.

178 *Argentina's federal transfers:* By the end of the 1990s, 56 percent of total resources received by the provinces came from the common pool of taxes collected by the federal government. See Mariano Tommasi, Sebastian Saiegh, and Pablo San-

guinetti, "Fiscal Federalism in Argentina: Fiscal Policies, Politics and Institutional Reforms," *Economia (Journal of the Latin American and Caribbean Economic Association)* (Spring 2001): 151.

178 *Additionally, the size of government:* Victor Bulmer-Thomas rightly indicates that the retreat of the state in the 1990s from areas in which it was previously active shifted the burden of investment policies to the private sector, which is dependent on borrowing through bond issues and on equity investment abroad for much of its investment capital. The foreign perception of risk in Latin American countries because of government irresponsibility therefore hurts the economy. See "Economic Performance and the State," p. 28.

180 *The region's participation in world trade:* "Panorama de la inserción internacional de América Latina y el Caribe, 2000–2001" (Santiago de Chile: CEPAL, March 2002), pp. 17, 18.

180–81 *The 2003 negotiations:* Manuel F. Ayau, "An Unfree Trade Agreement for Central America," *Wall Street Journal*, August 8, 2003.

182 *In Mexico, it is estimated:* The consultancy NAFTA Ventures estimates that the labor regulations raise the hourly cost of labor from $3 to $5.70. Quoted in "Mexico's Economy: The Sucking Sound from the East," p. 36.

183 *In a region that is still:* Elizabeth McQuerry looks at the failure of economic reform to reduce poverty in any significant way. See "In Search of Better Reform in Latin America," *EconSouth* 4, no. 2 (Second Quarter, 2002): 14–19.

183 *In contrast, East Asia:* In the last thirty years, East Asia's per capita income has grown four and a half times more than Latin America's. See Büchi and Fontaine, "Agenda para América Latina," p. 29.

184 *It should come as no surprise:* In 1999, the last year of growth before the long slump that started in the year 2000, domestic investment amounted to 21.5 percent of GDP. See "Estudio económico de América Latina y el Caribe, 1999–2000" (Santiago de Chile: CEPAL, August 2000), p. 82; Sebastian Edwards, "The Disturbing Underperformance of the Latin American Economies," Sol M. Linowitz Forum, Tenth Plenary Session of the Inter-American Dialogue, January 1997, p. 3.

184 *Consequently, the rate of growth of capital:* Hofman, "Economic Growth and Performance," p. 21.

184 *Under such conditions and with low productivity:* Paunovic, "Growth and Reforms in Latin America," p. 10.

186 *In fact, lack of business opportunity:* "The Paradox of Privatization," *Políticas económicas de América Latina* 18 (Washington, DC: Inter-American Development Bank, 2002), p. 3.

187 *In trying to steer a middle:* Octavio Paz, *El ogro filantrópico: Historia y política 1971–1978* (Barcelona: Editorial Seix Barral, 1979).

188 *During the reform years:* Birdsall, Lustig, and O'Connell, "The United States and the Social Challenge in Latin America," p. 83.

188 *In France, Germany, the United Kingdom:* Ibid., pp. 81, 107.

189 *Socialism was so strong:* The quote is from Donald T. Brash, "New Zealand's Remarkable Reforms," Fifth Annual Hayek Memorial Lecture (London: Institute of Economic Affairs, 1996), p. 17.

190–91 *Tax reform translated into low:* Ibid., p. 16.

191 *Polish researcher Grzegorz W. Kolodko:* Grzegorz W. Kolodko, *Ten Years of Post-Socialist Transition: Lessons for Policy Reforms,* Policy Research Working Paper 2095 (Washington, DC: World Bank, April 1999), p. 9.

191 *Only Chile has been able:* For the reasons explained earlier, oil-producing countries such as Venezuela and Ecuador tend to see their savings rates increase when oil prices are high, but it is the state that controls and therefore directs those increased investment resources.

Chapter 9: Corruption and the Ethical Abyss

193 *Recently, Latin American nations:* "Global Corruption Report 2003," *Transparency International.* See www.transparency.org.

193 *Andres Oppenheimer describes Latin American:* One graphic example of the mercantilist connections between the president of Mexico and the top businessmen during Carlos Salinas's administration is the banquet at which some of the biggest beneficiaries of government divestitures and various concessions pledged $750 million in order to help the PRI get reelected. See Oppenheimer, *Bordering on Chaos,* pp. 85–87.

194–95 *James M. Buchanan and Gordon Tullock's:* See James M. Buchanan and Gordon Tullock, *The Calculus of Consent: Logical Foundations of Constitutional Democracy* (Ann Arbor: University of Michigan Press, 1965).

195 *What it does encourage is much higher levels:* Simeon Djankov, Rafael La Porta, Florencio López de Silanes, and Andrei Schleifer, "The Regulation of Entry," Harvard Institute of Economic Research, Discussion Paper Number 1904 (Cambridge, MA: Harvard University, 2000), pp. 19, 20, 41. See http://post.economics.harvard.edu/hier/2000papers/2000list.html.

195 *In Mexico, it takes 112 business days:* Ibid., pp. 38–39.

195 *Corruption is the natural creature:* There is no Latin American equivalent to the efforts of the Indian state of Andhra Pradesh, where twenty-eight "eSeva" centers have been set up in Hyderabad, with clerks at computer terminals completing, quickly and online, thirty-two types of transactions with the government. See "Government by Computer," *The Economist,* March 22, 2003, pp. 38–39.

196 *In Peru and Mexico:* José Matos Mar, *Desborde popular y crisis del Estado: El nuevo rostro del Perú en la década de 1980* (Lima: Instituto de Estudios Peruanos, 1984), pp. 48, 75–91.

197 *According to the Community Associations Institute:* David T. Beito, Peter Gordon, and Alexander Tabarrok, "Toward a Rebirth of Civil Society," in *The Voluntary City,* p. 5.

198 *The idea of people helping:* John Locke, *The Second Treatise of Government*; David Hume, A *Treatise of Human Nature*; Adam Smith, *The Theory of Moral Sentiments.*

199 *Andreski's words, written many:* Andreski, *Parasitism and Subversion,* p. 11.

200–1 *But the amount of money politicians:* The government of President Menem, for instance, increased the number of Supreme Court justices from five to nine, obtaining the control of a key institution. Corruption plagued his government, based to a large extent on rule by decree, but the subservience of the Supreme Court prevented the judiciary from acting as a safeguard against its unethical practices and political excesses.

201 *The countries in which the justice:* Laurence Whitehead has referred to Chile's advantages over other Latin American countries regarding judicial institutions in their increasing role as substitutes of the governments' other branches in a privatized economy. He argues that the "neo-liberal" trend might be reversed if the legal system is not strong enough to support the demands of the market economy. See "Privatization and the Public Interest," pp. 266–67, 270–71.

201 *Conservative estimates by multilateral bodies:* William Prillaman, *The Judiciary and Democratic Decay in Latin America: Declining Confidence in the Rule of Law* (Westport, CT: Praeger, 2000), p. 3.

202 *The result of greater access:* Eduardo Buscaglia, Maria Dakolias, and William Ratliff, *Judicial Reform in Latin America: A Framework for National Development* (Stanford, CA: Hoover Institution Press, 1995), p. 23. Eduardo Buscaglia and William Ratliff also indicate that between 1973 and 1985, the median delay in first-instance Brazilian courts experienced a change of 4 percent, whereas between 1986 and 1997, the median delay experienced a change of 38.1 percent. See Buscaglia and Ratliff, *Law and Economics in Developing Countries*, p. 57.

202 *In Ecuador, there are:* Buscaglia, Dakolias, and Ratliff, *Judicial Reform in Latin America*, p. 9.

203–4 *A survey of U.S. firms:* The survey was conducted by Eduardo Buscaglia and J. L. Guerrero in 1995 and is cited in Buscaglia and Ratliff, eds., *Law and Economics in Developing Countries*, p. 26.

Chapter 10: Liberty for Latin America

212 *There are those who say:* Alan Reynolds, "The Case for Radical Tax Reforms in Latin America," in Goodman and Morotz-Baden, eds., *Fighting the War of Ideas in Latin America*, pp. 235–36.

212 *And, clearly, if the cost of doing business:* Djankov, La Porta, López de Silanes, and Schleifer, "The Regulation of Entry," pp. 1, 35–37.

214–15 *Millions depend on various forms:* For a comparative analysis of the dismal state of public education in Latin America vis-à-vis East Asia, where the focus has been on developing human capital rather than redistributing wealth, see William Ratliff, *Doing It Wrong and Doing It Right: Education in Latin America and East Asia* (Stanford, CA: Hoover Institution Press, 2003).

217 *A recent study indicates that productivity:* Douglas Kruse, "Research Evidence on Prevalence and Effects of Employee Ownership," testimony before the Subcommittee on Employer-Employee Relations, Committee on Education and the Workforce, U.S. House of Representatives, February 13, 2002. See http://www.nceo.org/library/kruse_testimony.html.

217 *Albert Gallatin, Jefferson's secretary:* Quoted ibid.

217 *"If the representative takes office":* Isabel Paterson, *The God of the Machine* (New York: Putnam, 1943), p. 288.

218 *The system was not imported in the South:* Hummel, *Emancipating Free Slaves*, p. 315.

219 *These in turn are part*: Birdsall, Lustig, and O'Connell, "The United States and the Social Challenge," p. 95.

219 *The result is increased choices*: Bauer, *Economic Analysis and Policy in Underdeveloped Countries*, p. 113.

220 *Because reform has not gone:* For comparative research on the various types of schools in Chile, see Marvia Olaski, "Compassion in Chile: School Vouchers in Chile Yield Results," *Compassion & Culture* (Washington, DC: Capital Research Center, January 2003).

221 *The British statesman Edmund Burke:* Quoted by Gregory Wolfe, *A New Dawn of Liberty: The Story of the American Founding* (Century City, CA: Henry Salvatori Foundation, 1992), p. 13.

Appendix

The various statistics included in the Appendix are interesting and credible references. I would, however, caution against too much reliance on general economic statistics because they tend to look at society in terms of aggregates rather than individuals, they include the government's participation in the economy as part of a country's total production when government "production" is also a cost to society, and they miss the myriad ways a government affects the lives and the property of citizens without it being immediately obvious in terms of performance. The various tables, compiled by the author, are based on data taken from the sources quoted in each case.

Acknowledgments

In the wee hours of a misty morning in 2002, I flew out of persecution's way in Peru, my native country. It was not my first venture into exile, but it was ironic that this time the people harassing me and my family were some of those with whom I had recently struggled to bring down a dictatorship and who constituted the new government of the nation.

Some time later, my newly found freedom directed me, through my friend Carlos Ball, to an unlikely place: the Independent Institute in California's East Bay area, where I had never set foot before. When David and Mary Theroux showed interest in me, I did not yet know them but I already knew what book I would write under the research fellowship they were offering me. This work has been possible thanks to the generous funding provided by Peter Howley and by the John Templeton Foundation, and, particularly, to David and Mary's encouragement. Their devotion to the cause of liberty has been a source of inspiration to me.

I am also indebted to a number of other people. Alexander Tabarrok, William Ratliff, and Lawrence Harrison, who had access to the original manuscript, made valuable suggestions. Comments made by Paul Elie and Kathryn Lewis, at Farrar, Straus and Giroux, were equally insightful.

Sanjeev Saini helped me obtain access to a number of books and periodicals.

Finally, I thank all my friends at the Independent Institute for their support—and for their discretion, a virtue I value above most others. I particularly appreciated my discussions with Argentinean analyst Gabriel Gasave.

None of the aforementioned people bear any responsibility for the content of the book, of which I am the sole culprit.

Alvaro Vargas Llosa

Index

THE INDEPENDENT INSTITUTE is a nonprofit, nonpartisan, scholarly research and educational organization that sponsors comprehensive studies of the political economy of critical social and economic issues.

The politicization of decision making in society has too often confined public debate to the narrow reconsideration of existing policies. Given the prevailing influence of partisan interests, little social innovation has occurred. In order to understand both the nature of and possible solutions to major public issues, The Independent Institute's program adheres to the highest standards of independent inquiry and is pursued regardless of political or social biases and conventions. The resulting studies are widely distributed as books and other publications, and are publicly debated through numerous conference and media programs. Through this uncommon independence, depth, and clarity, The Independent Institute expands the frontiers of our knowledge, redefines the debate over public issues, and fosters new and effective directions for government reform.

THE INDEPENDENT INSTITUTE
100 Swan Way, Oakland, California 94621-1428, U.S.A.
Telephone: 510-632-1366 Facsimile: 510-568-6040
E-mail: info@independent.org Web site: www.independent.org

INDEPENDENT STUDIES IN POLITICAL ECONOMY

THE ACADEMY IN CRISIS: The Political Economy of Higher Education | ed. John W. Sommer

AGAINST LEVIATHAN: Government Power and a Free Society | Robert Higgs

AGRICULTURE AND THE STATE: Market Processes and Bureaucracy | E. C. Pasour, Jr.

ALIENATION AND THE SOVIET ECONOMY: The Collapse of the Socialist Era | Paul Craig Roberts

AMERICAN HEALTH CARE: Government, Market Processes and the Public Interest | ed. Roger D. Feldman

ANTITRUST AND MONOPOLY: Anatomy of a Policy Failure | D. T. Armentano

ARMS, POLITICS, AND THE ECONOMY: Historical and Contemporary Perspective | ed. Robert Higgs

BEYOND POLITICS: Markets, Welfare and the Failure of Bureaucracy | William C. Mitchell & Randy T. Simmons

THE CAPITALIST REVOLUTION IN LATIN AMERICA | Paul Craig Roberts & Karen LaFollette Araujo

CHANGING THE GUARD: Private Prisons and the Control of Crime | ed. Alexander Tabarrok

CUTTING GREEN TAPE: Toxic Pollutants, Environmental Regulation and the Law | ed. Richard Stroup & Roger E. Meiners

THE DIVERSITY MYTH: Multiculturalism and Political Intolerance on Campus | David O. Sacks & Peter A. Thiel

DRUG WAR CRIMES: The Consequences of Prohibition | Jeffrey A. Miron

THE EMPIRE HAS NO CLOTHES: U.S. Foreign Policy Exposed | Ivan Eland

ENTREPRENEURIAL ECONOMICS: Bright Ideas from the Dismal Science | ed. Alexander Tabarrok

FAULTY TOWERS: Tenure and the Structure of Higher Education | Ryan C. Amacher & Roger E. Meiners

FREEDOM, FEMINISM, AND THE STATE: An Overview of Individualist Feminism | ed. Wendy McElroy

HAZARDOUS TO OUR HEALTH?: FDA Regulation of Health Care Products | ed. Robert Higgs

HOT TALK, COLD SCIENCE: Global Warming's Unfinished Debate | S. Fred Singer

LIBERTY FOR WOMEN: Freedom and Feminism in the Twenty-first Century | ed. Wendy McElroy

MARKET FAILURE OR SUCCESS: The New Debate | ed. Tyler Cowen & Eric Crampton

MONEY AND THE NATION STATE: The Financial Revolution, Government and the World Monetary System | ed. Kevin Dowd & Richard H. Timberlake, Jr.

OUT OF WORK: Unemployment and Government in Twentieth-Century America | Richard Vedder & Lowell E. Gallaway

A POVERTY OF REASON: Sustainable Development and Economic Growth | Wilfred Beckerman

PRIVATE RIGHTS & PUBLIC ILLUSIONS | Tibor R. Machan

RECLAIMING THE AMERICAN REVOLUTION: The Kentucky & Virginia Resolutions and Their Legacy | William J. Watkins, Jr.

REGULATION AND THE REAGAN ERA: Politics, Bureaucracy and the Public Interest | ed. Roger Meiners & Bruce Yandle

RESTORING FREE SPEECH AND LIBERTY ON CAMPUS | Donald A. Downs

RE-THINKING GREEN: Alternatives to Environmental Bureaucracy | ed. Robert Higgs & Carl P. Close

SCHOOL CHOICES: True and False | John D. Merrifield

STRANGE BREW: Alcohol and Government Monopoly | Douglas Glen Whitman

TAXING CHOICE: The Predatory Politics of Fiscal Discrimination | ed. William F. Shughart II

TAXING ENERGY: Oil Severance Taxation and the Economy | Robert Deacon, Stephen DeCanio, H. E. Frech III & M. Bruce Johnson

THAT EVERY MAN BE ARMED: The Evolution of a Constitutional Right | Stephen P. Halbrook

TO SERVE AND PROTECT: Privatization and Community in Criminal Justice | Bruce L. Benson

THE VOLUNTARY CITY: Choice, Community and Civil Society | ed. David T. Beito, Peter Gordon & Alexander Tabarrok

WINNERS, LOSERS & MICROSOFT: Competition and Antitrust in High Technology | Stan J. Liebowitz & Stephen E. Margolis

WRITING OFF IDEAS: Taxation, Foundations & Philanthropy in America | Randall G. Holcombe